CONTEMPLATIVE PRACTICES AND ACTS OF RESISTANCE IN HIGHER EDUCATION

The contributors to this volume – educators, student affairs practitioners, and higher education staff – heartfully share a broad range of contemplative practices and acts of resistance used within the confines of shattered systems and institutions for themselves, their colleagues, and their students. The narratives in this volume broadly imagine, inspire, recount, and guide readers toward the fullness of their humanity and wholeness within institutions of higher education. At the same time, these accounts navigate the operational realities of daunting demands on the mind, body, and spirit, the growing turbulence of working on higher education campuses across the country, and a sense of urgency toward collective life affirmation within modern higher education institutions. Each chapter features critical framing of a concept, personal stories of this concept in action, and descriptions of contemplative practices for readers to use in their own contexts. Together, chapter authors demonstrate what it means to be a contemplative practitioner attentive to issues of power, racism, and marginalization in higher education today. With a deep breath and mindful awareness, this book invites faculty and staff at colleges and universities on a transformational journey with the contributors toward fullness in pursuit of becoming whole and inspiring change.

Michelle C. Chatman is Associate Professor of Crime, Justice, and Security Studies, Director of the Violence Prevention and Community Wellness Program, and Founding Director of the Mindfulness and Courageous Action (MICA) Lab at the University of the District of Columbia, Washington, DC.

LeeRay Costa is Executive Director of Leadership Studies and the Batten Leadership Institute, and Professor of Gender and Women's Studies/Anthropology at Hollins University, Roanoke, VA.

David W. Robinson-Morris is former Executive Director of the Center for Contemplative Mind in Society (CMind), the Founder of The REImaginelution, and inaugural Executive Director of the Institute for Black Intellectual and Cultural Life at Dartmouth College, Hanover, NH.

"This book is a wise and wildly creative guide to transforming higher education into a place where we can truly explore what it means to be human and work toward healing, toward becoming whole. Edited and written by some of the most experienced, committed, and grounded practitioners in the field, it includes fearless explorations of the contemplative to increase appreciation of interconnection, impermanence, community, the body, and pedagogies of love. It is the inspiration we need to meet the formidable demands of this time and turn the campus into a home where we all belong."

Mirabai Bush, Founder, *Center for Contemplative Mind in Society and Association for Contemplative Mind in Higher Education, USA*

"In this beautifully written volume, the essayists generously offer their reflections and contemplative practices to academics feeling pressured to show up as fragmented, disembodied versions of themselves. With testimonials and a range of contemplative rituals, this guide can ground readers and bolster their capacity to (re)connect with and rely on their inner wisdom. Mindfully being in conversation with the authors' insights and engaging in their suggested practices positions academics to move towards wholeness and enhance the fortitude that is necessary to effect systemic change within our institutions and our society."

Veronica Womack, Associate Director, Inclusive Learning Communities, *Searle Center for Advancing Learning and Teaching, Northwestern University, USA*

"This collection is a balm for an educator's soul. Full of practical and wise essays, it addresses current challenges in higher education through diverse stories and healing contemplative practices. The anthology offers ways to re-connect with ourselves and one another, re-invigorate our passion for educating, heal from the toxicity of systemic higher education, and re-imagine possibility. As I read, I felt my exhausted spirit re-integrate with hope. I found myself jotting down ideas for how to bring the wise insights of this collection into my life, teaching, and work. I will be sitting with this collection for a while with deep, deep gratitude."

Beth Berila, Director, Gender and Women's Studies, *St. Cloud State University, USA*

CONTEMPLATIVE PRACTICES AND ACTS OF RESISTANCE IN HIGHER EDUCATION

Narratives Toward Wholeness

Edited by Michelle C. Chatman, LeeRay Costa, and David W. Robinson-Morris

NEW YORK AND LONDON

Designed cover image: © Sabiyha Prince

First published 2025
by Routledge
605 Third Avenue, New York, NY 10158

and by Routledge
4 Park Square, Milton Park, Abingdon, Oxon, OX14 4RN

Routledge is an imprint of the Taylor & Francis Group, an informa business

© 2025 selection and editorial matter, Michelle C. Chatman, LeeRay Costa, David W. Robinson-Morris; individual chapters, the contributors

The right of Michelle C. Chatman, LeeRay Costa, and David W. Robinson-Morris to be identified as the authors of the editorial material, and of the authors for their individual chapters, has been asserted in accordance with sections 77 and 78 of the Copyright, Designs and Patents Act 1988.

All rights reserved. No part of this book may be reprinted or reproduced or utilised in any form or by any electronic, mechanical, or other means, now known or hereafter invented, including photocopying and recording, or in any information storage or retrieval system, without permission in writing from the publishers.

Trademark notice: Product or corporate names may be trademarks or registered trademarks, and are used only for identification and explanation without intent to infringe.

ISBN: 9781032727318 (hbk)
ISBN: 9781032725468 (pbk)
ISBN: 9781003416777 (ebk)

DOI: 10.4324/9781003416777

Typeset in Galliard
by KnowledgeWorks Global Ltd.

Preamble

As the co-editors, we returned repeatedly to these questions: How do we write about wholeness in academia when the very institutions within which we work stand atop indigenous burial grounds, upon stolen and raped land, cultivated by kidnapped and brutalized people from another continent. In the heaviness of this work, how might we possibly honor the stillness, silence, solidity, and sacredness within ourselves without acknowledging our interdependence with the earth, air, waters, mountains, trees, and beasts among us? With our elders? The interrelatedness of us all. How do we restore wholeness when we have been historically dis-membered? A narrative of wholeness is a mighty work. An aspirational dream. In our efforts, we must acknowledge the first violations and atone for the violences.

Somehow.

This volume would not be whole or complete without the voices of the original peoples of this land. We have invited our sisters to open this volume as representative voices of the Grand Mothers of this land and the embodiment of sacred wisdom.

May their words set us on a new path, nourish our spirits, soothe our souls, and provide us with necessary sustenance to make being whole a lived possibility.

AN INVOCATION OF SEVEN DIRECTIONS TOWARD WHOLENESS

April E. Lindala, Denise Cadeau, and Cueponcaxochitl D. Moreno Sandoval

We begin in the direction of the East,
the place where the sun peeks over the horizon to nourish all life.
We embody a deep sense of Meegwechiwendam, gratitude,
for all that is pulsating with life.

We turn to the direction of the South
where we center in
our purpose for walking on this tlalticpac, Earth,
to remember our responsibility
for protecting all beings of Creation.

Next, we face the West,
where we commit to the renewal of our ancestral ways.
We thank the strong, cleansing winds and thunderstorms.
We call on them to help us balance the forces of the world.

We face the direction of the North
where we make our offerings to the next seven generations
so that the faces that look up from under the skin of the Earth,
the unborn generations, anticipate their time here with great joy.

We rotate our bodies up to the Sky World,
where we acknowledge the Winged and Star Nations,
the Cosmos, Grandmother Moon, and Grandfather Sun
for guiding our path here on Earth.

They serve as a mirror, reminding us about the cycles of life
that continue to regenerate themselves.

We humble ourselves to touch Mother Earth,
And *re-member* the interdependence of all life.
We offer deep gratitude for her
nourishment, teachings and cycles of
life in all its forms.

Next, we touch our hearts,
we close our eyes, and look inward with grace.
We reverently recognize our place in the world,
and our responsibilities to ensure that we
reciprocate the Earth's bountiful gifts.

We invite you, dear readers, to imagine yourselves in this collective kitchen from each of our ancestral homelands. We gather at this feast. We *re-member* these foods as our relatives. The aroma of broth and food medicine for our hearts, minds, bodies, and spirits nourish us. The thickness of root vegetables from the Earth grounds us, and the warmth of their goodness feeds us and awakens our senses. The coarseness of these gifts of the Earth come alive as we harvest them and prepare them together.

The meal is prepared. Our bodies gather into a circle. We are ready. We first start by feeding the spirits that are here to help us live with collective dignity. We gather a pinch from each of the foods, prepared by our hands, warmed by our hearts. We make these offerings to the spirits by carefully placing them in each of the elements, the Earth, fire, and water, as if feeding our babies with deep affection. We pray they will be received in a good way.

We hope this invocation opens up this anthology in sacredness. As you hold it, may it open your hearts, minds, bodies, and spirits to the messages collected in this book. This book carries much contemplative medicine for these unrelenting times in higher education. May our story bundles of resistance and ancestral brilliance grow with each line, each paragraph, and each page toward the wholeness we all need. Thank you for subversively walking in beauty.

CONTENTS

Preface	*xv*
Acknowledgments	*xx*
Meet the Contributors	*xxii*

1 Introduction: Contemplative Practice Is an Act of Resistance   1
   Michelle C. Chatman, LeeRay Costa,
   and David W. Robinson-Morris

PART I
Ever Present and Interconnected: Symphonic
Journeys, Rooted Practices   **23**

Michelle C. Chatman

2 Teaching Best What you Most Want to Learn:
   The Way of the Crows   27
   Brandon LA Hutchinson

3 Unsettling the Colonial Shadows of Contemplative Practice   36
   JuPong Lin

4 Cajitas as My Contemplative Practice   47
   Alberto López Pulido

5 Contemplative Practices Through a Black Feminist
   Lens: Badassery, For Real Love and Fellowship   56
   Emerald Templeton

6 Deepening Belonging: A Contemplative Practice
   of Relational Flourishing   63
   Aizaiah G. Yong and Yohana Agra Junker

7 Reflections Beyond Fragmentation: A Fractal
   Reconfiguration   72
   Vaishali Mamgain

PART II
Conjuring Transformation: We Who—*Know*—Know   77
David W. Robinson-Morris

8 Revealing Healing, Wholeness, and Power: Sitting Zazen   81
   Monika L. Son

9 From Body Oppression to Body Sovereignty
   through Contact Improvisation   91
   Robin Raven Prichard

10 From Practice to Purpose: Contemplative Dance
   as a Method for Moving through Resistance   101
   Candice Salyers

11 Creative Envisioning: A Contemplative Practice
   That Promotes Healing, Personal Growth, and
   Professional Development   109
   Virginia Diaz-Mendoza

12 On Being (A) Contemplative in Higher Education:
   'Moving' through Familiar and Unfamiliar Spaces   118
   Emmanuelle Khoury

13 Conjuring Transformation: The Magic Is in the Process 127
   Maria Hamilton Abegunde

A PAUSE.   **131**

14 Cool Like Jazz: A Loving Dialogue on the
Multiplicity of Black Manhood   133
Bradford C. Grant and Michelle C. Chatman

PART III
**Rhizomatic Awakenings: New Plateaus: Rhizomes,
Connection, Ruptures, and Lines of Flight**   **143**
David W. Robinson-Morris

15 Showing up Audacious and Bad Ass from the Edges
and on the Margins Like My Ancestors   147
Phyllis M. Jeffers-Coly

16 Our Skins are Membranes, Not Walls: A Multiracial
Feminist Conversation   156
Zahra Ahmed, Anita Chari, and Becky Thompson

17 Dancing Barefoot in the University: From Burnout
to Radical Presence   166
Lela Mosemghvdlishvili

18 Alongside Aaron   175
Wendy Petersen-Boring

19 My Rhizomatic Awakening   184
Steven Thurston Oliver

PART IV
**Liberatory Relationality: Cultivating Collective
Compassion**   **189**
LeeRay Costa

20 Cultivating Belonging: Compassionate Practice
and Pedagogy   193
Renuka Gusain

21 Beloved Community as Practice: Grounding
Exercises, Care Teams, and Redefining Success 201
Meika Loe

22 *Why am I Talking?* Disrupting Dominant Narratives
in Higher Education 208
Deb Spragg

23 Contemplative Emergence: How My Contemplative
Practices Have Supported Transformative Change in
a Higher Education Space 218
Ericka Echavarria

24 Enacting an Indigenous Decolonial Contemplative
Mentorship in Higher Education: Meditations on the
Legacy of Plenty Fox 227
Michael Yellow Bird and Holly Hatton

25 Contemplative Resistance Amidst the Fires of Global
Suffering 237
Jennifer Cannon

26 Afterword: A Ritual for Resisting 242
*Michelle C. Chatman, LeeRay Costa, and
David W. Robinson-Morris*

Index *247*

PREFACE

At a historical moment when higher educational professionals are feeling overwhelmed by multiple attacks on higher education, growing social inequities, racial violence, political division, and the fallout from a global pandemic and multiple wars, this volume offers the personal stories and contemplative practices of a range of diverse contemplative practitioners, with the intent to bolster personal and professional well-being and transform academic institutions from the inside out. These essays – characterized by honesty, vulnerability, pain, and love – invite college and university professionals to show up as whole and full human beings in their work. Collectively, these essays serve as inspiration and guide for people who wish to transform colleges and universities into life-affirming and liberatory sites, where humans, in all of their multiple identities and commitments, may flourish while sustaining themselves in the long and difficult work of systems change.

Published ten years after the foundational text *Contemplative Practices in Higher Education: Powerful Methods to Transform Teaching and Learning* written by Daniel P. Barbezat and Mirabai Bush (2014), this volume shifts the frame to focus on the teachers and higher education professionals who are engaged in contemplative practice, rather than students. Through the centering of stories written by contemplative practitioners, the collection explores more deeply the notion that one's own contemplative journey is a critical foundation for undertaking transformational work in the academy and in the world, and that healing – personal, communal, institutional, and global – begins with oneself.

This book is an affirmation, guide, and resource for anyone working within higher education who seeks to make it more inclusive, humane, and just.

The volume's 24 essays will be of interest to higher education professionals who are already interested in and engaged with contemplative studies and contemplative practices, as well as those curious about contemplative approaches, including faculty, graduate students, staff/administrators, campus leaders, and community activists. The volume centers the stories, voices, and experiences of higher education professionals who have historically been marginalized within this context, especially people of color, and will be of particular interest to members of those groups. Additionally, the book will be of interest to students, providing insight into the motivations and struggles of their professors and university staff, and enabling them to understand these professionals as real people, fellow travelers, and compassionate beings committed to bettering the world and humanity. The 20+ practices offered in the volume will serve as a resource to readers including those already engaged in their own contemplative practices across a variety of traditions, cultures, and contexts, as well as those practitioners who have not yet engaged with the field of contemplative studies itself.

This book begins with an invocation that acknowledges and pays respect to the indigenous lands upon which our educational institutions are sited, and to the innumerable ways we are nourished by the earth in our pursuit of wholeness. The introduction, written by the volume's co-editors, provides a historical and theoretical context for the work, identifies some of the most pressing inequities within higher education and their negative impacts on well-being, and makes an argument for how and why contemplative practices, rooted in a wide range of cultural heritages, histories, and spiritual traditions, are needed more than ever. The remainder of the volume is organized into four main parts; each section includes a brief introduction written by one of the editors and a concluding, reflective essay written by a contemplative scholar who draws upon their unique personal history of contemplative practice and work in the academy to respond to the essays in their section.

The main chapters of the book are personal narratives, written in the first person, that share each author's engagement with contemplative practices as a form of transformative change within the academy. Each chapter concludes with a contemplative practice offered by the author, and an invitation to readers to engage with these practices in their professional work, their personal lives, and their community endeavors.

In Part I, *Ever Present and Interconnected*, authors share stories of how they courageously persist in academe in the face of oppression, inequity, anti-Blackness, and the legacies of colonial conquest. They discuss their diverse cultural, spiritual, and wisdom traditions and how these give shape to their unique and evolving contemplative identities that are foundational to wholeness and resistance. Brandon Hutchinson (Chapter 2) explores contemplative practices rooted in the everyday traditions of Black people, and the specific challenges she has faced as a Black woman in the academy. In Chapter 3, JuPong Lin draws on poetry, autoethnography, and qigong as she seeks to heal from her experiences as a displaced Taiwanese immigrant, and related internalized racism/colonialism, and intergenerational trauma. Alberto López Pulido (Chapter 4) challenges people of color and other marginalized people to recognize and embrace the disjunctures of our lives through the creation of personal "cajitas" (sacred boxes). In Chapter 5, Emerald Templeton uplifts Black feminism and fellowship (as evidenced in Black Christian faith traditions) as forms of refuge and sustenance in academic spaces. Co-authors Aizaiah Yong and Yohana Junker (Chapter 6) tell of their friendship and shared practices of Convivencia as crucial resources for navigating the multiple oppressions they experienced within Christian institutions of higher education as faculty of color. In her closing essay, Vaishali Mamgain (Chapter 7), employs the CourageRISE model to envision an educational system rooted in, and in service of community, and that celebrates global majority ontologies and imaginations.

In Part II, *Conjuring Transformation*, contributors provide insight into the various ways they "conjure," i.e., bring into being, embodied liberation and justice consciousness within institutional contexts that far too often deny the full humanity of higher education practitioners, especially those from historically marginalized groups. The rituals and practices they share highlight stillness, movement, space, intuitive knowing, and more as channels for refusing limitations and opening up new potentialities. In Chapter 8, Monika Son shares how her practice of sitting zazen has provided opportunities to investigate internalized oppression and habits of mind that reproduce institutional structures of harm, and offered a pathway toward internal transformation and "sensing into possibility." In Chapter Nine, dance professional Robin Raven Prichard offers the concept of body sovereignty, with its roots in Native American cultures, together with the practice of Contact Improvisation as potential avenues for transforming universities into more relational spaces. Drawing on her own Islamic practices and perspectives, Candice Salyers (Chapter 10) explores contemplative dance as a means of moving through resistance and toward individual and community care and well-being. In Chapter 11, Virginia Diaz Mendoza invites colleagues and students to slow down and open themselves up to new forms of knowing and being through the practice of creative envisioning. In Chapter 12, Emmanuelle Khoury charts the constellation of her journey into academe as an immigrant daughter from the Global South and the unique, spatial approach she brings to social work practice and pedagogy. Maria Hamilton Abegunde closes this section in Chapter 13, reminding us that the path toward wholeness and healing is not magic, but hard work that requires honesty, persistence, and being willing to engage with our deepest fears.

Between Parts II and III, we offer a moment of pause. Chapter 14 features a dialog between one of our editors, Michelle C. Chatman, and colleague Bradford Grant, who discuss how contemplative practices may serve as a healing resource for Black men dispirited by persistent racial oppression, and a path toward expanded self-awareness and self-acceptance for students and colleagues at Historically Black Colleges and Universities (HBCUs).

Part III, *Rhizomatic Awakenings,* explores subjectivity, the nature of becoming, and the multiple ways through which we conceive of ourselves and the world. Contributors invite us to enter onto their respective plateaus of awakening and, through their deep love and truth-telling, assist the reader in catalyzing their own rhizomatic awakenings. Phyllis Jeffers-Coly (Chapter 15) writes about her experience inhabiting the margins of the academy as a Black woman, communicating with the ancestors, and creating a "hush harbor" for the healing of Black people through her project Diasporic Soul. Chapter 16, co-authored by Zahra Ahmed, Anita Chari, and Becky Thompson, tells of their virtual gatherings during the COVID-19 pandemic to discuss teaching from a multiracial feminist perspective and their respective contemplative practices converging in the exploration of an embodied "sensing the field" practice. Lela Mosemghvdlishvili, in Chapter 17, shares a personal story of burnout that becomes a catalyst for leaving academe in pursuit of healing, and the discovery of Feeding Your Demons® that facilitates their return to the academy. In Chapter 18, Wendy Peterson-Boring writes about her experiences loving and caring for her son who is disabled, and how they inspire her to reimagine what justice, equity, and sustainability in higher education might look like. In his concluding essay (Chapter 19), Steven Thurston Oliver grapples with his own struggles for wholeness and well-being as a late-career, Black queer-identified man in higher education and reflects on the ways the individual essays have clarified aspects of his own contemplative journey.

In Part IV, *Liberatory Relationality: Cultivating Collective Compassion,* contributors document the challenging inner work that is foundational to transformative relationship building and structural change. This work can be painful and uncomfortable on many levels and is critical to disrupting white supremacy, racism, colonization, extractivism, and the multiple hierarchies that shape academe. Our authors tell of their own encounters with marginalization and devaluation, and their dedication to bringing into being a new vision of higher education characterized by self-reflexivity, critique, care, and compassion – for self and others. In Chapter 20, Renuka Gusain weaves together her experiences as an immigrant educator, her initial extractive orientation toward contemplative practice, and how the methodology of Racial Healing Circles transformed her work in the academy. Meika Loe (Chapter 21) invites colleagues and students to reimagine their (white supremacist) notions of success and wholeness through the creation of accountable communities of care and beloved community. In Chapter 22, Deb Spragg writes as a white woman seeking to disrupt white dominance in academic culture and offers a practice called *Why am I talking?* (W.A.I.T.) that engages white colleagues in self-reflection on unearned privilege as a foundation for change. Discussing the harms of white supremacy as she has experienced them as a woman of color, Ericka Echavarria (Chapter 23) offers contemplative emergence as an integrated practice that has helped her to better understand collective trauma, marshal her values as resources, and sustain resilience in stewarding justice. In Chapter 24, Michael Yellow Bird (Indigenous) and Holly Hatton (white) write about their cross-racial, decolonial mentoring relationship, grounded in the lessons that Yellow Bird learned from his great-grandfather, Plenty Fox, an Arikara holy man; drawing upon decolonized contemplative practices they seek to disrupt settler power and logic in the academy. In her closing essay (Chapter 25), Jennifer Cannon argues that contemplative practices are more important than ever as we witness global systems of domination and the profound suffering of the world. We must trust in contemplative practices and the knowledge they provide in order to reclaim humane values, engage in ethical action, and manifest justice in the academy and beyond.

An Afterword concludes the volume, offering a call to action, a ritual for blessing, and an invitation to higher ed professionals to carry this work forward into their own institutional spaces through contemplative communities of practice.

ACKNOWLEDGMENTS

An acknowledgments page is an insufficient representation of our immense gratitude for the many people who have helped make this volume possible, and for those who have taught us and accompanied us on our contemplative journeys in this plane and beyond. A deep bow of gratitude to each one of you.

Every project first needs a vision and a champion. Thank you to Karolyn Kinane for being that person, for your fidelity to advancing contemplative practice and community, and for your friendship.

This project would have been impossible without our contributors, their willingness to be vulnerable and honest in sharing their stories, and their commitment to bringing into being a more just and loving educational system.

We extend deep bows of gratitude to Mirabai Bush, the Center for Contemplative Mind in Society (CMind), and too many others to name. CMind was an energetic alembic that gathered us all together under the mantle of transforming society through contemplative practice. *We, and the globe, are indebted to Mirabai Bush, Daniel Barbezat, Arthur Zajonc, and their colleagues for the vision of integrating contemplative awareness into contemporary life toward the creation of a more just, compassionate, and reflective society.* We would particularly like to thank Maia Duerr, a former CMind staffer, who was largely responsible for creating the Tree of Contemplative Practices image that has given so many of us a generative way of thinking about the diversity of contemplative practices.

We would like to acknowledge Sabiyha Prince whose stunning artwork graces our book cover.

Michelle would like to thank The Acosta Institute Restored Warrior Fellowship for their support of her summer writing time.

LeeRay would like to thank Hollins University for a Provost Summer Research Award in support of this project.

David would like to thank the friends of The REImaginelution, The Center for the Human Spirit and Radical Reimagining, and The Institute for Black Intellectual and Cultural Life at Dartmouth College for their support of this project.

And most importantly, we would like to thank the students, faculty, and staff of higher educational institutions in the United States and globally who model the way of contemplative justice, transformative social action, and educational becoming.

MEET THE CONTRIBUTORS

Editors

Michelle C. Chatman is a cultural anthropologist, community ritualist, vocalist, educator, and contemplative practitioner. She is Associate Professor in the Crime, Justice, and Security Studies Program at The University of the District of Columbia where she also serves as Founding Director of the Mindful and Courageous Action (MICA) Lab which advances community-engaged research and training on culturally relevant mindfulness and contemplative approaches. She is committed to amplifying healing-centered approaches that enable us to create organizations, systems, and structures of justice, liberated learning, and equitable thriving.

LeeRay Costa is a lifelong contemplative practitioner and has been actively integrating contemplative practices into her teaching, research, and community work since 2012. Trained as a feminist cultural anthropologist, she is Executive Director of Leadership Studies and the Batten Leadership Institute, and Professor of Gender and Women's Studies/Anthropology at Hollins University, and the Co-founder of Girls Rock Roanoke (a youth empowerment non-profit). Her current interests include engaging spirituality, contemplative practices, and creative expression in the service of human flourishing, planetary healing, and transformative social change.

David W. Robinson-Morris is a scholar, activist, author, philosopher, human rights advocate, educator, organizer, DEI practitioner, higher education administrator, and student of contemplative practices. At the writing, Robinson-Morris was appointed the inaugural Executive Director of the Institute for Black Intellectual and Cultural Life at Dartmouth College. He is the Founder of The REImaginelution, a strategic consultant firm working to engender freedom of the human spirit and catalyze the power of the imagination to reweave organizations, systems, and the world toward collective healing and liberation. David served as the final Executive Director in service to the Center for Contemplative Mind in Society (CMind). He is the author of a research monograph titled, *Ubuntu and Buddhism in Higher Education: An Ontological (Re)Thinking* (2019, Routledge).

Contributors

Maria Hamilton Abegunde began studying and practicing Contemplative Practices over 40 years ago and continues to integrate them in her research, writing, teaching, and service to multiple communities. You may read her recent contemplative writing in *North Meridian Review; ASHE: Ritual Poetics in African Diasporic Expression*, and *Black Joy Unbound*.

Zahra Ahmed is a scholar-activist who has worked in community-based educational spaces for over 20 years. She currently serves as Assistant Professor of Politics at St. Mary's College of California where she studies social justice movement building and pedagogical practices that facilitate social action among students and people of color.

Denise Cadeau is Chair of the Department of Anishinaabe (Native American) Studies, which she helped launch in 2016, at Keweenaw Bay Ojibwa Community College in L'Anse, Michigan. Prior to serving as Chair, Denise was the Dean of Student Services at KBOCC.

Jen Cannon is a scholar of critical and contemplative pedagogies, embodied feminism, decolonial epistemologies, and emancipatory education. Her research falls within Critical Mindfulness Studies and includes models for liberatory mindfulness. Jennifer has taught as a lecturer at UMass Amherst, Westfield State University, and as adjunct faculty at Southern New Hampshire University.

Anita Chari is a political theorist, somatic practitioner, and Associate Professor of Political Science at the University of Oregon. She is the author of *A Political Economy of the Senses* (2015) and *A User's Manual to Claire Fontaine* (2024), and is co-founder of the organization Embodying Your Curriculum™.

Virginia Diaz-Mendoza has been a member of the Counseling Faculty in the SEEK Department at John Jay College of Criminal Justice – CUNY for over 20 years. She designs trauma-informed, anti-racist, anti-colonial, culturally relevant educational experiences for those seeking to engage in individual, social, and global change.

Ericka Echavarria, JD LMSW, is a dedicated and experienced contemplative leader with a strong focus on building capacity and resilience in social justice workers. Her work centers on supporting transformative change within social justice workers, thereby promoting more mindful, embodied, and justice-focused service to reduce harm to vulnerable communities.

Bradford C. Grant is Professor of Architecture and Interim Chair of the Department of Architecture of the College of Engineering and Architecture at Howard University. As a registered architect and a distinguished educator, he has extensive experience in universal design, contemplative practices in design education, and environmental justice in architecture.

Renuka Gusain is a global citizen and first-generation college graduate. Raised in different countries, Gusain has taught at universities in India, Brazil, and the United States. She has an MA and MPhil from the University of Delhi, India, and a PhD from Wayne State University. She co-edited *Global Humanities Reader: Vol 2* (2022).

Holly Hatton is Associate Professor and Extension Specialist in the Child, Youth, and Family Studies Department at the University of Nebraska-Lincoln. Holly's scholarship focuses on the use of reflective practice, mindfulness, compassion, and social-emotional learning drawing upon community-based participatory methods. She is committed to addressing issues of systemic inequities.

Brandon LA Hutchinson is Associate Professor of English, Affiliate Faculty in the Women and Gender Studies Department, and co-steers the Africana Studies minor. Because she believes learning about our patterns and behaviors is ongoing, Brandon roots her facilitation style in a slow process utilizing community building and reflection methods.

Phyllis M. Jeffers-Coly (CYT – 600 hour) is the Founder of Diasporic Soul, which offers heritage and healing experiences that integrate culture and contemplative practices. She is the author of *We Got Soul, We Can Heal: Overcoming Racial Trauma Through Leadership, Community and Resilience* and currently serves as the Assistant Director of the HBCU Radio Preservation Project.

Yohana Agra Junker (she/hers) is Assistant Professor of Art, Religion, and Culture at Claremont School of Theology. As an ongoing learner of ancient healing modalities, she investigates how artists, healers, and spiritual leaders create sacred spaces to reclaim our sense of agency even in the face of impossibility.

Emmanuelle Khoury is a licensed professional social worker, researcher, and professor with a particular focus on care, language, and body as situated interactions that influence therapeutic relationships and understandings of self as a helping professional. She assists colleagues in developing engaged and contemplative pedagogies, and transformative teaching and learning approaches.

JuPong Lin draws on Taiwanese ancestral traditions in socially engaged art that honors our beloved Earth. She is a poet for the *Writing the Land* project and works to transform local food systems. She teaches at Goddard College and is an environmental studies PhD candidate at Antioch University New England.

April E. Lindala, MFA and PhD, is Professor of Native American Studies at Northern Michigan University. She was Director of the Center for Native American Studies for 13 years. Lindala was a finalist for the Upper Peninsula Poet Laureate in 2021. Lindala is a bead artist and powwow dancer.

Meika Loe is Professor of Sociology, Women's Studies, and LGBTQ Studies at Colgate University. In her courses on health, the life course, death, and dying, she prioritizes staying human, redefining student notions of success, interrupting historical and generational silences, building, centering, and sustaining community care, and connecting public issues to how we live our lives.

Vaishali Mamgain is Associate Professor of Economics and Director of the Center for Compassion at the University of Southern Maine. She is passionate about decolonizing contemplative practice. A leader in equity training, she helps organizations create compassionate and inclusive spaces. In 2017, she completed a three-year meditation retreat.

L. (Lela) Mosemghvdlishvili (they/she) is Contemplative Educator working on the intersections of innovation, wisdom traditions, and embodied practices. At the University of Amsterdam, Lela is committed to bringing whole-student-cantered methods of teaching to higher education and offers an introductory course in Contemplative Pedagogy to lecturers at their university.

Steven Thurston Oliver, Professor of Education and Department Chair of Secondary and Higher Education at Salem State University, is a sociologist whose research and expertise focus on using Contemplative Pedagogy in K-12 teacher preparation and higher education programs as a catalyst for cultivating greater capacity to engage across human differences.

Wendy Petersen-Boring, Associate Professor of History at Willamette University, teaches courses in medieval history, contemplative studies, and women and gender studies and co-directs *The Conversation Project*. Her publications include *Teaching Sustainability: Perspectives from the Humanities and Social Sciences* and essays in theology, spirituality, food justice, and environmental history.

Robin Raven Prichard's least favorite comment as a student was "your problem is that you think too much: you need to shut up and dance." She has spent more than two decades as a dance professor proving that thinking is integral to dance and that dancers should never be quiet.

Alberto López Pulido is Founding Chair and Professor of Ethnic Studies at the University of San Diego. His work seeks to develop and define a community epistemology for communities of color that draws from contemplative practices.

Candice Salyers is Assistant Professor of Dance at The University of Southern Mississippi. Her work engages dance performance as humanitarian service and has been honored with an Alma Bucovaz Award for Urban Service, as well as Choreographic and Solo Performance Fellowships from Massachusetts Cultural Council and Mississippi Arts Commission.

Cueponcaxochitl D. Moreno Sandoval (Zacateco/Xicana/Izkalohteka Nations) (she/they) is Associate Professor of Native American and Mexican Indigenous Studies in the Ethnic Studies Department at Stanislaus State. Their most recent publication is *Planting Son Jarocho Fandango: A Culturally Decolonizing Pedagogy in Ethnic Studies* with undergraduate students as co-authors.

Monika L. Son's current project, Ser Entero, supports women and (BIWOC) who are reclaiming their wholeness – the parts of themselves that have been unseen, rejected, invisible, or dark. She is inspired by women who are choosing to uplift radical love, compassion, connection, and healing to transform the spaces they impact.

Deb Spragg (she/her/hers) is Associate Professor in the Department of Graduate Expressive Therapies at Lesley University, where she serves as the faculty director for clinical instructors. Deb brings contemplative and arts-based inquiry to anti-oppressive pedagogy and supervision and has been involved in a variety of cross-university social justice initiatives.

Emerald Templeton is a seasoned educator and public servant with experience in higher education, K12, and local government programs. Her praxis combines scholarship and practical wisdom informed by Black feminisms and liberatory frameworks.

Becky Thompson, MA, PhD, is a scholar, activist, poet, and yogi and the author of several books including *To Speak in Salt*; *Teaching with Tenderness: Toward an Embodied Practice*; and *Zero is the Whole I Fall into at Night*. She has adored working with Zahra and Anita on this chapter.

Michael Yellow Bird, PhD, is Dean and Professor, Faculty of Social Work, University of Manitoba, and is a member of the Mandan, Hidatsa, and Arikara Nation in North Dakota. His research focuses on colonization, decolonization, healthy Indigenous aging, mindfulness, Arikara ethnobotany and traditional agriculture, and the significance of Rez dogs.

Aizaiah G. Yong (he/him) serves as Assistant Professor of Spirituality at the Claremont School of Theology. He is a Facilitator in Engaged Compassion and an Internal Family Systems Practitioner. Growing up in a multiracial and immigrant family, he is committed to addressing social oppression with presence, passion, and peace.

1

INTRODUCTION

Contemplative Practice Is an Act of Resistance

Michelle C. Chatman, LeeRay Costa, and David W. Robinson-Morris

Higher education is in a fragile state, and its future contested as the human collective undergoes a political, social, and ontological turn. Caught up within this precarious system are faculty, staff, and administrators, exhausted by the unrelenting pressures intensified during the coronavirus disease 2019 (COVID-19) global pandemic and further exacerbated by the extrajudicial murders of Black and Brown human beings at the hands of American law enforcement. The resulting nationwide "racial reckoning" combined with a vitriolic political environment has heightened fears and fueled greater social division within and beyond higher education. Through various channels, we heard from friends and colleagues across the country who were being asked to maintain an impossible sense of normalcy amid global death and dying, to provide extra care and compassion for their students, and to quickly transition their teaching to virtual apparatuses—all while enduring their own anxieties, grief, and physical and mental health concerns. The despair was so palpable that David Robinson-Morris (coeditor of this volume and then-executive director of The Center for Contemplative Mind in Society) hosted a 2022 web series entitled "Healing Higher Ed" that recognized and named the multiple and intersectional affronts with which faculty, staff, and students were being assaulted. The series offered contemplative practices that were meant to soothe the soul, catalyze healing, and bring each of us back home to ourselves amid global chaos.

As the current volume began to take shape, we further endured the grief and suffering of multiple global wars, famine and hunger, unbridled violence, death, and what appears to be the implosion of systems writ large. And yet, we have also experienced hope through the glimmering eyes of

DOI: 10.4324/9781003416777-1

our students actively advocating for justice, peace, and institutional accountability in the name of our shared humanity. Clearly, those of us within higher education and all of us in the human family are craving the balms of healing, peace, and humanity-centered systemic transformation.

Contemplative practices are acts of resistance that sustain us and wrest us away, however fleetingly, from the fast-paced, demanding, dehumanizing nature of the world. Contemplative practice allows us to *be* free, to *be* healing, to *be* human, to *be* filled, to *be* peace, to *be* joy, and to *be* at home with ourselves so that we can *do* justice. To say this another way, contemplative practices allow us to experience freedom and know liberation, so that we can be in right relationship with ourselves and others in pursuit of wholeness. Perhaps, we need time-space-place to sit with our anger, befriend our grief, be still, and invite the generous information gleaned from our practice(s) to inform our desire for justice and transformation.

There is no magic fix. We want to state plainly that the transformative power of contemplative practice requires ongoing, lifelong applications of intention, awareness, commitment, introspection, understanding, stillness, surrender, and conscious action. The process of transformation is arduous, yet unlike the university it might just save your life. As Alexis Pauline Gumbs wrote:

> The university was not created to save my life. The university is not about the preservation of a bright brown body. The university will use me alive and use me dead. The university does not intend to love me. The university does not know how to love me. The university in fact, does not love me. But the universe does.
>
> *(2012, para. 13)*

Gumbs' words resonate with many of the contributions in this volume. They also surface a critical question: *Why do we hold the expectation that the university or any system of domination, for that matter, will love us, save our lives, or even care about the quality of one's life over the institution's or system's need for production and outputs?* Indeed, from a systems perspective, higher education was not created to save our lives. Perhaps *we* were created to save ourselves and one another, to shape our students, and to alter our beingness. It could be that higher education was created to bring us—we, kindreds of spirit, who need to find one another—into collective, energetic communion to create road maps to home and community.

Contemplative Practices and Acts of Resistance in Higher Education: Narratives Toward Wholeness invites readers on a journey to develop practices, methods, and rituals that facilitate becoming and being whole. We invite you, through the pages of this volume, to discover avenues toward wholeness and methods to bring the fullness of our humanity into our work and workplaces. Collectively, our desire is that these narratives serve as inspiration and guides for people who wish to transform colleges and universities into life-affirming and liberatory ecosystems that live up to their professed values where humans, in all of their diverse identities and commitments, may flourish while sustaining themselves in the long and difficult work of systems change (Robinson-Morris, 2018).

An Invitation Home

We invite you to come home.

As James Baldwin (1956/2013) reminds us, "… home is not a place but an irrevocable condition" (p. 92). Contemplative practices allow us to come home to ourselves by quieting the mind to settle back into the body, by acknowledging our interconnectedness—impermanence—imperceptibility, and transmuting our suffering into contemplative justice.

Our notions of home, like some physical homes, are broken. It is at home where we learn all virtues and vices, where we learn to experience, understand, and develop ideas of what love is and most often what it ain't. It is at home—the physical homes we grew up in, survived, escaped, and/or remain in fugitivity from—where we learned our value, internalized our worth, and took ownership of narratives of who we were meant to be by very human and incomplete people who loved us to the best of their ability. It is the safety of home where we retreat to heal.

In the full comfort of home, we work to heal our physical, mental, emotional, spiritual, and intellectual identities in the hope of realizing wholeness and reemerging into the world in our fullness. In a talk at the Connecticut Forum (Morrison, 2001), author-Ancestor Toni Morrison remarked, "Sometimes you do not survive whole, but you survive in part. But the grandeur of life is that attempt. It is not about the solution. It is about being as fearless as one can and behaving as beautifully as one can." What Morrison and this volume's contributors provide for each of us is a glimpse into being human; a glimpse into the rhizomatic process of healing and becoming whole while relishing in the not so simple beauty of survival, growth, and transformation. Morrison reminds us to release the outcome and relish in the journey; the process of surviving, healing, and becoming—the human condition.

We invite you to consciously venture into the process of transformation and healing. In the spirit of Howard Thurman (1980), we invite you to become still enough to awaken the sound of the genuine within. Contemplative practice invites us to illuminate that which is immutable within us. We invite you to celebrate, in Lucille Clifton's words, that you have survived "everything that has tried to kill [you], but has failed" (Clifton, 2012, p. 427).

In the spirit of contemplation, we invite you now to participate in a brief practice. As you read the meditation, imagine that there are others reading these words and engaging in this practice alongside you. Wherever you find yourself at this moment, we invite you to

> Inhale with gratitude and exhale with gladness.
> Take note of your interior – the feelings, sensations, and thoughts that are arising now.
> Slowly scan your environment by allowing your senses to wander the space you are in.
> Acknowledge earth, stars, water, and sky in a way that feels right for you—a nod, smile, dance.
> Imagine the love of your ancestors and the yet born enveloping you.
> Inhale with spaciousness and exhale with surrender.
> Bring awareness to the present moment.
> Like water, let the feelings flow.
> Invite curiosity, extend kindness.
> Allow your body to be at ease.
> Give thanks.

Being and Practice, Being as Practice

Welcome. The words that you will read in this volume contain truth(s), are powerful, and have been woven together to form narratives—the stories that speak and unspeak us in every moment of life. We, the editors and the contributors, have set out on a mission to share, demystify, and educate about the transformative acts of coming to self through contemplative practice. We have centered this volume on higher education—the location of teaching, learning, producing, and engaging in scholarship that serve as temples of human becoming. These beautiful campuses of concentrated creative energy, like all things, are balanced by a shadow aspect. You will read critiques of higher education as a system in this volume, and you will read simultaneously of the love of higher education as difficult but magical sites of being and becoming. This volume heightens awareness of both the light and the shadow of laboring within institutions of higher learning and extends the common characteristics and experiences of individual institutions to the larger system of higher education. Today, higher education is a greatly contested space and yet, for many, remains a site of hope and possibility for the students it educates and the society it influences. Conversely, there are faculty and staff who, laboring under the weight of impossible expectations, unrealistic workloads, and compassion fatigue, remain for their students due to an abiding belief in the power of the educational endeavor. Many faculty, staff, and even our students are in institutional survival mode while experiencing the spectrum of the human experience in their daily lives. Contemplative practices provide one possible form of healing and resisting the societal, institutional, and personal anguish that threatens to overtake us. Contemplative practice is an act of resistance.

Contemplative practitioners are both the heart of this book and our focus as fellow contemplative sojourners. In these narratives, contributors share the role of contemplative practice(s) in their own lives—professional and personal—and how these practices sustain them while working to transform themselves and deeply entrenched inequities. Each chapter concludes with an offering of a contemplative practice by the author, which is meant to provide potential entry points for readers and fellow higher education professionals to deepen their own awareness and growth.

Moving away from Western mindfulness and capitalist-informed understandings of contemplative practice, the practices herein seek to incite critical reflection and stretch our collective thinking of contemplative practice beyond tools of productivity, efficiency, and techniques for managing stress and persisting within exploitative environments (Fleming et al., 2022). As discussed by some of the contributors to this volume, we must move beyond the commodified and extractivist orientation of contemplative practice (see chapters by Gusain and Cannon). While contemplative practice is a method, we understand method to be an ontological decision (Robinson-Morris, 2019). Therefore, contemplative practice is an ontoepistemology—a chosen way of being-knowing-doing in the world. We understand contemplative practices as thresholds of embodied understanding and universal connectivity that allow us to cultivate necessary awareness and self-reflection for our interactions with others. These practices, we hope, will manifest compassion, care, and healing toward ourselves and in our professional relationships with students and colleagues.

Be-Do-Know

While we encourage you to explore the practices offered herein, we also want to emphasize the importance of sustained engagement before sharing them with students or others. We invite you to *be* with the practices, to *do* or actively engage with and grapple with what arises during the practices so that you may come to *know* the practice—and yourself—in a deeper or new way *before* placing these practices in service to your teaching, leading, service, research, and other forms of work. This suggestion extends from our disagreement with "instant mindfulness" trends, where one can simply enact practices they learned in a workshop or borrowed from a text without depth or understanding what the practice may conjure in and up for the practitioner.

Challenging notions of sitting on one's pillow or chanting ancient mantras, contemplative practices can be understood not only as the formal skills developed through gurus, certified courses, or training programs but also as the potent, rich moments and encounters from your own cultural or familial context. As some of the contributors share, early experiences like the repetitive meditation of cooking with family members (Hutchinson) are potent for the cultivation of inner awareness. Contemplative practices are living engagements and evolving understandings of what it might mean to be at home, human, interconnected, and whole. Unscripted and unrehearsed, these inherent practices can also be messy, organic, and true. These are the practice gems that help cultivate our inner vulnerability and courage; necessary tools as we work to ease suffering and assist the academy in living up to its professed highest ideals. Our sincerest hope is that you will delve into what is authentic to your own experience with contemplative practices and inner approaches. As you be-do-know with the practices contained in this volume, we encourage you to consider: What is the body of wisdom and experience from which you draw that revives and grounds you? What are the teachings and ways of being that enable you to challenge power imbalances, dehumanization, and ecological degradation? It is from those wells of wisdom and storehouses of power you will need to draw, and to return again and again, to do the critical work needed in this moment—and in each moment.

A Deeper Look: Meeting the Moment

Understanding the nature of institutions and systems, we come to know that fragmentation facilitated by confusion, chaos, and any number of incomprehensible moving parts is their modus operandi. For the humans who inhabit these systems, it means that complete systemic subjugation requires our brokenness and feeds off of our own fragmentation. Becoming whole in the face of oppressive fragmentation and dehumanization is an act of courageous resistance.

For many, the love of theory, of teaching, learning, researching, and scholarship that birthed our commitment to higher education has been overshadowed by the 'work' of the institution—serving on committees, interacting with difficult faculty colleagues, serving students with multiple needs, responding to external political pressures, and the politico-intellectual olympic pursuit of the golden ring of tenure. In short, educational institutions have often become sites of trauma and dehumanization rather than locations for healing and wholeness.[1]

Stefano Harvey and Fred Moten write in *The Undercommons: Fugitive Planning and Black Study* (2013) warning:

> The university needs what she bears but cannot bear what she brings. And on top of all that, she disappears. She disappears into the underground, the downlow low-down maroon community of the university, into the *undercommons of enlightenment*, where the work gets done, where the work gets subverted, where the revolution is still black, still strong.
>
> *(p. 26)*

This is the experience of many of our contributors to this volume. There is a general recognition that the arduous work of institutional transformation is necessary but unwelcomed by those in power. Pushing the work of transformation upon a system or institution that will only thrust it off is onto-epistemological death that, perhaps, is the pursuit of an ultimate liberation. That is to say, our experiences have taught us that to ask institutions or systems to align with the values they profess, and actively engage in its transformation, is present danger and sure erasure. This is the risk of transformative resistance. Subverting this figurative and sometimes literal death[2] requires us all to find and come home to ourselves in the stillness of being—to cope, manage, and reimagine ourselves as otherwise in the midst of chaos.

The contemporary context of institutions of higher education has illuminated the oppressive nature, unhealthy work practices, and stresses of higher education institutions that were intensified by the COVID-19 pandemic and every system's unpreparedness to deal with the multiple crises that remain present even today. For example, as we write in April 2024, university administrators and governing boards across the country are responding to peaceful student protests, solidarity rallies, and the exercise of first-amendment rights with aggression, violence, militarization, and even threats to call in the National Guard. Faculty and staff along with students have been arrested and seriously injured at the hands of police. Simultaneously, higher education and academic freedom are under attack by conservative politicians who have passed or introduced anti-DEI legislation in 30 states, resulting in the elimination of entire units on college campuses and the reversal of decades of progress on equity and inclusion. We have also seen university presidents (the majority of them women and women of color) interrogated in congressional hearings not unlike the political theater of the McCarthy era, resulting in the loss of their leadership positions and declining public belief in the value of higher education.

These events come on the heels of the supposed racial reckoning of 2020 after the murder of George Floyd at the hands of law enforcement, which forced an examination of every American institution and materialized indictments of racism, widespread inequity, and unbridled oppression—the bedrock of our American "democracy." Let us say this a different way, the country's racial reckoning coupled with COVID-19 brought to the forefront higher education's systemic legacies of white supremacy including the physical, emotional, and spiritual violence against people of color and marginalized persons within educational spaces. Not that working in the academy was not difficult before, but the global moments of death, dying, and awareness each of us experienced personally while working within systems that were operating "as usual" made it increasingly difficult to maintain one's own sense of well-being while simultaneously endeavoring both to support the well-being of one's students and colleagues and alchemize institutional inequities.

As numerous scholars and journalists have observed, these multiple stressors have converged, exacerbating the ill health and burnout of higher ed professionals (Halat et al., 2023; Pope-Ruark, 2022). As our contributor Emerald Templeton writes "labor is overextended in this field because 'higher education professionals have stress levels that rival those of emergency room doctors and nurses'" (citing Beer et al., 2015, p. 163). This has led to what some have labeled the Great Disengagement, the Great Resignation, and the Big Quit (Doležal, 2022; McClure & Fryar, 2022).

How might we address these challenges in order to protect employee well-being and retain those individuals who are committed to creating a more humane and inclusive higher education? The contributors to this volume offer their experience and wisdom working in complex, oppressive institutions and provide insights on how they find sustenance, inspiration, and community in their personal and collective contemplative practices. The practices described in this volume serve as a potent means of navigating the turbulence of the times, the slowness of social change, the unending pursuit of liberatory decolonization, and the daunting demands on mind, body, and spirit—of finding and coming home to self and becoming whole. More importantly, they provide relief to our overwrought nervous systems and help to transform trauma into fuel for systemic transfiguration. As individuals across higher education seek ways to deal with external pressures that are forcing institutional change, these collected stories and practices invite us to engage and reengage with the transformative potential of contemplative practices in intentional ways—to, in the words of Octavia Butler, "shape change" (1993) and catalyze transfiguration.

History of the Project

The seed of this volume was planted by contemplative educator and consultant, Dr. Karolyn Kinane. Having long been involved with the Center for Contemplative Mind in Society (CMind) and having served as Associate Director of Pedagogy and Faculty Engagement at the Contemplative Sciences Center at the University of Virginia, Karolyn was interested in developing a follow-up book to Daniel Barbezat and Mirabai Bush's landmark text *Contemplative Practices in Higher Education: Powerful Methods to Transform Teaching and Learning* (Barbezat & Bush, 2014). For many university faculty, this was a radical book that invited them to bring contemplation and reflection into their pedagogy and their interaction with students.

As initially imagined, our book would take into account significant developments within the field of contemplative studies over the past few decades, including the imperative that practitioners grapple with the white supremacy, racism, and other multiple oppressions that have shaped both contemplative studies and higher education more broadly. Karolyn reached out to fellow contemplative educators Dr. LeeRay Costa, Dr. Michelle C. Chatman, and Dr. David W. Robinson-Morris and together we imagined possibilities. As the vision of the book evolved, however, we became increasingly interested in how higher education professionals draw upon contemplative practices to sustain their commitment to and practice of institutional transformation amid a confluence of crises and the unrelenting demands they face. As the complexities of these issues showed up in our own lives and institutions, Karolyn made the difficult decision to step away from the project, entrusting the three of us to carry it forward to completion. We remain deeply indebted to Karolyn for breathing life into this book project and shepherding it in its early stages, and we are grateful for her vision of a more humane and just academy.

The initial working title of this volume was "Showing Up in Our Fullness" and was meant to provide a textual space for university professionals to explore the ways that higher education does and does not encourage us to show up as the complex, multiple, diverse humans that we are, and the ways that contemplative practices aid us in reclaiming, asserting, and living into that fullness. Thus, this phrase appears in some of the individual essays. Although our book title has since changed, our commitment to creating space for us all to live into our fullness amid what are too often hostile, harmful, and hierarchical spaces remains. We hope that this volume will serve as inspiration for others to publish additional volumes centering the voices of contemplative practitioners within higher education.

Stories from the Editors

How did we, the editors, come to this work? What is our relationship to contemplative practices and transformational change in higher education? While our initial plan included each of us writing our own chapter, upon receiving so many powerful submissions we made the decision to prioritize the voices and stories of our colleagues. Thus, in this section we each briefly share insights into what compels and sustains us in the arduous work of systems change.

Michelle C. Chatman

Teaching has always felt to me like sacred work, a chance to nurture students' holistic growth (Chatman, 2019). My undergraduate years at UDC were incredibly formative, so when the opportunity to teach there arose, I was ecstatic. I wanted to challenge my students' perceptions about the "other" and deepen their understanding of our shared humanity through anthropology. My personal mission was to dismantle stereotypes and negative perceptions about Africa and its people, shedding light on how colonization, racism, and current systems of oppression perpetuate these harmful ideas and keep us disconnected from one another.

In my early years as a faculty member, I was energized by my work but also faced challenges. Managing a four-course teaching load, supporting diverse student needs, navigating faculty dynamics, and understanding the unwritten rules of the academic hierarchy was exhausting. Just months into my appointment, I found myself in a conflict with a senior faculty member. Despite my attempts at reconciliation, they were vehemently denied. They refused to speak to or even look at me. Our prior collegiality abruptly ended, and whenever I saw them on campus, my body bristled with trauma. Feeling betrayed, we never found our way back to each other. Yet, this conflict inspired a deep reflection on my part, an examination of the ways in which I needed to emotionally and spiritually fortify myself and remain cognizant of the ways that I, too, cause harm.

No formal institutional support was provided to help me process or persist through this painful experience that occurred so early in my academic career. I had to figure it out on my own as many are left to do. I turned to contemplative practices with which I was most familiar, those rooted in Black culture and African spirituality. Prayer, journaling, communing with nature, music, and rituals helped me expel the pain and heaviness accumulating in my body. To ground myself, I created a small altar on my desk: a candle, flowers, incense, and photos of my ancestors. Small icons of the Yoruba divinities and a tabletop water fountain soothed and reassured me. Eventually my office became the place where students and colleagues came to decompress and rest from the stressors they were facing in higher education.

My spiritual family, close kin, therapist, and CMIND colleagues provided much-needed solace. The CMIND/ACMHE Summer Sessions, in particular, allowed me to cultivate meaningful connections with other higher education professionals of like mind. As we learned, shared meals, living quarters, and practices together, we restored ourselves. Our annual talent shows and karaoke nights at Fitzwilly's (shout out to Earth, Wind, and Fire!) in downtown Northampton, Massachusetts, were pure bliss, reminding us that joy is a radical contemplative practice!

Academia can be alienating and trauma-inducing for people of color and other marginalized identities. Unfortunately, even our beloved Historically Black Colleges and Universities (HBCUs) often mirror the oppressive hierarchies and harms of predominantly white institutions. As much as I love being part of the higher education ecosystem, its adversarial and transactional nature, a carryover of our colonial past, often breeds mistrust, toxicity, and abuse. Rather than addressing these issues, we normalize and perpetuate them. Endemic to the racial hierarchy that dominates broader US society and higher education are the ways in which white supremacy culture shapes behavior that reinscribes the false hierarchy (Christopher, 2022; Okun, 2001). To liberate higher education, we must acknowledge our complicity in its issues and cultivate the courage and collective will to dismantle harmful practices. Faculty need emotional maturity to foster positive relationships and manage conflicts, ensuring that our personal wounds do not negatively impact our teaching and interactions with students and colleagues. To heal academia, we must center ways of being that invite deeper self-awareness, authentic relationality, and truth. This is the only way we will transmute the individual and collective racial trauma we have sustained (Menakem, 2017).

It is not easy to live as a healed and free Black woman in any US institution. This nation was literally established upon the dehumanization and brutal subjugation of Black female bodies. The historic and contemporary trauma we continue to face divorces us from our true nature to honor and serve one another. Contemplative practices, rooted in anti-racist, liberatory community and collective action, help me heal and keep an open heart. They allow me to show up in academia in authentic relationality with myself and others, living from a place of courageous joy. This is the basis upon which my teaching, faculty development, community healing, and social justice work rest.

Recently, I saw my colleague with whom I'd had the conflict years ago as I was shopping in Costco. I'm unsure if she saw me. Immediately, I felt my face brighten and smile. My body was at ease. I silently extended them loving kindness. My ancestors were pleased. I wish this healing for all in higher education and beyond. I truly believe that contemplative practices can support us in this pursuit.

LeeRay Costa

Becoming an academic was not what my parents envisioned for me. As much as they valued education as an avenue toward desired class mobility, it was also a path that created distance and misunderstanding between us as I became increasingly socialized into academic culture. I loved learning, and as an undergraduate, I embraced the idea that by becoming a professor I would never have to stop learning, and I could share that learning with others. Except for my whiteness, my identities (working class, first-generation, spiritual, woman) were not optimal for "success" in the secular, elite academy. In order to make it, I learned how to conform, to hide my shame and imposter syndrome, and to wear overwork and perfectionism as badges of honor, even when it meant severing important parts of myself, primary among them, my body and spirit. This distancing and separation pose a specific problem for white folks like me whose socialized disembodiment and dispiritedness have enabled 400+ years of violence and the entrenchment of white supremacy, which manifests in higher education in numerous ways. I learned to endure sexism, diminishment, and hazing by graduate school faculty, journal reviewers, select colleagues, and a few administrators who refused to address bullying or conflict among our colleagues, even as I continued to strive for reaching every benchmark in the academic hierarchy.

My undergraduate honors thesis, which explored whether sociologists who were also members of the spiritual communities they studied could do rigorous, "objective" analysis, became a harbinger of the divided self I would eventually be forced to confront (Costa, 2018; Palmer, 2009). It took a panic attack, hospitalization, and a spiritual crisis for me to intentionally shift how I work in higher education and to prioritize my own wholeness.

Finding CMind and fellow contemplative teachers felt heaven-sent. Here was a community in which my lifelong contemplative practices and interest in spirituality were understood as *central* to being and knowing. For me, prayer, meditation, journaling, walking, mushroom hunting, making earth altars, art, yoga, and kirtan are grounding practices that slow down time, and open space for deep reflection and self-inquiry. This inner work has been essential both to my well-being and wholeness and to my efforts to live my commitments to equity, antiracism, and justice in the academy because, as Truesdell et al. (2018) assert, we cannot intellectualize our way out of the problem of whiteness or the necessity of antiracist work (see also Magee, 2019; Williams et al., 2016).

As fraught as my own experiences in the academy have been, they pale in comparison to those of BIPOC and other marginalized colleagues, as documented in our contributor essays, and in numerous other books, blogs, and LACRELA webinars.[3] Through my ongoing contemplative journey and in studying the work of women of color contemplatives in particular (e.g., Anzaldúa, 2002; Fernandes, 2003; Maparyan, 2012; Rendón, 2014), I have learned that I must be willing to confront my own complicity (intended or not) in the multiple harms committed within the academic institutions I am part of, to embrace humility, and to sit with the discomfort and vulnerability I *feel* in my body and heart as necessary steps toward personal and collective change. It means doing the necessary personal work of self-examination with curiosity and courage.

Because we are all interconnected, seeking wholeness for ourselves is meaningless without simultaneously seeking wholeness for others, and as a white woman who now has educational, class, and rank privilege as a tenured full professor, it is imperative that I put that privilege in service of more just and humane academic institutions. This has manifested, for example, in my advocacy for faculty well-being, coordination of a faculty-staff contemplative collective, creation of a mentoring collaborative rooted in antiracist principles at my home institution, and integration of pedagogies of invitation (Keating, 2013) and tenderness (Thompson, 2017) into my cherished work with students. Additionally, working on this volume, bearing witness to the struggles of my colleagues, and amplifying their generative, liberatory, and heart-full visions of higher education gives me hope that our collective efforts will bring about meaningful and sustainable change. I will be forever grateful to all of my contemplative colleagues who model a more loving and healing way of being in higher education, and who inspire my compassionate approach to education and leadership.

David W. Robinson-Morris

Contemplative practice has helped me to remember, as Cynthia Dillard (2012) says, what we have learned to forget: we shape the future just as the future is shaping us. Dwelling in the present moment, I situate my spirit in the future and place my imagination in service of new world-building. Therefore, I will not discuss the influence of my time as executive director in service to the Center for Contemplative Mind in Society, the violence of the education system, nor the many assaults I have suffered as a student, staff person, faculty member, and administrator within the system of higher education. Nor will I regale you with stories of my post high school years as a novice Josephite seminarian, or my enamorment of Ignatian spirituality as an undergraduate student at a Jesuit university. I came to contemplative practice, as we commonly understand it, while trying to sedate the racing of my mind as a doctoral student writing his dissertation and dealing with the departmental politics rife in graduate programs across the country. Meditation, lectio divina, automatic writing, art making, kitchen dancing, bearing witness, being in community, maintaining communion, and walking have helped me calm my nervous system and make conscious decisions as I advanced in my career within and outside of higher education; encountered racial prejudice and size discrimination; and lived through the devastation of death and the constant surprises of grief.

Born Black and male in the American South, practice has allowed me to imagine and envision freedom in an oppressive society and has enabled me to transform the myriad of traumas I must endure in this raced and gendered body into power and a focus on Black aliveness (Quashie, 2021). Practice allows me to touch the richness of liberation that fuels an ability to create, disrupt, and transform. Liberation is knowledge of self-colliding with the freedom of beingness, healing intersecting with power, soaked in love, in a void of fearlessness and limitless possibility—*l' énergie* or the capacity to effect transformation. Or as my grandmother, Grand, would remark, "liberation is freeing your mind and spirit, so your ass can follow." True liberation, we know, can only be birthed through the collective.

Power. I believe, like Winona LaDuke, "Power is not brute force and money, power is in your spirit. Power is in your soul. It is what your ancestors, your old people gave you. Power is in the earth. It is in your relationship to the earth" (Thompson, 2015). It is your relationship to yourself, to all things seen and unseen. It is your relationship with your purpose and how you encounter and endure the lessons your soul is meant to learn in this iteration, on this plane, at this moment in the history of the universe.

My Grand is ever-present in spirit; she comes to mind for several reasons, but most poignantly for a simple question she asked me one day when I called home for advice about a situation I faced as a university administrator. After thirty minutes of listening to me explain the situation, complain about unfair treatment, and devise a strategy of defense, my Grand asked: *Is this what you want to waste your power on?*

It is a question I have come back to repeatedly within my career as a faculty member, administrator, nonprofit executive, and entrepreneur. It is not a question asked only when conflict arises, it is a liberatory question of purpose, a question of emancipation, a question of agency, and a deep question of remembrance.

In her way, she was asking me: Do you know, do you remember who you are? Do you see yourself as yourself—regal, valiant, intelligent, righteously rageful, liberated, and whole? Do you understand that you are love itself created? Do you understand that the unseen walk with you, go before, stand beside, intervene, and intercede on your behalf? Do you know that like Blackness, you are limitless, uncontainable, and always already engaged in the act of (r)evolution just because you are here? These questions have become practice and gateways to deeper being, clearer knowing, and righteous doing when my humanness provokes me to angry destruction.

Within the systems and institutions within which we find ourselves engaged, there is no shortage of opportunities to waste or rise within one's power. I had to learn the hard way; the way one answers Grand's question can diminish us or it can move us toward wholeness, flow, connection, and love. Us: it is also a constant reminder of Ubuntu—we are links in a chain of humanity; there is nothing that I can do that will not impact others. Grand's question corrects our vision and focuses our energy away from petty squabbles or distracting institutional conflicts—it helps us to re-member ourselves home.

For me, working within higher education and the various other politically charged systemic assemblages, I understand that Grand's question is one of cartography, of mapmaking rather than a tracing. It is a reminder that we—individually and even more so collectively—have *l' énergie* to create new futures and new ways of being together. We have *l' énergie* to live in a way that consciously aligns our purpose, values, and actions to repair the work or create a new one. We have *l' énergie* to refuse exploitation and division. We have *l' énergie* to create a politics of hope in our being, teaching, research, and scholarship.

Through the practice of Grand's question, I have been able to ask: How do I want to use my power? How might I become my power? These questions have allowed me to shape an authentic life, to resist where resistance is needed, to raise hell where thoughts of heaven will not due, and to move through the world with purpose. Perhaps more importantly, they have incited my imagination, fueled my journey of personal transformation, deepened mindful awareness, and empowered me to resist and reimagine harmful structures and systems.

Grand continues to teach from the great beyond; I am grateful. From her simple question, I have learned resistance is a practice and the cultivation of courage a necessary endeavor. May my—may our being and doing be a testament to placing one's power in service to justice, to equity, and uplifting the human spirit toward meaningful self and institutional transformation.

Diverse Voices

In response to our initial call for contributions to the volume, we received a significant number of proposals, which demonstrated the considerable interest in and need for such a volume that shares the voices and experiences of contemplative practitioners in higher education, especially those historically marginalized and harmed in the academy. Reflecting the diverse landscape of contemplative educators, the majority of our contributors are women of color, with additional representation of white women and men of color. Our authors come from a variety of institutions ranging from PWIs, HBCUs, and small liberal arts schools to Research I institutions and encompass both permanent and contingent faculty. These scholars bring diverse disciplinary backgrounds, geographical origins, and academic ranks. Some have even relinquished their academic positions during the two years it took to complete this project, largely due to the problems discussed in this volume. These essays are not conventional academic pieces, and we intentionally included a wide range of stylistic approaches to allow for an authentic voice and sharing of experiences. Here, you will find works that are biographical, autoethnographic, personal, and creative, incorporating poetry, movement, art, and more.

The Risk

We acknowledge the risk and vulnerability involved in sharing personal stories and practices, especially for scholars from historically marginalized and oppressed groups in the academy. By centering and amplifying these scholars, we aim to interrogate how our sense of safety and risk shifts based on our positionality. We applaud the scholars who dared to delve deep and expose themselves in these essays, especially during this time of intense scrutiny, censorship, and punishment within higher education.

As researchers ourselves, we noticed how some of the contributors stepped timidly into the waters of their own internal wading pools of consciousness. We questioned, probed, and provoked each of them to step outside of the disciplinary boundaries of the academy to greet themselves arriving—to locate and return home. The sense of fear and danger was palpable, which unfortunately confirmed Robinson-Morris' (2019) assertion that institutions of higher education have become epistemological subregimes characterized by fear and driven by the market.

To subvert the shackles of institutionalization, we encouraged the contributors to delve as deeply as possible into themselves and their practices; to let go of the weight of academic jargon, identity politics, and the illusion of objectivity. Instead, we urged them to approach their writing as seekers, as practitioners, with hearts full of curiosity and passion, aiming to heal and transform the harmful institutions and systems within which they worked. For some, this came naturally, their inner wellsprings already nourished by years of dedicated practice akin to sacred pilgrimage. Others struggled to center themselves in their contemplative narrative and integrate it with their justice efforts, fearing the risk of sharing such personal stories with the world (Anzaldúa, 2002; Keating, 2000). Many were strategic in what they felt safe sharing, mindful of potential retribution.

As we reflected on the risks and the challenges of this work, we noticed an interesting phenomenon: there are only three Black men and no white male contributors. We found this to be a curious occurrence and pondered why this might be so. How do we engage more male identified persons and especially more white and male identified persons in understanding their critical role and responsibility in fostering more just institutions? And how might contemplative practices serve as one potential avenue in that effort?

As we considered the dearth of self-identified Black men as contributors, we began to understand even more the great risk of showing up in one's fullness within institutions and systems not built for one's survival. Black men *and* Black women have had to create "hush hollows" of freedom (in the words of contributor Jeffers-Coly) where they can be fully themselves—free and liberated—away from the prying eyes of the oppressive overseer, a topic also taken up by Templeton in Chapter 6. That is to say, we are well aware that higher educational institutions across the country continue to perpetuate plantation politics and colonizer ideologies (Bell, 2021; Dancy et al., 2018). Perhaps, the Black male identified contemplatives understood that, in the words of Angela Davis, "freedom is always stalked by death" and were unwilling to place themselves publicly and institutionally in harm's way when they are always already walking societal targets. How might we support Black and Brown identified men in coming home to themselves—safely and wholly—within the very institutions that utilize practices of dehumanization? And how might engaging in contemplative practice serve to disrupt racist and toxic masculinity narratives that shape Black and Brown men's self-images, as discussed by Bradford Grant and Michelle Chatman in Chapter 15?

Organization of the Book

The volume is organized into four main parts. Each section includes a brief introduction written by one of the editors and a concluding essay written by a contemplative scholar who draws upon their unique personal history of contemplative work in the academy to engage with and respond to the essays in their section. We acknowledge that these groupings are somewhat artificial, insofar as similar themes and concerns are threaded throughout all of the essays. We grouped chapters around a particular idea or theme, though they could have been grouped in multiple alternative ways. We invite you to make your own connections across the essays.

In Part I, *Ever Present and Interconnected*, authors share stories of how they courageously persist in academe in the face of oppression, inequity, anti-Blackness, and the legacies of colonization. They discuss their diverse cultural, spiritual, and wisdom traditions and how these give shape to their unique and evolving contemplative identities that are foundational to wholeness and resistance. Authors speak from their unique social locations, histories, and intersectional identities, sharing what it is like to navigate white supremacy, racism, and other forms of hierarchy and othering within academe as a Black woman, a displaced Taiwanese immigrant, and a Chicano. Two of our contributors write of the particular challenges of navigating these oppressions within Christian institutions of higher education as early-career faculty of color raised within Christian traditions. In detailing their individual journeys, contributors in this section claim elements core to their being: creativity, collectivity, embodiment, and the sacred, just to name a few. Through practices of fellowship, Convivencia, poetry, qigong, and the creation of personal "cajitas" (Pulido), these higher education professionals cultivate presence and interconnection as paths toward healing. In the closing chapter, Vaishali Mamgain employs the CourageRISE model to envision an educational system rooted in, and in service of community, that celebrates global majority ontologies and imaginations.

In Part II, *Conjuring Transformation*, contributors provide insight into the various ways they "conjure," i.e., bring into being, embodied liberation and justice consciousness within institutional contexts that far too often deny the full humanity of higher education practitioners, especially those from historically marginalized groups. Again, authors draw upon their specific intersectional identities and cultural frameworks to inform their approach toward cultivating change, from the concept of Native American body sovereignty to Islamic teachings on faith and care, to the spatial experience of immigrating across cultural and national borders. They write of rage, loss, grief, isolation, and trauma across their personal and professional lives, and how somatic practices—stillness, movement, and dance—open a portal for regulating emotions, discerning internalized narratives and power relations, and shifting energy toward new fecund potentialities. This includes learning to access the creative energy of both oneself and universe/spirit/creator as processes of "creative envisioning" (Diaz-Mendoza) and "sensing into possibility" (Son) that help to shift our relationships with ourselves and those we care about: students, colleagues, and community members. Maria Hamilton Abegunde closes this section, reminding us that the path toward wholeness and healing is not magic, but hard work that requires honesty, persistence, and being willing to engage with our deepest fears.

Between Parts II and III, we offer a moment of pause. Chapter 14 features a loving dialog between one of our editors, Michelle C. Chatman, and colleague Bradford Grant. They discuss how contemplative practices may serve as a healing resource for Black men dispirited by persistent racial oppression, and a path toward expanded self-awareness and self-acceptance for students and colleagues at HBCUs. Grant discusses his own contemplative practice of art making and shares one of his drawings. Their conversation reminds us of the solace, love, and insight to be found in contemplative companionship, a theme threaded throughout the volume.

In Part III, authors of *Rhizomatic Awakenings* explore subjectivity, the nature of becoming, and the multiple ways through which we conceive of ourselves and the world. Contributors invite us to enter onto their respective plateaus of awakening as they travel across and through territories of marginalization, anti-Black violence, virtual distancing and disembodiment, burnout and illness, and ableism. They tell of communicating with the ancestors, crafting a multiracial feminist community, "sensing the intercorporeal field" (Ahmed et al.), Feeding Your Demons® (Mosemghvdlishvili), and caring for a loved one with developmental disabilities as modes of contemplative discovery and emergence. These stories reflect authors' deep love for and truth-telling about *both* their beloveds (ancestors, family, friends) *and* higher education (students, colleagues, community members, and mission). The honesty and vulnerability demonstrated by these contributors is revelatory, and these personal narratives serve as generous invitations to readers to pursue their own rhizomatic awakenings. In the concluding chapter, Steven Thurston Oliver grapples with his own struggles for wholeness and well-being as a late-career, Black queer identified man in higher education and reflects on the ways the individual essays have clarified aspects of his own contemplative journey.

In Part IV, contributors of *Liberatory Relationality* document the challenging inner work that is foundational to transformational relationship building and structural change. This work can be painful and uncomfortable on many levels and is critical to disrupting white supremacy, racism, colonization, and the multiple hierarchies that shape academe. Accountability is a key theme in this section—accountability for the harms we inflict on others (whether intentional or not), and accountability for bringing into being a new vision of higher education characterized by self-reflexivity, critique, care, and compassion. Essays critique extractive approaches to contemplation that reinforce dominant notions of productivity, reproduce settler logics and power relations, and reinforce white supremacist and capitalist ideas of "success" in the academy. They also highlight the specific work required of white people. Authors reimagine the shape and quality of interpersonal relationships within higher education through Racial Healing Circles, the creation of beloved community, sustained self-reflection on unearned white privilege, and cross-racial, decolonial mentoring relationships grounded in Native American teachings. Jennifer Cannon closes this section, drawing our attention to the present moment of multiple, converging crises. She reiterates that contemplative practices are more important than ever as we witness global systems of domination and the profound suffering of the world. We must trust in contemplative practices, the knowledge they provide, and the ways they call us to courage and integrity. Through the plethora of contemplative practices offered here, we may reclaim humane values, engage in ethical action, and manifest justice in the academy and beyond as we pilgrimage together toward wholeness.

Our concluding chapter offers a call to action, a ritual for blessing, and a few ideas for how higher education professionals might carry this work forward individually and collectively, into their own institutional spaces and their lives beyond the academy.

A Portal Home

There are no conclusions, only new plateaus (Robinson-Morris, 2019). This volume is a tool and a portal that leads us back to self in/with/through love while continuing to labor within the system of higher education. It is an experiential, multiperspectival map leading us home in accordance with our respective conceptions of home.

As you read the words of our contributors, know that each word is soaked with generative intention. Each letter crowded together infused with the spirit of liberatory transformation and contemplative justice. The pages are imbued with the intention that you locate, enter, and be at home with yourself just as you are and in the fullness of your humanity. We call forth generative disruption and the transformation of self and system.

May you place in service what speaks to your soul.

Notes

1 See, for example, Ferguson (2012), Niemman et al. (2020), Wooten et al. (2020).
2 We are thinking here of the many scholars and staff of color who have died as a result of the harms and pressures of discriminatory and oppressive institutions. A recent example is the tragic suicide of Antoinette Candia-Bailey of Lincoln University, which occurred during the preparation of this volume.
3 See, for example, Niemann et al. (2020), Whitaker and Grollman (2020), Matthew (2016); *Inside Higher Ed's* column Conditionally Accepted. LACRELA is the Liberal Arts Racial Equity Leadership Alliance hosted by the USC Race and Equity Center, which my institution was a member of for several years.

Reference List

Anzaldúa, G. (2002). Now let us shift...the path of conocimiento...inner work, public acts. In G. Anzaldúa, & A. Keating (Eds.), *This bridge we call home: Radical visions for transformation* (pp. 540–578). Routledge.

Baldwin, J. (2013). *Giovanni's room* (1st ed). Vintage International. Original work published in 1956.

Barbezat, D., & Bush, M. (2014). *Contemplative practices in higher education: Powerful methods to transform teaching and learning.* Jossey-Bass.

Bell, D. (2021). Becoming an anti-racist intuitions: The challenges facing higher education. *International Journal of Multiple Research Approaches, 13*(1), 22–25. https://doi.org/10.29034/ijmra.v13n1commentary2.

Butler, O. (1993). *Parable of the Sower.* Four Walls Eight Windows.

Chatman, M. (2019). Advancing black youth justice and healing through contemplative practices and African spiritual wisdom. *Journal of Contemplative Inquiry, 6*(1), 27–45.

Christopher, G. (2022). *Rx for racial healing: A guide to embracing our humanity.* American Association of Colleges and Universities.

Clifton, L. (2012). Won't you celebrate with me. In Kevin Young, & Michel S. Glaser (Eds.), *The collected poems of Lucille Clifton, 1965–2010.* BOA Editions.

Costa, L. (2018). Sabbatical as sacred time: Contemplative practice and meaning in the neoliberal academy. *Journal of Contemplative Inquiry, 5*(1), 65–85.

Dancy, T. E., Edwards, K. T., & Earl Davis, J. (2018). Historically white universities and plantation politics: Anti-blackness and higher education in the black lives matter era. *Urban Education, 53*(2), 176–195. https://doi.org/10.1177/0042085918754328.

Dillard, C. B. (2012). *Learning to (re)member the things we've learned to forget: Endarkened feminisms, spirituality, and the sacred nature of research and teaching.* Peter Lang, Inc.

Doležal, J. (2022). The big quit: Even tenure-line professors are leaving academe. *The Chronicle of Higher Education.* https://www.chronicle.com/article/the-big-quit?cid=facebook,linkedin,twitter&utm_campaign=20220601&utm_content=opinion:_thinking_of_leav&utm_medium=Chronicle±of±Higher±Education,The±Chronicle±of±Higher±Education,chronicle&utm_source=facebook,linkedin,twitter.

Ferguson, R. (2012). *The reorder of things: The university and its pedagogies of minority difference.* Minnesota University Press.

Fernandes, L. (2003). *Transforming feminist practice: Non-violence, social justice and the possibilities of a spiritualized feminism.* Aunt Lute Books.

Fleming, C. M., Womack, V. Y., & Proulx, J. (Eds.). (2022). *Beyond white mindfulness.* Routledge. https://doi.org/10.4324/9781003090922

Gumbs, A. P. (2012). The shape of my impact. *The Feminist Wire.* https://thefeministwire.com/2012/10/the-shape-of-my-impact/.

Halat, D. H., Soltani, A., Dalli, R., Alsarrai, L., & Malki, A. (2023). Understanding and fostering mental health and well-being among university faculty: A narrative review. *Journal of Clinical Medicine, 12*(13), 4425. https://doi.org/10.3390/jcm12134425.

Harvey, S., & Moten, F. (2013). *The undercommons: Fugitive planning and black study.* Minor Compositions.

Keating, A. (2000). Risking the personal: An introduction. In *Interviews/Entrevistas: Gloria e. Anzaldúa.* (pp. 1–15). Routledge.

Keating, A. (2013). *Transformation now! Toward a post-oppositional politics of change.* University of Illinois Press.

Magee, R. (2019). *The inner work of racial justice: Healing ourselves and transforming our communities through mindfulness.* TarcherPerigree.

Maparyan, L. (2012). *The womanist idea.* Routledge.

Matthew, P. A. (Ed.) 2016). *Written/unwritten: Diversity and the hidden truths of tenure.* University of North Carolina Press Books.

McClure, K., & Fryar, A. H. (2022). The Great Faculty Disengagement. *Chronicle of Higher Ed*, January 19. https://www.chronicle.com/article/the-great-faculty-disengagement

Menakem, R. (2017). *My Grandmother's hands: Racialized trauma and the pathway to mending our hearts and bodies.* Central Recovery Press.

Morrison, T. (2001). The Connecticut Forum. Toni Morrison on Trauma, Survival, and Finding Meaning. https://youtu.be/5xvJYrSsXPA?si=v4Y0Xna2GPXGR2QH.

Niemman, Y., y Muhs, G. G., González, C., & Harris, A. (Eds.) (2020). *Presumed incompetent II: Race, class, power and resistance of women in academia.* Utah State University Press.

Okun, T. (2021). *(Divorcing) white supremacy culture: Coming home to who we really are.* https://www.whitesupremacyculture.info/.

Palmer, P. (2009). *A hidden wholeness: The journey toward an undivided life.* Jossey-Bass.

Pope-Ruark, R. (2022). *Unraveling faculty burnout: Pathways to reckoning and renewal.* Johns Hopkins University Press.

Qaushie, K. (2021). *Black aliveness or a poetics of being.* Duke University Press.

Rendón, L. (2014). *Sentipensante (sensing/thinking) pedagogy.* Routledge.

Robinson-Morris, D. W. (2018). Curriculum reform: The aims and purposes of higher education. In J. Blanchard (Ed.), *Controversies on campus: Debating the issues confronting American universities in the 21st century* (pp. 143–161). ABC-CLIO.

Robinson-Morris, D. W. (2019). *Ubuntu and Buddhism in higher education: An ontological rethinking.* Routledge.

Thompson, L. (2015). Winona LaDuke inspires audience at Greenfest. *East County Magazine.*

Thompson, B. (2017). *Teaching with tenderness: Toward an embodied practice.* University of Illinois Press.

Thurman, H. (1980). The sound of the genuine. Baccalaureate address delivered at Spelman College. https://thurman.pitts.emory.edu/items/show/838.

Truesdell, N., Carr, J., & Orr, C. (2018). The role of Combahee in anti-diversity work. *Souls: A Critical Journal of Black Politics, Culture, and Society, 19*(3), 359–376. https://doi.org/10.1080/10999949.2017.1389632.

Whitaker, M., & Grollman, E. (Eds.) (2020). *Counternarratives from women of color academics: Bravery, vulnerability, and resistance.* Routledge.

Williams, Rev. A. K., Owens, L. R., & Syedullah, J. (2016). *Radical dharma: Talking race, love, and liberation.* North Atlantic Books.

Wooten, C., Babb, J., Costello, K., Navickas, K., & Macciche, L. (2020). *The things we carry: Strategies for recognizing and negotiating emotional labor in writing program administration.* Utah State University Press.

PART I
Ever Present and Interconnected
Symphonic Journeys, Rooted Practices
Michelle C. Chatman

In this opening section, *Ever Present and Interconnected*, we embark upon a deep exploration of contemplative scholar identity, which is often overshadowed by our roles as specific disciplinary experts which academia heralds. A departure from your typical academic essay, these authors share their symphonic and transformative journeys toward wholeness drawing inspiration from contemplative practices rooted in their diverse cultural, spiritual, and wisdom traditions.

They share how their wealth of cultural capital broadens the scope of contemplative practices, reaffirms their worthiness, and creates possibilities for healing and integration within hierarchical and oppressive systems of learning. Their testimonies highlight ancestral wisdom and presence through memories, stories, spiritual connection, and deep relationality. These authors disrupt the idea that we are divorced from the revered cultural ways of knowing that have sustained people of color for multiple generations. They share the ways in which they have found safe harbor in the practices and ways of being of their kin which stokes the fire of their resistance against overwhelm, extraction, and burnout.

In these works, you will bear witness to their truth-telling of the harm often caused in academia alongside the reverential creativity of storytelling, kinship, and embodied practices. As an anthropologist, I delight in this deeper narrative work as I know it is essential for our transformation of higher education. We grow up with a hopeful valence of the academy, acculturated with the ideas of its benevolence. And while our lecture halls and labs can most assuredly be places of profound inspiration, deep learning, and transformative innovation for solving social ills, they also contain preferential policies, overt assaults, microaggressions, and various forms of othering.

To retain one's wholeness within a culture and system with a legacy of colonial conquest, inequity, anti-Blackness, and oppression is an act of profound courage and care. The contributors here share the myriad ways they persist in academia where ideologies of racial hierarchy are encoded into policy, put into practice, and felt in lecture halls and board rooms. These scholar educators seek to bring a fuller version of themselves to their vocation as they resist affronts to their humanity. Steadfast in their contemplative practices which act as armor against the commodification of their bodies, souls, and minds.

Further, these practices evoke the sacred as they reclaim the sensory, ancestral, imaginative, collective, and ceremonial aspects that are central to our wholeness. Not as whimsical, past-time engagements but as core to our deeper, liberated beingness. Hutchinson offers guidance for tending to the self with curiosity and gentleness knowing that the body of a Black woman is often unprotected in academia. The self-awareness she invites far exceeds the navel gazing of which inner approaches are often accused. Rather, it serves as an opportunity for continuous attunement so that our work may be grounded and generative. Through practice, poetry, theorizing, and testifying, Lin takes us on a cyclical, non-linear healing journey that mirrors the bumpy and iterative process of claiming wholeness. Pulido challenges us to consider how the architecture of our personal "cajitas" as higher education professionals supports us in discerning how they convey the feelings and connections of home. Templeton uplifts Black feminism and fellowship in academic spaces, celebrating the freedom found in the knowing looks, reaffirming nods, and shared identity and ideologies of Black women. Yong and Junker reclaim the dance between emotion and somatic truths that we are taught to abandon in favor of analytical reasoning and logic. Together, they are the provocation and the promise for how we might live more freely and transform our institutions for equity, healing, and true connection.

As you take in these offerings, I invite you to acknowledge what is alive in you. What disjunctures have you experienced directly or observed in the spaces where you serve? What are the deeply embedded ways of being that emerge from your cultural, spiritual, or wisdom traditions that enable you to enliven your teaching, service, and leadership from a place of wholeness? How can you put those gifts in service to freedom and the eradication of harm in higher education?

I wish you spaciousness and curiosity as you hold these questions and indulge in the works of our contributors.

A Prayer for Teachers

May we, the teachers,

Remain.

Ever present to the

Truth of our worthiness

Right to health and wholeness,

Joyful and Just service.

Knowledge of wisdom much older than us. Potent and Strong.

Interconnectedness of all beings

Our healing. Earth's healing

Bounded destinies

Collective power

A complex and glorious dance of awakening

2

TEACHING BEST WHAT YOU MOST WANT TO LEARN

The Way of the Crows

Brandon LA Hutchinson

A Way In(troduction)

I discussed this project with a friend and shared my initial trouble getting started. I didn't realize until we spoke what the problem was. So much of how I approached this entry had been rooted in the sneaky and (al)luring stink of whiteness.

This is why I was stuck.

I was trying to forge all of who I am and what or how I practice into the realm of a singular contemplative genre when I am so much more expansive. Might something about that be amiss, given I am a child of the diaspora? I am a descendant of many people whom I don't know yet, all of whom I am sure have been enriched by the practices of everyday traditions that just *were*. They hadn't been co-opted and renamed. It was just how Grandaddy sang that note that opened up room for tears. It was just how Big Ma healed. It was through that dance and stomp that a curse had been broken. It was the intervention that followed a neighbor's dream. It was the Sunday night before a hair braiding session with Blue Magic grease, sitting between some mama's legs, which helped me see myself clearly through my very own eyes. In. My. Own. Fullness.

My friend, David, said, "Cleaning greens and snapping peas is a contemplative practice, Brandon." Just like that, my heart opened, and I remembered again.

Whiteness can help you forget who you are and who you've been across millennia. I tell stories. I was trained at the dinner table and under trees on hot days with garden-ripened tomatoes sprinkled with Lawry's in sticky hands. I hold stories, too. I listen deeply from my toes, straight up, inviting spaces for generative pauses; lean into curiosity; reflect on the things I behold; and practice giving people back to themselves, all with truth twisted up with kindness.

Whether in the classroom or the relationships I have cultivated with Black women, I put these practices into "everyday use" (Walker, 1983) for my well-being and liberation, with everything else being ancillary.

Crows: They Always Know

Recently, I was given a memory of myself. Now, it's mine to keep and use to understand me and my ways of being better. As told by my mom, it was a sunny day, and I had on a snowsuit of sorts—a toddler standing in the middle of crows.

And "I mean a lot," she said.

She knew not to worry because I wasn't. I was right where I belonged.

Many decades later, the crow still teaches me about truth, so much so that I wear one on my arm. Etched in my skin and positioned on my left shoulder, I remember that there is magic in the world and that it's always possible to find my path even when I don't think I can (Baron Reid, 2018, pp. 52–54).

We are called together in other ways, too.

Today, I visited my uncle, whom I hadn't seen in years. It always happens this way. I wind up getting things other than what I came for. It was a long time coming, but I went to get my father's ashes—he died when I was in seventh grade, but now I am forty-eight. While sitting in his lovely gardens, I noticed that my maker spirit, which often shows up in how I create beauty and peaceful dwellings, is a special gift my Uncle Carlos and I share. We swapped stories, some of which focused on my tattooed animal totem, and wouldn't you know, I learned that both my grandfather and my dad claimed the Crow as their animal. In their growing-up years, the sound of my grandfather making the crow call was their version of "you better be close to home, if not walking in the door, when the porch lights come on." I was called to Montague, MA, not just for the ashes, which would mark the first gift on my ancestor's altar, but to learn more about my relationship with the Crow.

Can't you see it? We were connected way before that bright day.

When I pull the Crow in the oracle, I am taught, "Crow is the keeper of universal law, the law of truth. Crow teaches us to walk our talk, to find congruence between who we say we are and who we know ourselves to be. This winged one insists that we speak truth, that we create truth instead of searching for it, and that we bring truth to every situation we find ourselves in" (Marc 2018 para. 1). I wonder if my mom knew even then that she was being conspired, brought directly into what would be my life's work (so far). Mommie and the Crows intend to help me remember that I am a creator and that I know my truth. I don't have to search for it.

The Practice of Seeing and Being Seen

About four decades ago, I was introduced to that learning. I'm still in the middle of it. Strange things happened with my schedule when I began teaching twenty-two years ago. As one of two Black women in my department, both of us under thirty and newly hired, I was uncertain how to advocate for myself. Unlike what was languaged to me at my point of hire, I ultimately wound up teaching courses outside my subject area. It was a disaster in some ways. At the time, I was still writing my dissertation, and up until that point, I had previously only taught one class, having chosen to be a research assistant semester after semester (grading papers ad nauseam without the break of anything else task-related) to avoid standing in front of students. So busy trying not to fail and to appear like I had it going on, I was doing "the most," mostly without reflection and with worry. I tried adopting other people's teaching styles, but it was not working.

And the reason was simple. I was out of alignment with who I knew myself to be. Slowly, it registered in my mind and heart; it couldn't be that I continued to show up how my husband did—an expert educator of elementary school kiddos—or do things the way my more experienced colleagues got things done. Operating from my own self-study, I got more explicit about my purpose and about what it was that I, first and foremost, was to be doing in the classroom. It took time, deep reflection, and practice, but what I grew to be good at was what made absolute sense to me: creating life-affirming containers for learning, which *had* to be relational. Once this truly kicked in, I felt liberated and inspired by what I could create by being attuned to my purpose. It sounds simple, but it was groundbreaking. Liberatory, even.

When students feel like they can show up and settle in, they can more easily make meaning from what they are learning. In my role as an educator, my first duty is to put out a bid to students for connection. It's simple for me—maybe it's because I have Black girls whose names are often mispronounced or because I have seen the shrinking in a person's body when they must restate their name over and over and still have it reverberate in ways so unlike what is known to them. A basic tenant of this liberatory and relational community is the belief that people should be referred to by their names—with proper pronunciation. I want students to know that I am sincere in getting it right, so much so that I write names down phonetically and practice outside of the class. Erasure can happen so quickly. A person must hear who they are.

An Attunement to Enough

As a Black woman, I worry about being enough in the world, in academia—rigorous enough, smart enough, professional enough. Because this feels so weighty, I try to reduce my participation in a cycle that perpetuates the same stress on others by providing spaciousness and grace to students. This is why I try very hard to lead from curiosity when students do not meet the expectations that I have established. Much of this ease stems from being tenured and winning a prestigious teaching award at my university. Still, an equally significant part comes from my attunement and soul's calling to practice (be)holding coupled with curiosity and deep listening. I try to break down barriers that might keep students from revealing themselves to me. As. They. Are. I show that I am interested in knowing what might have shifted their behavior. I make myself available for appointments. I extend deadlines when appropriate.

The Privilege of Caring

To look upon, to marvel, and to see are all characteristics of beholding. Many people do not feel seen but want to be. In practice, beholding takes the shape of noticing. Some people say that they don't remember faces, but I do. I also pay attention to things like fresh haircuts, and for Black girls especially, I let them know how much I like their braids, twists, color, or edges. I notice when someone isn't looking quite like themselves. In discreet conversations, I ask about what is happening and write down details after they leave to follow up. And I do. I might email a student to let them know I am checking in, catch them on campus at another point, and create a space to see how things are playing out.

Like standing amid the crows, these things feel natural. My practice of beholding, leading with curiosity, and making time to listen empathetically is affirmed by students who say, "Thank you for asking how I was" or "Thank you for following up. That has never happened in my four years here." I can think of a parent of a student I ran into in the grocery store who repeatedly thanked me for the kind of care I extended to her daughter when her good friend died.

Embodied Black and Woman

While the practices impact students meaningfully, the goal is not primarily outward facing. As a Black woman tenured faculty member, I know that I am a "rare species" to borrow Sheryl Lee Ralph's words sung during her Emmy award speech. I tote this reality around everywhere. It's in every fiber of my body. Like the lady in orange from

Ntozake Shange's groundbreaking and still resonant *for colored girls*, I can even feel it in the bottom of my shoe (Shange, 1977). For sustainability, I must intentionally curate environments that feel affirming to my being and help foster a feeling of belonging. Conscious that multitudes of Black women, out of necessity, have been at the forefront of creating generative spaces for their wellness, I draw upon their wisdom. It was in 1892 when Anna Julia Cooper wrote in *A Voice from the South*, "only the BLACK WOMAN can say when and where I enter, in the quiet, undisputed dignity of my womanhood, without violence and without suing or special patronage, then and there the whole Negro race enters with me" (Lemert & Bahn, 1998). Cooper set a stage that centered Black womanness in such a striking way. Written over a century ago, it is a teaching tool for me today. Cooper embodied a lofty responsibility to uplift her entire race and herself by illuminating the potent power of scanning and self-awareness. As Cooper suggests, the Black woman must lead from a place of deep knowing.

It is a comforting feeling to see evidence of this ancestral wisdom taking shape in my higher education spaces. With intention, I, too, create a path to enter fully.

Holding Space, and Then Some

Last year, I taught in my university's honors program for the first time. What a delight to click "join" and see several faces of color, most of the bunch of five being Black women. Never forgetting what it was like to be Black and a woman at a predominately white institution, I recognized the gem of the opportunity I had been given. I knew that my role extended beyond helping them to meet curriculum goals. I hoped they would feel affirmed by the material, which centered on young Black adolescents coming of age *and* in their relationships with me. On purpose, I straddled two practices. I created spaciousness to witness and to be witnessed, which required a degree of vulnerability I had been more prone to share, primarily with Black female colleagues.

Witnessing as Love

Over the semester, I was called to connect with these students in multiple ways. Some were more familiar. For example, our one-to-one meetings were not only about brainstorming ideas; they became opportunities for me to learn about some aspects of their lives. I made sure that they knew I was rooting for their wholeness. While supporting their endeavors for academic success, I encouraged them to make room for rest, to find joy, and to spend time with friends while they were fully planted in eldest daughter caretaking and full-time college student roles. I sent emails. I remember affirming one student's lovely hot pink hijab, which couldn't help but accentuate her deep chocolate-buttered skin tone. Another celebrated a successful interview turned summer internship, which we hoped would lead to further entrepreneurial opportunities.

While I knew I was in alignment regarding relationship building, deep listening, and providing spaces for others to enter completely, it became evident rather quickly that more was required of me. Unexpectedly, I was asked to reflect on the impact of my working in higher education for nearly twenty-two years. And it broke me open mostly because I was forced to confront how I had been handling the onslaught of being Black and a woman in academia. And, because I could feel the sentiment of my favorite quote in my body, which goes something like, "You teach best what you most need to learn."

Two instances come to mind. The first happened when I met one student in person for the first time at an Honors College event. She held nothing back and shared her initial hesitancy toward me. Even though another one of my colleagues, who she enjoyed and respected as her professor, kept encouraging her to set up times to talk with me, she was not sure if online meetups and virtual class time could be engaging enough. After talking for a spell, she said that while in-person classes were her preference, our meeting times had been "surprisingly" helpful and even fun. Next, she honed in on what she wanted me to answer: "But professor, why are you teaching virtually?" She couldn't believe I enjoyed it. Now, it was time for me to admit some things. I noticed that my heart rate was accelerating. My body was signaling that I had something to say. I recognized the offering to reveal myself honestly and took it.

So, I began. I told her that before the pandemic, I would have never agreed with anyone who might have thought I would be good at creating a virtual community, let alone enjoy it. But I could not have been more wrong. It changed my life, and the repercussions were stunning. In the virtual space, there was a marked distance from microaggressions and the feelings of loneliness in being one of few Black women faculty on campus. As I convened class, I burned sage and sat beside Magnus, my dog. I tended to myself more lovingly. I moved less quickly.

It felt good to share my reflections on what I learned and how I felt my wholeness so clearly. Standing across from my student and looking into her eyes, I was helping her to understand who I am. I was also remembering what I missed as a young college student. Recalling my time as an undergraduate at a predominantly white institution (PWI) in upstate New York, my capacity *to see* the only three Black women professors was nil to none.

I wondered why they weren't around much or looked so beaten. I did not know what was happening in their lives or understand the weight of trying to gain promotion and tenure. I did not think about what it meant for them to *be* among colleagues at the primarily white affluent college. My criticism and frustration toward them emanated from my isolation, even though I didn't know that then. After all these years, what I lacked in attunement toward truly seeing them still feels raw.

The second instance, with a different Black student, happened at the close of an in-person honor's program event. We chatted as we walked, becoming familiar with each other's presence side by side—in the flesh and not through virtual squares. We happened upon two of my white colleagues, whom I greeted as we proceeded toward the stairs. Of the two, one hollered an out-of-pocket joke across the hallways. It was one of those off ones. It was the type that made you say to yourself, with your head semi-cocked, "What"? It's not a quick "what," either. It's drawn out, seconds long, because you can't believe *that* just happened.

At that moment, it was as if our gait—if footsteps could feel—understood the immediacy of breaking away quick-fast and in a hurry. My student was embarrassed and tucked her head down, her chin almost touching the tip of her sternum bone. Once downstairs, I looked up into my student's eyes, my head having found itself into a tuck of its own. Right before our embrace, I noticed the tears in her eyes. "I'm sorry, professor," she said.

"I'm sorry, too," I said.

Both sorries hung in the air like clothes pinned crookedly on a clothesline, each of us caught in a vulnerable moment we hadn't prepared for. Walking out the door, in the car ride home, and even after, I wasn't sure what my student was sorry for. I could feel poignantly who I was early in my career and felt some remorse about that. *And* I was also in touch with who I had become. Then, I humped along, laughing at jokes that weren't funny. I sacrificed ease in my body to be a part of the group. This time, I didn't default to eclipsing my well-being; instead, I spoke up. He looked stunned when I responded to his, "But you used to always think this kind of stuff was funny," with, "It was only because I felt I had to."

Reflecting on that Sunday afternoon, I see myself standing right in the middle of practice, affirming the value of my worth. Practicing self-disclosure with vulnerability and honesty, creating new patterns of being with my students, and telling the honest-to-goodness truth. Like Anna Julia Cooper, I make room for both me and others to enter spaces alongside me in their wholeness. Through personal moments of awareness and courage, I unabashedly choose liberation for myself over and over, making room for the collective to be and do the same.

Practice: Wholeness as an Action Verb

To be in my wholeness requires that I "be" in a particular state of mind, intentionally pulling toward me the good I need to thrive. My contemplative practices combine like the fixings in a soup that won't become delicious all by themselves. A careful eye and lots of stirring are crucial.

To show up in my fullness as a Black woman in higher education, I must

1. Listen deeply and compassionately, both to myself and others.
2. Create spaces that feel life-affirming and allow me to tap into my wisdom.
3. Even amid grind culture, invite in spaciousness; make room to slow down.
4. Be curious about myself and check how I feel in my body to know how to move throughout my day.
5. Practice self-disclosure with honesty.
6. Trust that vulnerability is an essential bridge to building meaningful relationships of support.

Every day, I must remember to stir together all the following, each in good measure. And whenever something is a little off, I take a minute, scan what's there, and perhaps add something else.

It may need a lot of shakes of loving kindness.

Or a walk in nature.

Or a deep rest practice.

I keep adding and combining the ingredients, making it just right for the day.

How can YOU make wholeness an action verb? Here are some questions to guide your reflection.

1. How can you practice listening more deeply and compassionately to yourself and others?
2. Where are the places you frequent that align you with your purpose? Draw upon your feelings in those environments and ask yourself, how can I, alone or with community, create atmospheres of vibrancy and peace?
3. What might a commitment to several daily conscious pauses look like for you?
4. How can you encourage self-awareness in your body and begin to trust its guidance?
5. How can you chip away at the messaging preventing you from sharing how you are?
6. Who might your accountability partners be? How do you remind each other to show up not in performance but vulnerably and as enough?

Reference List

Baron-Reid, C. (2018). *The spirit animal oracle: Guidebook* (pp. 52–54). Hay House.
Lemert, C., & Bahn, E. (Eds.). (1998). *The voice of Anna Julia Cooper (VAJC)*. Rowan & Littlefield Publishers.
Shange, N. (1977). *For colored girls who have considered suicide, when the rainbow is enuf: A choreopoem.* Book club ed. MacMillan.
Walker, A. (1983). *In search of our Mothers' gardens: Womanist prose.* Harcourt Brace Jovanovich.

3
UNSETTLING THE COLONIAL SHADOWS OF CONTEMPLATIVE PRACTICE

JuPong Lin

Sunrise Walk

Dawn light breaks through thickly vined limbs
tangled in, strangled by bittersweet—the "invasive" one. Bright
speckles skitter across pond. Low drone of motors exhaling up
fumes to a choir of chirps, peeps, warbles, whistles.

Four-legged Odessa sniffs mown grass, traces
of a neighbor's furry one tickles her nostrils
muttering mowers keep suburban lawns neat, noxious
gas blends into breezes blowing over sovereign soils

Foreign soil when we were tots, now familiar as
the shadow my body casts. My unsheathed feet touch
the Earth. Toes sense spring shoots asleep in her damp chill
Pores open to wormy leaf mold, edged by machine-blown mounds.

Facing a stand of pines beyond the pond, arms lift and Dragon
meets Tiger. Moans of mowers and blowers muffle laughter
from the other side. Feet become barn owls' ears. Listen down low
for critters hunted by great birds sharing breath with their prey

Mist rises from pond like warm breath. Odessa barks me to
breakfast duty. Sapsucker crunches a bug, shits on grass. We walk home
to stories of mass shootings, climate chaos, everyday woundings. Water
becomes air becomes breath of every waking sleeping critter.

DOI: 10.4324/9781003416777-4

Walking wounded we warm-bloodeds exhale gas —poison to our own
Bodies, nectar to trees; our bodies soften into each other at dawn.

Not My BornPlace

This was not the land where I was born 出生. This is not the land of my people, my ancestors 故鄉. These are not the birdsongs I first heard when I arrived on Earth 土地. When I let myself pause and *be* in stillness, allowing my full presence to connect with this land where I now live, Nipmuc, Nonotuck, and Pocumtuc land, my *bodymindspirit* remembers that this place/ground/earth 土地 is not the land of my BornPlace 出生地.

> *I learn from my parents and the Maryknoll Language Service Center Taiwanese-English Dictionary that there are many words for "birthplace" in Taiwanese Hokkien;* 誕生地*;1) birthplace, formal;* 出生地 *2) includes the character for "go out," two mountains stacked on top of each other;* 故鄉 *3) the place of my ancestors.*

I awaken to the complexity of the space between belonging and not belonging, between oppression and liberation, alienation and kinship. Contemplative practice awakens me to the nonduality of living, breathing, walking the ground underneath, which lies a minefield of rigidified patterns of thinking and being that academia trains us to follow. Higher education schools us well in critical thinking, argumentation, rational resistance, and dissent, but for me it is the arts and imagination that hold space for the wholeness of *being*, embodied spirit, and emotional intelligence. It is poetry that allows us to free ourselves of the traps of rhetorical debate, the dualisms and hierarchies of good and evil, human and nonhuman, right and wrong. I follow the tradition of Audre Lorde, who asserted (1984), "For women, then, poetry is not a luxury. It is a vital necessity of our existence … Poetry is the way we help give name to the nameless so it can be thought" (p. 37). I open my exploratory journey with the question, "how can I make good relations with this land that is not my BornPlace? What can I do to repair the violence, harm, injustices inflicted on this land and the Indigenous People who lived in good relations for tens of thousands of years?"

What the academy now calls "contemplative practices" originated in places where lineages of the sacred have been honored, cultivated, and passed down through many, many generations. The transport of culturally rooted, sacred practices into the colonial United States broke the continuity of these lineages, commodifying and stripping the traditions from their original cultural, social, ancestral roots, and political contexts. As an artist-educator fighting for my own reconnection with cultural and spiritual lineages—for revitalization of my heritage practices—the road to embracing contemplative practice has been anything but smooth. I've struggled with internalized colonialism (Liu, 2020), grief, and rage triggered by the loss of language, identity, and culture of my diasporic Taiwanese family. The struggle to decolonize my bodymind/being shapes how I parent, how I teach, how I live my life.

When my older son was about 8 years old, we took Taekwondo classes together for a year. After he passed the green belt, he stopped going to class with me because he didn't want to be viewed as a living stereotype of the Karate Kid. Writing those words arouses a painful awareness of how the idea of racial inferiority gets embodied individually, collectively, and intergenerationally. Wrapped up in that sliver of a story is the larger story of assimilation, cultural appropriation, white supremacy, and how those braid together to form the colonial fabric of "North America," the name that European invaders imposed on the land that was, and still is, home to millions of Indigenous people. The genocide of Indigenous peoples, some Indigenous scholars have argued, begins the era that geoscientists have called the Anthropocene (Davis & Todd, 2017) "the epoch under which 'humanity' – but more accurately, extractive, petrochemical industries, capitalism, and colonialism – have had such a large impact on the planet that radionuclides, coal, plutonium, plastic, concrete, genocide and other markers are now visible in the geologic strata" (pp. 761–762). Those words of Zoe Todd and Heather Davis bear contemplation; they nudge me further into a decades-long inquiry into the wounds of colonization on People and Land, and the role of Asian immigrants in the colonization of Turtle Island. As a descendent of colonized Taiwanese, I call on ancestral memory to help me understand how colonization has shaped and harmed me and my kin, and our complicity with the colonial milieu that granted us citizenship. I reconnect with the heritage practices of *qigong*[1] to learn from the teachings of intergenerational wounds that led my ancestors to develop these practices.

Here I invite you, Dear Reader, to pause and practice. Four performance scores—instructions to guide contemplative practice—will interrupt this essay, an invitation to pause and practice. This first practice is a Qigong warm-up to open energetic and emotional channels.

Score #1 Tuning the Body, Breath, Mind

- Do the two-year-old bounce (standing, bounce gently on heels, letting body jiggle head to toe, loosening all the meridians). Give yourself a *qi* shower.
- Practice Tuning the Body, "wei wu wei," or "doing without doing" (5+ minutes, standing or sitting; increase time as you practice). Breathing, notice outside air mixing with inside.

- "Qigong practitioners learn to control the stress response by practicing Tuning the Body, Breath, and Mind at least ten minutes every day. The Three Tunings calm the sympathetic nervous system's 'fight or flight' stress reaction—which the Chinese call excess yang, and activates the relaxation response of the parasympathetic system, which the Chinese consider yin…Find the balance between effort and effortlessness. Taoists call this 'doing without doing' (wei wu wei)." (Cohen, 2005, p. 13).
- Speak lines below from *Tao Te Ching*. Notice how your body feels to "do nothing."

HUSHING

Not praising the praiseworthy
keeps people uncompetitive.

Not prizing rare treasures
keeps people from stealing.

Not looking at the desirable
keeps the mind quiet.
…
When you do not-doing,
nothing's out of order…

"Doing not-doing. To act without acting. Action by inaction. You do nothing yet it gets done …. It's not a statement susceptible to logical interpretation …"

(Laozi, Le Guin 2017, p. 6)

Colonization and Decolonization (Re-definitions)

Some scholars have argued that invasion is not a singular event but a structure to enable the permanent takeover of settler colonizers who "come to stay" (Wolfe, 2006, p. 388). Indigenous scholars, Waziyatawin and Michael Yellow Bird, theorize that colonization not only refers to the initial process of subjugation, but that "Colonization is an all-encompassing presence in our lives" (2012, p. 3), underscoring the ongoing process that persists in contemporary life. In *The Black Shoals: Offshore Formations of Black and Indigenous Studies,* Tiffany Lethabo King's analysis further disrupts the concept of conquest as a singular event, one constantly rendered "historical." She critically reframes the dominance of Wolfe's famous line in settler colonial studies and amplifies Waziyatawin and Yellow Bird's presencing of colonialism's ongoing presence. King suggests that far from a thing of the past, "Conquest, as well as resistance to conquest, is a living, quotidian, and ever-present moment that actors can interact with and interrupt. It is not an event, not even a structure, but a milieu or active set of relations that we can push on, move around in, and redo from moment to moment" (King, 2019, p. 40). In King's formulation lies potential energy for movement and reformulation of the "all-encompassing presence" of colonizer-colonized relations. The analyses of Waziyatawin, Yellow Bird, and King suggest forms of decolonial praxis rooted in daily, "moment to moment" practices of pushing on, moving around, and un- and re-doing colonial relations. This is sacred work, what Yellow Bird calls "neurodecolonization" (Yellow Bird, 2012). In naming the ceremonies, prayerful rituals, songs, and dances of Indigenous peoples "neurodecolonization," Yellow Bird restores to contemplative practice all that the dominant culture and medical sciences have stripped away (Yellow Bird, 2012). Understanding these practices as neurodecolonization re-roots contemplative practices back into the rich soil of Indigenous cosmologies, epistemologies, and ontologies, and supports the resurgence of ancestral knowledge coming through living bodymindspirits.

> *I notice my forehead is pinched, butt clenched, mind struggling to connect with body. I catch myself reading extractively, pulling quotes to build up an argument, while my creative self resists rationality and linear process. I read Helena Liu's blog post on internalized racism where she summarizes Fanon's stages of colonialism. I notice I'm drawn to the numbered list of the stages of colonialism, parsed into four neat bullet points. Notice the discomfort of "explaining" colonialism, as if it were an abstract concept and not about Black and Indigenous death; or in my homeland, Asians brutalizing other Asians. How absurd to lump together people of such diverse cultures of "Asia." Adding PI to Asian Americans only exacerbates the erasure of Pacific Islanders; Native Hawaiians, the Chamorro, Samoans. Who does the lumping together of AAPI serve?*

King's and Yellow Bird's analyses make a critical shift in settler colonial studies, revealing how whiteness is re-asserted at the moment when Indigeneity steps into the foreground. King examines the etymology of "settlement" in settler colonial discourse and finds the white "settler" taking center stage in the colonial theater, pushing to dominate the field of Indigenous Studies, just as Indigenous scholarship moves to focus academic inquiry on the connections between the violent conquest of Indigenous people and land, and the enslavement of Black bodies. The rhetorical move of replacing the word "settler" with "conquistador" makes a powerful intervention. King writes, "*The Black Shoals* arrests settler colonialism's tendency to resuscitate older liberal humanist modes of thought to create new poststructural and postmodern forms of violent humanisms that feed off Indigenous genocide and Black social death" (2019, p. 10). Along this line of reasoning, King calls the humanities "conquistador humanism" (2019, p. 13).

A passage in which King builds on Rey Chow's theorizing of "the ascendancy of whiteness in the modern world" (2019, p. 3) nudges me to acknowledge I have been avoiding a close examination of my own fraught relationship with Taiwanese culture and people—especially my own immediate family. My parents raised my sisters and I to "ascend" to whiteness, to disavow the ceremonial practices and beliefs of their/our Taiwanese heritage. My father called his village's religious beliefs "superstitions." As soon as we began learning English at school, we began losing our ability to speak Hokkien. The greater our ability to speak English without an accent, the greater our loss of our first language.

Score #2: Embodied Reading: Noticing Conquistador and Colonial Selves

Warm up with two-year-old bounce.

- Read these words out loud:
    - "*The Black Shoals* arrests settler colonialism's tendency to resuscitate older liberal humanist modes of thought to create new poststructural and postmodern forms of violent humanisms that feed off Indigenous genocide and Black social death." (King, 2019, p. 10)
    - "Conquistador humanism" (King, 2019, p. 13)
    - "Ascendancy of whiteness in the modern world" (King, 2019, p. xii)
- Notice how you are reading. Take a pause from extracting information. How does your body feel; your heart? Consider the labor of the author. How have you honored them?
- Journal/creative prompt[2]:
    - Consider the question, how have you benefited from systems of colonization?
- Notice the soles of your feet held by the moist fertile earth, each toe cradled, every pore touching soil. Drink in the nourishment of *yin qi*.

There's a story that wants to be told, but I'm struggling to allow the words to form on the page/screen. I know this will be printed, published, made widely accessible. And the words I write will define me in ways that I can't predict.

I police my words, overquote other scholars, put off writing the story—the story of my failed relationship with "mindfulness."

Many years ago, I went to a [insert name of white-dominant meditation center] workshop that promised to address racism in the Buddhist movement. I walked in with trepidation. I have practiced meditation off and on for decades but kept getting turned off by roomfuls of whiteness blurring my connection with the dharma. Right away I notice I can count the number of People of the Global Majority on one hand. The floor is given to a researcher who presents her psychosocial research on reactions to facial expressions of racially marked people, specifically black- and brown-toned faces. Participants were asked to interpret the expressions (smiling to "neutral" to frowning.) My blood boils… I see where this is going. And then I tip over the edge. She says the study did not look at Asian faces. We're sitting at an altar to Buddha and Quan Yin, supposedly examining racism in the American Buddhist movement. And they choose to uplift the research and "expertise" of a white researcher who didn't think Asians were relevant to her research population???

I want to tell the story in a way that holds space for multiple audiences. No universal (white) reader assumed here. I'm holding in my mind my beloved Black & Indigenous friends, colleagues, co-conspirators. And I notice my resistance to identifying as "Asian American," the complexity of that grouping. My own kin, my sisters, have not fully shown up for each other in our lives. I sit and give in to the grief over how colonial academia has insinuated itself into our lives, drawn borders between us and our family. I vow to change this, Sisters.

In Tiffany Lethabo King's narrative of conquistador nation-building, Black and Indigenous struggles are connected. I return to the question of the role of Asians in the colonization of North America. Asian immigrants have suffered assimilationist policies, anti-immigrant citizenship laws, anti-Asian violence, and scholarship of these social justice issues is expansive and growing. Yet these narratives have not sufficiently countered the myth of Asians as a monolithic "model minority" with supposedly closer proximity to whiteness. Jean Wu's essay, "Teaching *Who Killed Vincent Chin?* 1991 and 2001," reveals the deficit of knowledge of Asian America among college students. Her scholarship asks educators: when will the story of Vincent Chin be taught in American history courses?

Decolonization, then, must confront and resist the multiple dimensions of the colonial milieu, as King has theorized. "Black abolition and Native decolonization as projects that frustrate liberal (and other) modes of humanism offer new forms of sociality and futurity." (King, 2019, p. xv). For Waziyatawin and Yellow Bird, the project begins with "questioning the legitimacy of colonization … decolonization is not passive, but rather it requires something called *praxis*." (Waziyatawin & Yellow Bird, 2012, p. 3). Decolonizing contemplative praxis must resist the cooptation of contemplative practices by the mindfulness-industrial-complex and metamorphose coloniality.

I suggest that decolonization for Asians needs to engage in a transnational project of global majority futurity. I take up this challenge as a person of Asian heritage, resisting the homogenizing label of AAPI. I offer a praxis that fuses the principles and practices of life-nurturance (qigong) with critical theory and action. I invite you, Dear Reader, to momentarily pull apart the strands of theory and practice integrated in decolonial praxis, so they can be re-braided back together into a stronger cord of solidarity.

Score #3: Repair the Wounds of Colonization—Reclaim Ancestral Knowledge and Heritage

- Two-year-old bounce warm-up.
- Practice 5 Elements Qigong for Fire with Mimi Kuo-Deemer (Kuo-Deemer, 2013), the elements of Wood, Fire, Earth, Metal, and Water and their associated organs and meridians. Each element is demonstrated with some instructions and repeated a few times. "In the **Cycle of Destruction (or Dissolution, Restraint, and Control)** *(Xiang Ke)*, wood penetrates and destroys earth, earth absorbs and destroys water, water puts out fire, fire melts metal, and metal chops wood" (Cohen, 2005, p. 23).
- Journal/creative prompt. Consider the questions:
  - How have you been harmed by systems of colonization?
  - What energy do you sense in the potentialities of the colonial milieu, the relations that can be moved, transformed?
  - What do you notice, inside your body and outside?

My family on my mother's side migrated to Taiwan six or seven generations ago, and on my father's side, more than seven generations ago. My parents grew up under Japanese occupation in a system of colonization based on the German method of "scientific colonization," an approach "based on the German passion for methodical research and investigation" (Liu, 2020, p. 19). In *Prescribing Colonization: The Role of Medical Practices and Policies in Japan-Ruled Taiwan, 1895–1945*, Michael Shiyung Liu states, "The health transition in colonial Taiwan echoes Megan Vons' argument that 'the power of colonial medicine lay not so much in its direct effects on the bodies of subjects … But in its ability to provide a 'naturalized' and pathologist account of these subjects" (Liu, 2020, p. 175).

What does a "transnational project of global majority futurity" look like? It would be a future peopled by the bodies and stories of those like my mother who survived colonial violence but passed on the intergenerational wounds inflicted on her. It would be a future in which my sons can find cracks in the world of the binary, rationalistic wall of whiteness they confront, and invoke connections with our ancestors who knew the medicine of plants and pressure points on the flesh.

I have been a spiritual seeker all my life, ever since we emigrated from Taiwan—my BornPlace (my parents explained that the word for "homeland" literally translates as "the old village of ancestors" and has one of the same characters for "birthplace")—and I was separated from my people's spiritual and cultural traditions. In resistance to internalized colonialism, I read and read and read about Taoism, Buddhism, and qigong. I talked with my parents about their childhoods under Japanese colonization. My father still says with pride, "we were born Japanese citizens." I read an article reporting that the Japanese built many Shinto shrines in Taiwan, and they encouraged the Taiwanese to worship with them. Many of these shrines still stand, whether actively used or not. But my father believes "most Taiwanese would not accept shintoism." Local religious practices blended Taoism and Buddhism (and sometimes Confucianism) with the worship of local deities. I am more than a little irritated with my parents that I knew nothing about these practices or beliefs, as I was raised in the whitespace of the Chicago suburbs. Only one other Taiwanese family lived in the town at the time. I am more than a little irritated with the white spiritual seekers who had the privilege of traveling to India or China or Tibet to study at the feet of [insert name of spiritual teacher] and found fulfillment or enlightenment and then returned to North America to spread the good word, initiating a movement of contemplatives. My story is much more disjointed and fractured.

Learning from Michael Yellow Bird's work on "neurodecolonization"—"the contemplative science of healing that starts from quieting the mind to restore balance"—I began to practice decolonization through poetry, papercraft, deep listening, and qigong-inspired community performance (Clarke & Yellow Bird, 2020, p. 149). The divisions between artmaking, theorizing, listening, and qigong movement softened, and I found that contemplative practice allowed me to go much deeper into the journey of reconnecting with my ancestors, human and more-than-human. I found that contemplative pedagogy also helped my students get unstuck and move on in their journeys of ancestral healing. Contemplative practice can link internalized colonization and external decolonial praxis. Decolonization will not be achieved through academic argumentation alone, but requires processes of engaging communities in creative, somatic, contemplative acts of imagination and compassion. Decolonization is not a metaphor (Tuck & Yang, 2012) but must be enacted and practiced in and through our bodies, individual and collective.

Score #4 for Repairing the Wounds of Colonization—Cultural Appropriation

- Practice Tuning the Breath (Cohen, 2005, p. 14)
- After at least a week of Tuning the Breath every day, read these words out loud:
  - Cultural appropriation
  - Orientalism
  - Epistemic violence
  - Cultural extractivism

- Journal prompt: What do you sense through your holographic being (see next paragraph), inside and outside your body; inside and outside of temporality?

Qigong practice is a somatic revitalization of ancestral knowledge for me. The *bodymindspirit* becomes a zone of "holographic co-becoming" with the elements (five elements) and animals. Here I borrow from Dr. Manulani Meyer's theorizing of holographic epistemology, where knowledge-making integrates the three "beams" of body (physical), mind (intellectual), and spirit (energetic) that are found in all the wisdom traditions (Meyer, 2020, pp. 3435–3443). In my vision of the future of contemplative environmental education, many more Black and Indigenous people show up living their collective dreams. In this vision, Asian people are honored for their multifaceted, diverse traditions of "contemplative" practice that continue to thrive and grow today. I can now share a qigong practice with generosity, because I am no longer afraid it will be taken from me.

I began this essay from a place of negativity—*not* my bornplace. *Not* the space of colonization that separates wholeness and connection from the mechanistic illusion of the world. We walked through practices of Tuning Body, Breath, Mind… to a space of co-becoming in a nondualistic (no positive-negative, right-wrong) noncolonial future. In this world, there are no universals. No one has the authority to speak for all beings. Any idea of universal goods or universal bads, universally accepted values, has no place here. This is a world of accountability to interspecies relationships, interspecies justice for all, where the "all" will always be complex and troubling, and we return continually to the breaking of dawn.

Notes

1 ˈchē-ˈgu̇ŋ.
2 A journal entry can take any form of expression and is not limited to verbal written words. It may include drawing, nonverbal gestures, or poetry, which while it is verbal engages the nonrational, emotional, and psychic aspects of the author.

Reference List

Clarke, K., & Yellow Bird, M. (2020). *Decolonizing pathways towards integrative healing in social work*. Routledge. https://doi.org/10.4324/9781315225234

Cohen, K. (2005). *The essential qigong training course: 100 days to increase energy, physical health, and spiritual well-being*. Sounds True.

Davis, H., & Todd, Z. (2017). On the importance of a date, or, decolonizing the anthropocene. *ACME: An International Journal for Critical Geographies, 16*(4). https://www.acme-journal.org/index.php/acme/article/view/1539

King, T. L. (2019). *The black shoals: Offshore formations of black and native studies*. Duke University Press. https://doi.org/10.1215/9781478005681

Kuo-Deemer, M. (Director). (2013, October 30). *5 Element Qigong Practice for Fire (heart, small intestine, pericardium, triple heater)*. https://www.youtube.com/watch?v=GR9A3AL1pgA

Laozi, Le Guin, U. K., & Seaton, J. P. (2019). *Tao Te Ching: A book about the way and the power of the way*. Shambhala.

Liu, H. (2020, December 20). 6 Signs of Internalized Racism (and How To Heal)—Disorient. *Disorient*. https://disorient.co/internalized-racism/

Lorde, A. (1984). *Sister outsider: Essays and speeches*. Crossing Press.

Maryknoll Language Service Center. (n.d.). *Taiwanese-English Dictionary*. Retrieved January 22, 2023, from https://mkdict.net/

Meyer, M. A. (2020). *Holographic epistemology: Native common sense* (pp. 5232–5240). https://doi.org/10.1007/978-3-030-30018-0_6

Qigong. 2021. In *Merriam-Webster.com*. Retrieved December 7, 2023, from https://www.merriam-webster.com/dictionary/qigong

Tuck, E., & Yang, K. W. (2012). Decolonization is not a metaphor. *Decolonization: Indigeneity, Education & Society, 1*(1), Article 1. https://jps.library.utoronto.ca/index.php/des/article/view/18630

Waziyatawin, & Yellow Bird, M. (2012). *For indigenous minds only: A decolonization handbook*. School for Advanced Research Press.

Wolfe, P. (2006). Settler colonialism and the elimination of the native. *Journal of Genocide Research, 8*(4), 387–409. https://doi.org/10.1080/14623520601056240.

Yellow Bird, M. (2012). Neurodecolonization: Using mindfulness practices to delete the neural networks of colonialism. In Waziyatawin and M. Yellow Bird (Eds.), *For indigenous minds only: A decolonization handbook*. School for Advanced Research Press.

4
CAJITAS AS MY CONTEMPLATIVE PRACTICE

Alberto López Pulido

Opening Reflection and Prayer

There was always a yearning deep within me – always a search – searching for a missing piece – an unanswerable question – that bothered me and kept me uneasy – an unsettled feeling deep inside in my quest for seeking answers and connections. It was in response to certain unveiled aspects of my family's intergenerational collective history, guarded by the quiet whispers of our parents from whom we sought answers.

This revealed itself within my Mexican/Chicano family situated along the U.S.-Mexico border, guided by immigrant parents who had made a survival pact to never trouble their children with stories of hardships and disjunctures in their lives. The objective was to extinguish such stories in an attempt to prevent the life-changing trauma(s) that would impact our lives.

Beginning the Journey: A Quest and the Desire

My emotional journey represents a life of fragments – the leftovers or the unspoken that you strove to breathe life into but with little to show for it. Rather, these fragments remain as unresolved disjunctures that I am compelled to search for – those pieces of the puzzle that I strive to put together, the confidence and courage I seek to ask questions in my search to be a complete human being. These disjunctures require observation, examination, and contemplation. This is the commencement of the contemplative path and journey in my life: contextualized and intergenerational personal reflection, exploration, prayer, and action.

DOI: 10.4324/9781003416777-5

Describing the Journey

I awake with the desire to both know and feel. My intellectual and personal journey has taught me that complete understanding requires getting in touch with both feelings and emotions. Our quest for fully understanding ourselves guides us toward discovering our hidden stories and narratives; stories that evoke both feelings of joy and happiness and also feelings of rejection and exclusion. This is a painful but necessary journey for members of all communities of color in their quest for full affirmation and self-determination on the path toward wholeness.

I first came to this realization over 20 years ago when I published an essay seeking guidance on how to craft an emotive scholarship that would guide me in discovering and accepting feelings of self-affirmation as a Chicano educator (Pulido, 2003). My task was to resist and reinscribe the sting of racism experienced growing up in this society. This revealed itself as a journey in search of an emotional epistemology described by Ronald Takaki (1998) as "narrative history" where one's experiences, feelings, adjustments, imaginings, hopes, uncertainties, dreams, fears, regrets, tragedies, and triumphs are welcomed and fully embraced. It acknowledges a *sentipensante* path where thinking and feeling are central to our personal and educational development (Rendón, 2009).[1] Complete and comprehensive knowledge draws from both how we think and how we feel about those life experiences that impact all of our lives.

Yet, traveling this path would not be easy, laden as it is with contradictions that guide and define our lives. On the surface, this quest feels counterintuitive and at odds with ourselves as we are impelled to ask: why would I want to explore my past if it is filled with contradictions and painful memories? Why must I stir up the past where the trauma suffered by my elders and relations is so painful that they were forced into silence and simply wanted to forget?

My journey has taught me that these painful tensions are and remain the consequences of colonialism and oppression to which our communities have been subjected throughout history by the powers that be. Du Bois (1968) describes it best in naming this as a "double consciousness" where "internal conflict" represents the residual consequences experienced by colonized groups in an oppressive society. I firmly believe that it is our destiny to accept these contradictions in order to be fully human, as we discover that we must live and navigate a world that is full of inconsistencies and negations. Such a choice does not in itself bring forth wholeness or resolution to these tensions and traumas. Rather, it puts us on a path toward self-realization and personal acceptance where, despite the contradictions and feelings of incongruity, we seek to recognize and embrace our knowing and feelings. Personally, this has helped me, and many people close to me, make sense of our lives.

Disjunctures and Application in Higher Education

These lived incongruities are best described as "disjunctures" – indicative of moments in our lives when we feel detached and disconnected from the dominant culture. They arise when "difference" is underscored, named, and institutionalized by the powers that be and are lived out at three levels: (1) at the level of our personal lives; (2) within the history of our nation; and (3) in the character and actions of our institutions. In addition, I have identified five sites of disjunctures experienced by communities of color in our unequal society that shape our lives lived out in a state of contradiction, compelling us to understand and to act.

1 The person I claim to be runs into direct contradiction with others who attempt to define and redefine who I am.
2 The stories that I uncover and embrace about myself run into direct contradiction with the stories that others tell about me.
3 The places and spaces I inhabit and that define and orient me as to who I am run into direct contradiction with others who seek to challenge and redefine my space and characterize it as unstable, contested, and extinguishable.
4 The social forces that I struggle toward challenging and changing in relation to those social forces that work systematically to control, silence, and erase me.
5 The political power I tap and demand access to in relation to political power that seeks to systematically control and disenfranchise me in order to sustain the status quo.

A recognition and deeper understanding of the disjunctures in our lives is deeply meaningful and transformative because it removes the internal doubts, insecurities, and instabilities we feel deep inside. Recognizing our disjunctured lives enables us to put a name to our feelings and guides us on a path toward wholeness. We better understand and accept our fragmented life journey as we identify all the disconnected strands and work to pull them together to better understand ourselves. In doing so, we must move beyond the feelings of "guilt, sin, and shame" that result from growing up fragmented in a society that is guided by a legacy of contact and conquest and that maintains its hegemony through practices of power, control, racism, and violence against the disenfranchised. Instead, we must work to uncover and embrace a life of transformation and wholeness (Abalos, 2007).

This journey of disjunctures began for me as early as kindergarten when I felt embarrassed about my cultural symbols and expressions of love. Deep inside I felt I was different from the rest of my classmates, and this led to feelings of shame (vergüenza) and inferiority that were self-inflicted. My mother's expressions of love – walking me to class and making me a hearty lunch – were seen as awkward and different from all the other white kids. This disjuncture would stay with me throughout my childhood and into my adulthood. Now, as a university professor, I have come to navigate this world of disjunctures and contradictions by recognizing and affirming alternative voices and paths validated by me in my role as an educator. Hence, experiential and community-based work that is rooted in my cajitas project (described below) recognizes alternative realities within the academic world that I first learned from my mentor, Julian Samora, the first Chicano sociologist in this nation. Professor Samora had a distinguished career at the University of Notre Dame where, over the years, he perfected a "signifying strategy" in which he could find humor in any situation in an attempt to derail the official narrative and orientation of academia. His form of expressing love and support for his students by offering an alternative reality via a trickster approach sent us a message that our lives mattered and that we were as important as the official narrative. Similarly, I have come to understand that the cajitas practice provides a different way of knowing, a unique epistemology that opens up new possibilities for students (and myself) by validating our stories and journeys and inviting all of us to embrace our intellectual and emotional selves as a legitimate academic exercise.

Complete knowledge and truth come from *both* knowing and feeling. As I have come to review my collective history alongside my personal journey, I realize that I must be able to comprehend it with a critical lens that strives toward a decolonial analysis and includes feelings and emotions. My journey has taught me that feelings and emotions may take a while to recognize as it takes more time to process and embrace what is going on within our heart and spirit. Such discoveries are sometimes too painful to process and articulate, so we must speak about them metaphorically through the use of art, storytelling, and music. This is a contemplative act where we fully embrace and speak about feelings utilizing color, imagery, light, or sound. We are invited to express our feelings via practice: writing, painting, building, creating, performing since it is too difficult to express ourselves in traditional ways. This helps explain the central role of cajitas in the lives of my students, in my community, and in my own personal life as an educator, ally, and activist.

My Contemplative Path: Cajitas as Situated and Intergenerational

Cajitas began as a classroom assignment where students were encouraged to learn about and affirm themselves by telling their stories as part of a larger personal, family, and collective history that spoke directly to their purpose and meaning in life. The exercise emerged from my desire to recognize and honor all relevant emotive knowledge rooted in community that those of us in ethnic studies refer to as community epistemology (Pulido, 2002). This resonated with my students of color and/or first-generation students who were granted permission to share their narratives and realities. As a result, they realized that their stories and experiences served as a foundation for personal and subjective knowledge that in turn shaped academic knowledge that was now being taught and analyzed in the academy. In my mind, this was and remains nothing short of revolutionary.

Cajitas are best defined as "sacred boxes" that serve as containers filled with personal and collective memories in relation to one's life journey. They represent vessels and repositories that preserve and protect personal and sacred belongings tied to one's personal orientation, grounded within memory, narrative, and place. The most significant role of the cajita is to offer its carriers guidance and orientation during a specific journey or over the span of a practitioner's lifetime, as they fulfill their desire for wholeness and healing from disjunctures and trauma.

The cajitas practice affirms that contemplation must come out of a situated context and must expand into an intergenerational reflection that includes parents and elders. Cajitas enable us to explore contemplation within a historized, politicized, and racialized context. When working with people of color and other marginalized groups, we must guide our contemplation into a living context that shapes our history, our story, and our specific experience to provide focus and guidance for our intersubjective mindful project. Additionally, since we are working on recognizing our personal traumas, we must be open to the fact that these disjunctured experiences are intergenerational and may move us beyond our individualistic path; they must be inclusive of those who came before us and affirm our collective historical experiences that span two generations or more. I have been awakened to the fact that my personal disjunctures described in this essay are directly related to the trauma my parents experienced, including their being uprooted upon their parents' death, and having to give away their own children. These life traumas of being uprooted and unwanted have directly impacted my own experiences and shaped my quest for clarity, orientation, and wholeness.

Formal education played another important role in creating disjunctures in my life as is the case for so many people of color who are erased from the formal educational process. Some of my earliest encounters with disjunctures in my life arose because the structures and lessons directed at me within formal public education were neither relevant nor adaptable to my life. There was a critical disconnect between the knowledge and guidance given to me by my parents, extended family, and community elders, and that given to me within formal public education.

The structures and lessons of formal public education were neither relevant nor adaptable to my life as a young man growing up in a strong traditional Chicano family. Absent in my formal education was the guidance and direction that mirrored the knowledge and wisdom given to me by my community. Words of guidance and practical life lessons offered within the Chicano community were meant to show us the way and provide instruction. They came in the form of "consejos" or advice to live by – both practical and personal. Consejos guided us in being "personas educadas" or well-mannered people who are respectful of others within a reciprocal framework. This was experiential advice guided by the value of "amar al prójimo" or *love thy neighbor* with an eye toward building community. We were taught to accept the truest sense of our being, opening ourselves up in search of personal validation, authenticity, affirmation, and transformation despite the numerous disjunctures encountered along the journey. Disjunctures led us to reject linear assumptions about life and instead recognize that life was a series of cyclical events that forced us to look back in order to move forward in search of our truest selves. This is a lifelong collective quest where some on the journey are further along than others – and where some have made the choice to exit the path, choosing a life of incoherence and deformation via assimilation and/or cooptation into the dominant culture.

The epistemological approach that I describe here affirms that the experience of disjuncture is the case for countless people of color and that our truths are discovered by looking both back and within in order to honor those "second sights" where we were endowed with a "double consciousness." Having been enlightened by numerous mentors within an ethical framework of reciprocity, both in formal higher education and in my community, requires that I teach and guide students, colleagues, and community members to recognize the disjunctures and traumas in their own journey. This process may aid them in better understanding themselves and overcoming the challenges of higher education and community disenfranchisement. Embarking on this journey, those who have been marginalized and erased are enabled to write their own stories and histories on the path toward wholeness and self-love.

My cajitas project has evolved into a contemplative practice that incorporates practitioners from all sectors and, in particular, faculty and professionals within higher education. Such a practice reminds us of the human dimension of our work and recognizes the frailties and struggles we need to face in order to be more effective teachers and educators. Cajitas also validate the work of educational practitioners as our professional lives are explained in relation to our biographies and communities. Engaging in this work transforms us into more mindfully grounded and compassionate guides and leaders for those who come after us.

The cajitas practice transforms and decolonizes higher education for marginalized and communities of color as knowledge and ways of knowing are not exclusively in the control of "experts," but rather in the hands of all. We incorporate ideas such as community epistemology; what this offers us is a knowledge base where we are not erased and our ideas are validated. The stories we tell via our cajitas are equally as valid as new academic theories that attempt to explain our cultures and traditions. More importantly, the cajitas stories arise from our own experiences and help us to better explain and understand ourselves.

Final Reflection

I began my work with Cajitas over twenty years ago. There are many people who have enlightened and guided me in better understanding my work as a contemplative project. I consider this present narrative as the foundation for a larger and more profound project on the power of teaching the value of cajitas as a contemplative project. I trust the guidelines below will help you in crafting a coherent contemplative practice that is both situated and intergenerational, with an eye toward transforming our fragmented and disjunctured lives into wholeness and offering an emotionally informed understanding of our past in order to strengthen ourselves and those that will follow.

Practice

Cajitas ("sacred boxes") are usually small wooden boxes filled with significant personal and sacred belongings as well as family "artifacts" carried by Mexican migrants during travels, including movement across real and symbolic borders and borderlands during the mid to late 20th century. These boxes offer an orientation (a sense of place and belonging) as people in motion traverse new and unfamiliar spaces. Always in movement, the boxes contain anything from personal family items (e.g., family pictures, dishes, documents) to replicas of religious saints. Our objective with the cajitas project is to capture the feelings and connections in our lives.

In this activity, students and their faculty mentors create diorama-like boxes related to their own journeys and identities. Think of this project in terms of the framing metaphors of "journey" and "pilgrimage," with specific attention to the unique disjunctures and sacred spaces experienced in our biographical journeys. This is a powerful, personal contemplative activity that I have done myself and with students many times over the years. Although it was originally designed for students, in this iteration I invite all higher education professionals to explore and to grapple with their own disjunctures in order to become better at the work they do within higher education and to guide others on the contemplative path.

The following cajitas guidelines will aid you in your contemplative journey:

Create a box, whether found or made, that will serve as the background, canvas, framework, landscape, microcosm, and/or stage for/of your story. What types of materials, shape, and structure accurately and authentically express your identity and journey?

Recall key events, moments, people, places, and the like related to your identity and journey. Are there specific objects (e.g., photographs) that represent or remind you of these? Begin to add and arrange them in your cajita. Be mindful of how you utilize the space of your cajita in conveying meaning that speaks to your identity and journey in relation to your feelings, connections, or disjunctures.

Reflect on significant experiences, feelings, memories, and the like related to the previous elements. Are there associated smells, sounds, tastes, and/or textures? Can they be expressed by or represented by additional materials, objects, or metaphors? Continue to select, add, and arrange the contents of your sacred box.

Complete the initial selection and arrangement. Consider to what extent this cajita is your own cajita, a material expression of your identity and journey. Is your identity and journey rooted in you, the individual? Or is it more rooted in the collective, or both? Is your identity and journey deeply personal and private, or is it more public with a community orientation? Feel free to remove any contents and/or add new ones.

Imaginatively inhabit your sacred box. Does it "feel like home"? Is it an accurate material approximation, expression, and/or representation of your spiritual landscape? If so, then finalize the project. If not, reflect on any feelings of disconnection or discomfort. Then adjust the cajita accordingly. Do not shy away from encountering and contemplating the disjunctures and contradictions that may arise in your work.

Finalize the contents and arrangement. Perhaps consider a title or framing theme. Reflect on the larger story being told and prepare an oral narrative that can be shared with others as they view your cajita, and as they explore your story through engagement and dialogue. In your written narrative, consider whether your journey-story is linear or cyclical, and what that might teach you about yourself and your experiences.

Note

1 Sentipensante pedagogy is a culturally validating, deep learning experience that addresses the harmonic balance between intellectual, social, emotional, and inner-life skill development. The pedagogy also connects the learning experience to issues of equity and justice. To foster deep learning, illuminative learning tools/"prácticas de conocimiento" are employed to open the senses. Examples include periods of silence, music, poetry, arts-based projects, testimonios, socially driven art and photography, ritual, and cultural immersions, among others.

Reference List

Abalos, D. T. (2007). *Latinos in the United States: The sacred and the political.* University of Notre Dame Press.

Du Bois, W. E. B. (1968). *The souls of black folk: Essays and sketches.* Johnson Reprint Corp.

Pulido, A. L. (2002). "The living color of Students' lives: Bringing *cajitas* into the classroom". *Religion and Education, 29*(2), 69–77. https://doi.org/10.1080/15507394.2002.10012310.

Pulido, A. L. (2003). "Engraving emotions: Memory and identity in the quest for emotive scholarship. *Crosscurrents, 54*(2), 45–50.

Rendón, L. (2009). *Sentipensante (sensing/thinking) pedagogy: Educating for wholeness, social justice and liberation.* Stylus.

Takaki, R. (1998). *A larger memory: A history of our diversity with voices.* Little Brown & Co.

5
CONTEMPLATIVE PRACTICES THROUGH A BLACK FEMINIST LENS

Badassery, For Real Love and Fellowship

Emerald Templeton

Introduction

The epistemological, ontological, and ideological approaches of Black Women in higher education have often been ignored, undermined, and/or erased despite the wealth of knowledge and intellectual capacity we bring. Black women have sustained rigorous and elevated scholarship in the midst of being devalued or reduced to insignificant others (Evans-Winters & Love, 2015; Patton et al., 2022; Perlow et al., 2018). Patton et al. (2022) posit that while Black women are noted as the fastest-growing group to be educated in America, this emerging statistic does not negate that this group continues to face harsh treatment consequent to gendered racism and *still* succeeds with severely lacking support. Dillard (2000), when describing *Endarkened Feminist Epistemology*, suggests that if higher education practitioners and leaders truly hope to transform the field, there is a grave need to situate Black women's knowing and understanding in new ways that account for the "historical, political, and cultural," (p. 670). For Black women, we navigate shifting spaces and narratives in higher education that require us to draw from our cultural capital to sustain ourselves, and to remain present and aware.

Cultural capital often includes contemplative practices that extend beyond simply deep thinking in the mind and transcend to the embodiment of introspection in tangible ways. These practices are sustaining, empowering, and transformative. Beer et al. (2015) describe contemplative practices as "exercises and pursuits that aid participants in achieving a state of calm and alertness, balancing work and personal identities, and performing work tasks with a high degree of self-awareness and self-respect" (p. 164). These practices can take many forms, from the physical to metaphysical, and can be practiced alone or in community (Beer et al., 2015).

Sustaining Forms of Contemplative Practices

As a Black woman navigating the complexities of interlocking oppressions (i.e., race, gender, class) in a higher education setting, I engage in contemplative practices that are grounded in spiritual practice, cultural knowledge, lived experience, and situatedness to the sociopolitical histories of my Black womanness. Already maneuvering within the constraints of a supremacist and patriarchal system, labor is overextended in this field because "higher education professionals have stress levels that rival those of emergency room doctors and nurses" (Beer et al., 2015, p. 163). So, to engage in transformative work that honors my experiences as a Black woman (Dillard, 2000) and creates an environment of stability and respect (Beer et al., 2015), I engage several formal and informal contemplative practices: prayer, meditation, writing, and fellowship.

Prayer

Prayer can be described as a spiritual practice wherein one submits petitions regarding their concerns and seeks connectedness, peace, and/or assuredness. As someone with a faith-based perspective, I consider prayer an essential part of being in relationship with God. I rely on guidance from God, and my primary venue for communicating and receiving assurance is through the act of praying.

Meditation

Often conflated with prayer, I engage in meditation when I want to center my focus on joy, commitment, peace, or other positive aspects of my experience. This contemplative practice allows me to disrupt the grind and hustle of work that can lead to high levels of stress and stagnation, while allowing me to hold onto the promises and possibilities in my work.

Writing

The process of writing often includes several parts: reading, reflection, outlining, and scribing. As a contemplative practice, writing takes many forms for me and often leads to clarity, release, and innovation. In informal ways of writing, I use journaling, concept mapping, and word bubbles to manage confusion and to get unstuck. Formally, I engage in scholarly writing as a way to influence and intervene in research and practice related to the concerns of Black women in higher education.

Fellowship

When I engage in contemplative practices on my own, I find that I have a deeper understanding of myself. However, engaging in contemplative practices in community opens the door for deeper inter- and intrapersonal connections. Grant and Thompson (2018) describe reflexive praxis as individual and communal reflection wherein deeper understanding about the impact of work on community can be gained. Fellowship, or shared community, is an opportunity to connect to shared purpose and goals. As a contemplative practice, specifically in spiritual spaces, I engage in communal worship and exaltation through music, hearing a "word," being in agreement (saying "Amen"), and witnessing/with-nessing possibilities for change. This practice is incorporated in my daily work as I reflect on my fellowship experiences for sustenance and engage in fellowship with likeminded people in the workplace.

Together, these practices lead to opportunities for rest, liberation, and radical love for self and community. For the purposes of this essay, I will focus on the sustaining and healing effects I experience from the practice of fellowship. Within this practice can exist the other contemplative practices of prayer, meditation, and writing.

"Fellowship" and Black Feminism in Practice

In Black Christian faith traditions, there is a common practice that typically follows a worship service or is embedded into an event known as the "fellowship service," or simply "fellowship." This is an opportunity to connect with fellow congregants and get caught up on the latest news. Folx will share stories, laughs, encouraging words, guidance, and warm embraces over a meal. Not necessarily a formal activity, fellowship often extends beyond the planned time for an event and, at times, carries over to people's homes. Beyond faith traditions, fellowship can look like "water cooler chat" at work, or communing during an employee affinity group meeting where folx find refuge and regeneration in a shared experience. It can look like advocacy, and sharing hidden yet important information about promotions or other workplace benefits and details. It may also be found in the nurturing relationships built in one formal environment that then develop into lasting connections in other informal environments. Fellowship offers safety, belongingness, and visibility that congregants often do not find in other non-Black spaces.

Porter et al. (2023) describe Black feminisms as understanding the ways of knowing, doing, and being within the construct of Blackness by centering Black women. Black feminist approaches such as Endarkened Feminist Epistemology (Cynthia Dillard), Black Feminist Thought (Patricia Hill Collins, 2000), and Critical Race Black Feminism (Nikol G. Alexander-Floyd, 2010) underscore the alternative knowledges Black women have and how their utility is in the social, political, and cultural astuteness that can only be found in community with others. Relying upon community—or fellowship—for sustenance, reflection, advocacy, and even strategizing responses to oppression is not at all uncommon for Black, and other historically oppressed communities. A cornerstone in Black feminisms is collective wisdom wherein Black women can exist as their full selves with accountability, care, and compassion (Morton, 2020).

The practice of fellowship is the lifeblood of Black feminism. As a scholar-practitioner in higher education, I often navigate predominantly white spaces as one of few, or the only Black-identified person. Existing in a world that marginalizes and defames my race and gender, it can be rather exhausting justifying my humanity and resisting systems of oppression, particularly when the actual work I do centers equity and justice for the marginalized. Taking a neutral stance to this work is almost impossible, and dare I say irresponsible, since I have cultural, sociopolitical, and historical connections to issues these communities face and situational understanding that cannot be learned through theory only. As a manager supporting programs that serve hyper-marginalized students such as adult learners and incarcerated individuals, collaboration is as integral to this work as fellowship is to sustaining myself while doing this work. I often work alongside others who have little culturally relevant or responsive knowledge to the communities being served, and who fail to see the conflict that exists between our equity mission and the need to be a profitable institution. So, connecting to and reflecting upon shared understanding within a culturally responsive community has been healing and energizing—a balm in a system that is known for its harshness to historically oppressed communities. I engage fellowship as a contemplative practice with other Black colleagues at my institution and in other professional networks. In my practice, I find support and encouragement as well as advocacy and mentorship.

Contemplative Practice for Liberation

In Beverly Tatum's seminal work, *Why Are All the Black Kids Sitting Together in the Cafeteria?* (2002), she artfully describes how even young people combat the contempt of racism by finding refuge in fellowship with their peers. Their shared racial identity and experience navigating white supremacy bound them together providing support, self-definition, and strength to traverse the rocky terrain. Similarly, Black leaders and educators need to develop their own communities that are spiritual, cultural, radical, loving, and sustaining. Exercising fellowship fulfills these needs while also providing space for self-awareness and communal vigilance in the face of oppression. This depth of connection has been necessary in the history of social justice movements (Perlow et al., 2018) and will be essential for institutional transformation and liberation, particularly in higher education, which can be seen as a site wherein movements begin.

What Black feminisms help us understand is what Monique Lane (in Patton et al., 2022) describes as *badassery* and *for real love*—Black women's ability to walk the line between resistance and institutional priorities while expressing a deep care for others beyond a singular dimension. The contemplative practice of fellowship embodies Black feminism as it situates the knowledges and lived experiences of the oppressed at the center with the goal of justice and liberation.

Final Thoughts

As a contemplative practice, fellowship offers practitioners, educators, and administrators in higher education an opportunity for deep, communal rumination and delineation. Using fellowship as an analytical and practical tool for implementing change, these actors can be responsive by co-constructing the culture, policies, and practices that reflect the ontologies and epistemologies of the communities they serve. Being careful not to disrupt the integrity, meaning, and essence of spaces that provide a safe haven for affinity groups, higher education leaders and practitioners who recognize and/or encourage the use of fellowship as a contemplative practice must avoid cultural appropriation and usurping spaces wherein folx with marginalized identities often operate with a sense of fugitivity, as described in Jarvis Givens' book *Fugitive Pedagogy*. Givens (2021) discusses how the "secret places" in which Black people learned during and after US chattel slavery were criminalized yet necessary for survival and connection. Similarly, spaces where fellowship happens might be misunderstood by dominant groups as divisive or even criminal, or in some cases, they may be sanctioned as a diversity tactic. This approach whitewashes or strips away the cultural appropriateness and richness of fellowship.

Instead of meeting the practice of fellowship with censorship, higher education leaders can offer resources such as time, space, and budget for marginalized communities—staff and students alike—to engage in fellowship. Allow these communities to lead these spaces without intervention or infiltration. Defer to marginalized communities about their needs for safety and belonging, and then be responsive to those needs recognizing that in many cases, the organization's culture is so steeped in systemic racism and structural oppressions that communities must find solace and fellowship within fugitivity (Givens, 2021) and/or outside of the organization.

In Patton et al. (2022), the authors describe how Black girls are often policed and under a constant white gaze—their actions, expressions, and language misunderstood and misconstrued as deviance. However, Black girls *and* women have a shared cadence to their talk, and rhythm to the ways they move that are rooted in love, community, and resistance to people and systems that intend to subjugate them. Like these Black girls and women, historically oppressed communities on college and university campuses often share sacred, spiritual, and cultural practices where fellowship happens. With institutional support for these spaces and respect for the full representations of individuals' identities, these communities can lead the change that is so important for transforming higher education.

Practice: Reflections on Fugitivity

What spaces do you hold as sacred and secure? What characteristics, artifacts, or understandings help you to recognize that you belong and can find safety there?

How might you locate safe spaces to engage the practice of fellowship? Do you see possibilities of engaging this practice in your higher education setting?

For BIPOC/Global Majority readers: How can you proactively embrace fugitivity to foster wholeness in your educational or professional context? Who are potential co-conspirators?

For non-BIPOC/non-Global Majority readers: How did the essay make you feel? Did you experience confusion, surprise, sadness, or anger? Reflect on these emotions and their insights into the need for liberatory and safe spaces.

Reference List

Alexander-Floyd, N. G. (2010). Critical race Black feminism: A 'jurisprudence of resistance' and the transformation of the academy. *Journal of Women in Culture and Society, 35*(4), 810–820. https://doi.org/10.1086/651036.

Beer, L. E., Rodriguez, K., Taylor, C., Martinez-Jones, N., Griffin, J., Smith, T. R., Lamar, M., & Anaya, R. (2015). Awareness, integration and interconnectedness: Contemplative practices of higher education professionals. *Journal of Transformative Education, 13*(2), 161–185. https://doi.org/10.1177/1541344615572850

Dillard, C. B. (2000). The substance of things hoped for, the evidence of things not seen: Examining an endarkened feminist epistemology in educational research and leadership. *International Journal of Qualitative Studies in Education (Education, 13*(6), 661–681. https://doi.org/10.1080/09518390050211565

Evans-Winters, V., & Love, B. L. (2015). *Black feminism in education: Black women speak back, up, and out (Black studies and critical thinking)*. Peter Lang Inc., International Academic Publishers.

Givens, J. R. (2021). *Fugitive pedagogy book subtitle: Carter G. Woodson and the art of black teaching book*. Harvard University Press.

Grant, M., & Thompson, S. (2018). Reflective praxis: Accelerating knowledge generation through reflecting on our research and practice. *Cities & Health, 2*(2), 91–95. https://doi.org/10.1080/23748834.2019.1598711

Hill Collins, P. (2000). Black feminist thought knowledge, consciousness, and the politics of empowerment. Routledge. http://public.eblib.com/EBLPublic/PublicView.do?ptiID=178421

Morton (2020). (Re)centering the spirit: A spiritual Black feminist take on cultivating right relationships in qualitative research. *Journal of College Student Development, 61*(6), 765–780. https://doi.org/10.1353/csd.2020.0074

Patton, L. D., Evans-Winters, V., & Jacobs, C. (2022). *Investing in the educational success of Black women and girls*. Stylus Publishing.

Perlow, O. N., Wheeler, D. I., Bethea, S. L., & Scott, B. M. (2018). *Black women's liberatory pedagogies: Resistance, transformation, and healing within and beyond the academy*. Springer Nature.

Porter, C. J., Sule, V. T., & Croom, N. (2023). *Black feminist epistemology, research, and praxis: Narratives in and through the academy*. Routledge.

Tatum, B. D. (2002). *Why are all the Black kids sitting together in the cafeteria* (5th ed.). Basic Books.

6

DEEPENING BELONGING

A Contemplative Practice of Relational Flourishing

Aizaiah G. Yong and
Yohana Agra Junker

Meeting in Times of Catastrophe

We met each other as professors within a Christian higher education institution in Northern California. As we were both appointed around the same time, we were still learning and sensing how the institution structured its educational and leadership model to reflect its values and commitments. While we felt initially aligned with how the institution touted efforts and devotion toward racial and social justice, equity, and radical belonging, we quickly experienced intensified religious and cultural violence woven into historically white and Christian higher educational institutions. In such spaces, intimidation, manipulation, and ostracization tactics were all too prevalent. The school continuously named it wanted to move toward participatory governance while asking staff and faculty to go above and beyond their initial contracts, sometimes with no additional compensation. While we both sought to use our voices in private and group settings to offer feedback and incite change, our comments were regularly taken out of context and used to perpetuate the status quo of white supremacy and hegemony prevalent within the institution. While we worked tirelessly with others to decenter whiteness, normativity, settler-colonialism, and racial capitalism, our efforts landed us at odds with the leadership, and they became visibly frustrated with us. When one of us tried to advance and protect the rights of students facing insecurities of all tenors, the culture of intimidation, power-hoarding, fear, and scarcity prevailed. The work some of us created was stolen from us, and senior scholars were given credit. We were also expected to acquiesce and adapt to top-down styles of governance, to teach outside our areas of expertise, and to dilute class content so it could be used as a recruiting strategy to increase fiscal revenue. Our work was instrumentalized to generate more income without proper compensation, recognition, or regard.

In this context it became clear that what sustained us was the relationship we had built as colleagues and friends, our spiritual practices, and the creation of spaces for deep listening and Convivencia (or "living-with," elaborated on further below). It was evident that movements of reciprocity and mutuality transformed into a practice that helped us collaborate and show up to the classroom as co-instructors, inviting our students to do the same. In the fall of 2020, we were asked to co-teach a class on contemplative practices and spiritual formation. As one can imagine, we were just five months into the global pandemic, and our bodies, spirits, and hearts were processing how COVID-19 and uprisings against anti-Black racism and violence would change our lives forever (Junker, 2020). Against this backdrop and as co-instructors, we attempted to create spaces where participants, including ourselves, had a chance to let the heaviness present all around us sink in one breath deeper. We both understood that our collective bodies needed space to metabolize the fear, rage, anxiety, trauma, and numerous unknowns. We discovered that, through our Convivencia, we were leaning into contemplative practices to survive the experiences of marginalization, struggle, and isolation. These practices helped us reclaim personal and collective courage and work toward healing amid such a challenging reality. During this time, Aizaiah spent extensive time gleaning from the spiritual teachings and wisdom of a great interreligious and intercultural ancestor, Raimon Panikkar; the philosopher, theologian, and monk who articulated the "Cosmotheandric Vision" or the intuition that all reality consists of rich diversity, including matter (the cosmic), the sacred (theos), and the human (Anthropos as consciousness) (Yong, 2023). Yohana turned to the arts and ancient healing modalities to develop "Breathing-Drawing-Meditations" as generative tools to access the visceral and somatic life of the body, its reflexes, intuition, desires, and needs (Junker, 2021). Together, and through the context of co-teaching, we co-created a new contemplative practice that involved ongoing shared check-ins, conversations, and a desire to thrive even amid oppressive histories and ongoing challenges of structural harm.

Origins and Commitments to Liberation

I (Aizaiah) was raised in a family as a third-generation convert to Pentecostal Christianity. My grandparents on my father's side were Chinese and Buddhist, and my grandparents on my mother's side were Mexican-American and Catholic. White missionaries from the United States came to my family's home communities on a mission to convert "heathens." And my grandparents first learned about Christianity from those missionaries and felt initially touched by their ministries, understanding them to have brought physical, emotional, and spiritual healing to their bodies. Yet, while the initial healing experience was deeply embodied, experiential, and affirming to them as human beings, the interpretations of Christianity that they received later became very problematic and culturally oppressive. As my grandparents chose to study and be guided under the tutelage of white, cishet, Christian men, they began to internalize the idea that their own cultures, beliefs, and rituals of origin were "demonic." This tragedy was passed to my parents intergenerationally, and I was raised with the assumption that to live with the divine meant to align with whiteness—all couched in the veil of "Christian religion." While I spent almost a decade in congregational and young adult ministry, much of that time was driven by questions around how to reclaim my sense of spirituality that affirms the mysticism of Jesus Christ while also rejecting religious teachings and practices that promote superiority, exclusivism, violence, and oppression. Further, I aim to re-integrate aspects of my ancestral and cultural wisdom lineages that were dismissed and left behind in my grandparents' conversion experience so that I can live in greater solidarity with communities on the edges of empire/s and partner together with the rich cultural and spiritual diversity of the world for the sake of collective healing and flourishing.

I (Yohana) was born in Brazil while the country still lived under a military dictatorship. My families on both sides were active in Brazilian Protestant churches as musicians, pastors, educators, and artists. As the years of the military dictatorship advanced, some of my family members became more entrenched in governmental initiatives and less committed to the values of the liberation movements burgeoning in the trenches. As the 1980s advanced, along with oppressive political tactics, my parents found spaces of generativity within theological education in Latin America committed to conscientização and liberation movements. We had the opportunity to live and study in Argentina and the United States while my parents advanced in their academic pursuits. Meanwhile, back in Brazil in the 1990s, neo-Pentecostal and neo-capitalistic movements began to enter into the Protestant churches that had formed me. As I reflect on those decades, the geopolitical territories we traversed, and the educational institutions we encountered, I become more convinced that our deep commitment to justice, freedom, and community allowed us to survive. This journey has not been easy. As a family, we absorbed the impact of continued harm and violence perpetrated by Christian theological institutions that were built upon and continued profiting from racial-capitalist, hegemonic, colonial, and transactional structures. Ours has become a commitment to undoing such compounding harm by building relationships predicated on values of mutuality, justice, and radical belonging.

While we are both professors within Christian higher education, we continue to struggle toward its potential transformation. As has been documented, the Christian university has had mixed historical impacts on society and, at its worst, has been a tool aiding the purposes of settler colonialism, white supremacist violence, and a false sense of religious superiority above all others who are not Christian (Panikkar, 2015). Therefore, it is not an overgeneralization to recognize that the Christian university has in many ways been a primary weapon of the oppressor to rationalize theologically and justify behaviors of exclusion and violence against all "non-normative" bodies. Some have given names to this kind of Christianity [what Jonathan Wilson-Hartgrove calls "slaveholder religion" (2020) and Yvette Flunder calls "oppression sickness from bad religion" (2005, p. 2)], and it has surely had devastating impacts on us; we are still only now (in our 30s and 40s) learning to disentangle from this religious toxicity. Yet, we remain committed to practices of healing that transform these spaces. Moreover, we know that we can only achieve this when we courageously tell our own stories with fullness.

Introducing A Contemplative Practice of Relational Flourishing

Our emergent co-created contemplative practice is called Deepening Belonging: a Contemplative Practice of Relational Flourishing because the cultivation of belonging sustained us through the challenges we have faced individually and collectively over the last three years. As this practice began to take shape, we noticed that it was grounded on mutuality, reciprocity, and co-flourishing. Indeed, this practice aligns with the wealth of ancestral wisdom passed down to us as Latin Americans through the traditions of Convivencia, a word that reflects our diverse Latin American contexts as it exists both in Spanish and Portuguese. Convivencia translated in Spanish is the action of living-with. In Portuguese, it connotes a life that is lived communally, with frequency, intimacy, and a sense of deepening "familiarity," that is, to make family-with, to construct families beyond what is typically understood as one. We build upon these traditional understandings, and in our work, we expand Convivencia to include the ongoing co-shared relational work of co-liberation (as we seek to make peace within ourselves and others spiritually, materially, psychologically, emotionally, and physically). For us, creating a space of Convivencia emerged organically because of our situatedness and cultural backgrounds, which allowed us to be open to cultivating personal and communal grounding, discernment, nourishment, and empowerment as we navigated a historically white and Christian institution that had a long history of being instrumentalized in the oppression of people like us.

We understand Convivencia as a liberative, embodied, relational, and intercultural way of being that calls us to interact with ourselves, one another, our ancestors, the earth, and our vocational work through *compassionate listening, deep witnessing*, and *embodied ritual-making*. What is vital to name is that while this practice is deeply personal, it is also profoundly communal. In this way, we seek to overcome the privatized and individualized Western and Eurocentric forms of contemplative practices that primarily focus on idiosyncratic interiority and neglect our systemic, intergenerational, ancestral, and collective needs and longings. In this practice, we realize that life is inter-in-dependent (both unique and inextricably interwoven with all others) and that every being is sacred (Panikkar, 2003). Deepening Belonging calls us to offer *compassionate listening* by holding space for the tender interior movements that surface in our experiences that are multiple and dynamic, especially around encounters where we have experienced suffering or oppression. And our practice extends compassionate listening beyond the self as it also involves listening to one another and others who we are in community with (including storytelling, dream work, the arts, music, and being in and with nature). *Deep witnessing* is about how respect, freedom, agency, and individuation are acknowledged within ourselves and others. Deep witnessing requires consent, is willing to move with patience and forbearance, and accepts grief, mourning, and rage from living in and through oppressive systems. *Embodied ritual making* is a way to process via the arts, which has a tremendous power to disclose to us that which is sublimated in embodied, visceral, and striking ways. Embodied ritual-making allows us to create processes for rehearsing speculative possibilities before intervening in the world. By amalgamating our bodies' contemplative, somatic, intuitive, and intellectual wisdom in ritual practices, we can recalibrate, assign new meaning, and integrate our lived experiences. It also allows us to compost the traumatic experiences that continue to perpetrate harm toward our bodies and souls. Embodied ritual-making provides us space to not only reorganize and retell our individual stories, but also for the mutual processing of experiences of trauma, grief, and angst all while reassuring us of the insidious ways in which we are, collectively, victims of institutional violence.

Four agreements that are vital to share in understanding more fully the nature of our practice and the ways we went about creating psychological safety are as follows: (1) the non-linearity of transformation, (2) the power of non-judgment, (3) the emphasis on the process along with outcome, and (4) the call to both solitude and solidarity. When it comes to *non-linearity*, we recognize that transformational work often feels like two steps forward and three steps back. Our practice seeks to embrace this felt experience of "messy," and, rather than making war with it, use it so that our lives can become more compassionate and tender. An agreement with non-linearity also helps us to be more radically honest with ourselves and engage in shadow work where and when necessary, opening ourselves and our communities to critique and greater accountability. Speaking to the agreement of *the power of non-judgment,* we recognize that we live in extremely polarized times where judgment and blame are often the first immediate reactivity present and that this mostly hinders creative possibilities. So, our practice aims to acknowledge the presence of both obstacles by normalizing the experience and creating space from them so that we can be more fully present with other experiences that blame and judgments can often protect us from. For us, a non-judgmental posture does not mean we leave out the importance of discernment (which we flesh out later). Still, it does mean that we seek to let go of preconceived ideas, notions, or scripts that often govern our actions and relationships unconsciously. Third, another binding agreement for our practice is an emphasis on the *process and the outcome.* This agreement is a commitment to living with courage and integrity as well as resisting hypocrisy. To accomplish this, we accept that the change process is just as important (if not more) as the outcome. And through this agreement, we look at our process and the fruit of it carefully and attentively. The agreement of embracing the process also allows us to be sensitive to our pacing (attempting to resist the ever-increasing acceleration of the consumer and technocratic age) so that we can be sure to take space for rest and digestion. In this agreement, we value time to pause, wait, and let things settle before acting. Taking time and space to process and reflect also creates opportunities for acknowledgment of failure or when there is a need for relational repair. Finally, an agreement on the paradox of *solitude and solidarity* is our way of recognizing that each being is infinitely unique and simultaneously invited to live in relational harmony with the rest of Life. We appreciate the teaching of Thich Nhat Hanh, who coined the term "inter-being," which he described profoundly as the truth that "everything relies on everything else to manifest" (Hanh, 2017). Our contemplative practice builds upon this sense and hopes to cultivate harmonious relationships by embracing space for the radical individuation of each person (without falling into individualism). Our approach contends that through embracing the radical solitude of one's life, one is empowered to hold and respect the freedom and diversity of others. So, our practice again seeks to integrate the personal with the communal. All four of these assumptions counter the logic of oppression and help foster a different orientation toward our lives and deepest yearnings.

As we see it, Deepening Belonging invites us to live from our deepest identity and to become co-creators in the adventure of Life through embodied, dynamic, and open connections. Our practice asks us to be patient with Life through the journey, which includes the ups and downs of the journey, and aligns with the post-humanist and African animist wisdom of "slowing down" (Akomolafe, 2022), where little by little, breath by breath we can learn to name, resist, and undo all that is violent and harmful. Our practice is as much for the individual as it involves the wisdom from and for the collective. Our practice is always asking that we make more space to hear the new sound resonating deep within us and trusts that when we befriend that, we will become more of who we are: free, generous, and in communion with all. Our practice has kept us alive and offered hope, comfort, and strength. And we hope that it will take new shapes and forms as our lives change and the world is continuously re-made.

Conclusion and Further Invitations

Deepening Belonging is a contemplative practice that is committed to potentializing and igniting relational flourishing. It invites us to ground ourselves in the totality of our experiences while creating opportunities to offer support, creative embodiment, and integration so we can tap into the power of our wisdom and creative vigor amid our unique social locations, our places of work, and/or relationships to spirituality. Deepening Belonging allows us to sense how our psychosomatic beings absorb the impact of compounding oppression, or, as Alexis Pauline Gumbs names it, to resist "the worst muck of racialized, ableist heterocapital" and settler-colonialism (Gumbs, 2020, p. 2). By becoming anchored in our bodies, we exercise what Gloria Anzaldúa names as touching "what most links us with life" (Anzaldua, 2009, p. 34). Through this contemplative practice not only do we experience spiritual and intellectual growth, but we are also able to sense how our souls and our bodies—individually and collectively construed—are important in the process of expansion, seeking harmony, and understanding that as above, so below. It is our hope that our offering can continue to offer strategies and stories of how presence, regard, mutuality, and reciprocity can allow us to flourish collectively as we continue to create spaces that allow us to intimate and befriend ourselves, each other, and this world in a radically different way.

Practice: Deepening Belonging: A Contemplative Practice of Relational Flourishing

Our contemplative practice comprised five movements that are more like threads that interweave together to co-create new life. Each movement within our practice should be understood not as a linear progression but rather as a dance in and with Life. The five movements of our practice include (1) *accepting* what is, (2) *befriending*, (3) *checking in*, (4) *discerning* the next steps, and (5) *extending* gratitude through embodied ritual and blessing.

In *accepting* what is, we affirm the need for truth-telling. So often, institutions within higher education deny and dismiss the emotional, spiritual, or somatic truths and privilege an intellectual-only approach to reality. This reductionist bias represses some of the deepest knowings available to us that are directly needed in our work toward liberation. So, our movement of *accepting* what is works as one way to give ourselves the permission to say and feel what has not yet been given space to be said or felt.

In the movement of *befriending*, it is the call not to do more harm and/or violence to one another while we are in the ongoing process of transformation. At times, we expect ourselves and others to be further along the road of healing and this can lead to bitterness and cynicism. *Befriending* is the alternative invitation to tend to the vulnerabilities and frustrations that are inherent to our lived experiences, and especially to meet our raw places with hospitality and compassion.

In the movement of *checking in*, it is the invitation to dialogue with others who can hold spaces for listening and processing. It is about being and becoming the kind of people who can truly hear or sense with us (not for us) and allow for creative and adaptive responses to begin to take shape. *Checking in* is all about engaging the moment with reverence, curiosity, and a sense that our lives and our work are sacred and, ultimately, asking what is arising so we can more fully partner toward cultivating communities of belonging.

Discerning next steps is about remaining open and willing to try and explore new ways of moving, being, and becoming that were not at first in purview. When we discern, we are making a concerted effort to act concretely. At times, this action may mean doubling down and strengthening efforts in a particular way, or at other times, it might mean letting go of where we were headed and attempting something different.

Finally, the movement of *extending gratitude and blessing* emphasizes the importance of ritual, marking our insights received, and taking time to remember and extend thanks to what has most deeply touched us. In some ways, this movement helps to harvest all the unique insights that are bubbling up through our spiritual journeys, offering gratitude and blessings from it that can spill over onto the lives of others. In this movement, we recognize that every transformation we receive is not solely for us, or even this moment, but is something for All reality to enjoy and partake in.

Reference List

Akomolafe, B. (2022). *A Slower Urgency.* https://www.bayoakomolafe.net/post/a-slower-urgency

Anzaldua, G. (2009). Speaking in tongues: A letter to third world women writers. In A. Keating (Ed). *The Gloria Anzaldúa reader*. Duke University Press. https://doi.org/10.1215/9780822391272-008

Flunder, Y. A. (2005). *Where the edge gathers: Building a community of radical inclusion*. Pilgrim Press.

Gumbs, A. (2020). Foreword. In E. Dixon, & L. L. Piepzna-Samarasinha (Eds.). *Beyond survival: Strategies and stories from the transformative justice movement*. AK Press.

Hanh, T. N. (2017). *The Insight of Interbeing*. https://www.garrisoninstitute.org/blog/insight-of-interbeing/

Junker, Y. (2020). On covid-19, U.S. Uprisings, and black lives: A mandate to regenerate all our relations. *Journal of Feminist Studies in Religion, 36*(2), 117–129. https://doi.org/10.2979/jfemistudreli.36.2.09

Junker, Y. (2021). *Breathing | Being | Praying Meditations: The Generative Possibilities of the Arts*. https://rsn.aarweb.org/spotlight-on/teaching/trauma-informed-pedagogies/breathing-being-praying-meditations

Panikkar, R. (2003). Human dialogue and religious inter-independence: Fire and crystal. *Faith and Development, 310*(4), 1–4.

Panikkar, R. (2015). *Christianity. Part two: A Christophany*. Orbis Books.

Wilson-Hartgrove, J. (2020). *Reconstructing the gospel: Finding freedom from slaveholder religion*. Intervarsity Press.

Yong, A. G. (2023). *Multiracial cosmotheandrism: A practical theology of multiracial experiences*. Orbis Books.

7

REFLECTIONS BEYOND FRAGMENTATION

A Fractal Reconfiguration

Vaishali Mamgain

These essays, accounts of deeply personal journeys, have been a joy to "receive." I use the verb "receive" intentionally, to acknowledge *"sentipensante,"* a "culturally validating, deep learning experience," that marries sensory, emotional, and intellectual knowing (Rendón, 2021, para. 1). Each author explores themes of identities and experiences of marginalization; they situate education in the context of their own journeys. I resonate wholly with this approach.

In the spirit of mutuality, I offer this reflection wherein multiple fragmentations act as a kaleidoscope, shattering our conception of the nature of knowing, of being itself! Yes, much about our educational system is broken, but we can *choose* how we reconstitute. Today, a college degree is a prerequisite to a living wage, yet the price is astronomical! Because of racism, global majority students typically do not receive intergenerational transfers of wealth. They rely heavily on loans. The Brookings Institution reported that the disparity in Black-White student debt more than triples four years after graduation (Scott-Clayton & Li, 2016). This financial reality makes it crucial that institutions ensure student success.

I employ the CourageRISE model to envision an educational system that is rooted in, and in service of community. I question the ethics of a profit-driven model of education and ask how we can promote an equitable sharing of resources without abandoning the resistance and creativity of the borderlands (Anzaldúa, 2012). Finally, perhaps paradoxically, I remind readers of the wisdom of transcending identity, and embracing an expansive, nondual awareness.

But first, *Who. Am. I?* Asian Indian, Hindu, Buddhist, economist, lover of Trees and Seas, and a settler colonial, I live in Dawnland-Maine. I am enlivened by the complex, rich, moment-by-moment encounter we call "teaching and learning." I also acknowledge that these encounters happen in charged spaces where histories of oppression are alive, in bodies and systems. Ironically, despite recent research that points to the importance of "extra-neural" learning – through feelings, sensations, movement, community, and even physical space itself (Paul, 2021) – the Cartesian split between body and mind dominates academia. Add to this the ruptures caused by colonialism, racism, and homophobia. No wonder many global majority folx disassociate, finding it hard to succeed in a system that doesn't acknowledge the fullness of us. To truly transform our educational system, each teaching moment must strive to bridge this separation!

Contemplative Education and Epistemology

As educators, we have long known that teaching and learning are not linear, disembodied, individualized processes. Instead, they are rich, sensory, relational ways of being! Dependent on time, place, and identities, but also uncharted, and full of possibilities. Contemplation offers a pause, a spaciousness that allows us to question, afresh – who learns? what? from whom? and to what purpose? Querying epistemology is not merely an intellectual exercise; it can serve as a koan – a repetitive, revelatory, and transformative process that untethers the habitual mind from ossified, unhelpful patterns. Although liberatory, it can also be very ungrounding – without a community to support us, we will likely falter.

A Courageous Community

My love-justice kin are the Courage of Care coalition. Their model CourageRISE (Lavelle et al., 2021) lays out a trajectory of transformation: a compassionate community gives us courage to reveal injustice, *and* to heal. It inspires us to sense and create more loving and just societies. Although presented sequentially, the Courage RISE model is holarchical; each stage deepens an understanding of the whole.

Courage (from cor – heart): to transform, we need to acknowledge who we are – including the painful alienation we feel from ourselves and each other. Such vulnerability is particularly difficult for us who have experienced marginalization. These essays, from skillful and loving teachers, offer Black fellowship, communing with nature, Qigong, and Convivencia, as ways forward. Each modality – compassionate and culturally appropriate – shows us how to come home to ourselves.

R(eveal) truths: as academics, we are trained in theories and histories of injustice and oppression, but we have neglected to acknowledge that teaching and learning these histories comes at a personal cost to those who inhabit marginalized identities. For instance, the authors describe poignantly, feelings of hypervigilance, erasure, shame, and exhaustion. The CourageRISE model uses insights from attachment theory and reminds us that when we are grounded in compassion, we feel safe enough to explore internalized oppression. Pulido asks: Who am I in relation to a socio-political system that denies my humanity? How can I *know* and *feel* these multiple identities, without descending into "incoherence and deformation" forced to assimilate and adapt?

I(nvest) in healing: these essays offer alternatives to assimilation, teaching us to acknowledge the fissures and richness of the global majority experience. Pulido, for example, employs *cajitas*, allowing imagination and creativity to access alternate realities, where art and storytelling help mediate difficult truths, and connect individuals to their ancestors. But sometimes, it can be difficult to face our own complicity. Lin explores the complexity of healing when one's own placemaking is fraught in the role of "settler colonial." For her, a decolonial praxis is not a one-time thing. It is an undoing that requires constant engagement.

S(ense) alternatives: we can look to liminal spaces for inspiration, as sites of inquiry and resistance. Although our current systems are dysfunctional and unjust, there also exist caring and collaborative relationships, and mutual aid organizations that promote flourishing. But we have to "sense" into these alternative futures and advocate for equitable sharing of resources. We can also harness the imagination and wisdom of folx relegated to the borderlands – for they can clearly see the dysfunction of systems from which they are excluded. These liminal, sometimes fugitive spaces have historically been sites of inquiry and resistance – employing art, theater, and humor (the trickster!) to subvert the dominant narrative. Anzaldúa (2012) cautions against romanticizing the borderlands, yet the resistance and creativity of these spaces can inspire us to imagine and create wildly different, more loving societies. However, as Templeton warns, we must be alive to the dangers of co-optation and cultural appropriation. Yong and Junker remind us that solidarity requires that we practice radical honesty while being committed to process and outcome. They offer a framework to acknowledge failure and attend to repair. Practicing solitude and solidarity, as they put it, are both essential to deepen our wisdom and to counter oppression. Reforming Academia is a social movement; we must learn to navigate conflict well!

E(mbody) and transform education rooted in Dr. King's vision of a beloved community: central to this is the understanding that teaching-learning are not market-based transactions! On the contrary, they are situated in cultural, intellectual, and spiritual lineages – we *receive* knowledge(s) from mentors, ancestors, and earth; we transmit through word, song, qi-showers, and Convivencia. In such a dynamic and multi-directional process, knowledge creation is not the domain of experts alone. Community epistemology is honored, and erasure is resisted. Most importantly, learning is in service of love and justice. "Knowledge grants humility," I learned as a child, in India. Humility inspires us to benefit others, to be a "community person," ordinary, really! In Buddhism, it's called the "wisdom of ordinariness," in the Tao, "nothing special"; Hutchinson talks of the everyday sacred: "cleaning greens and snapping peas." My teacher Dzigar Kongtrul Rinpoche tells stories about his grandmother, a wise meditator. Her path? Pause, reflect, and just be... all while milking a female yak!

Knowing Identities, Reach Beyond

Contemplative practices connect us to ourselves and others, to experiences of love, compassion, and awe – a sense of vastness that inspires and renews our experience of what Thich Nhat Hanh called "interbeing." For marginalized folx, it is important that we honor and celebrate our identities. *And* it is crucial we know these identities to be impermanent, alive only in relation to labels, often assigned by the oppressor (Akómoláfé, 2015). These too must be transcended to experience and manifest our full potential.

These essays evoke in me a reverence for the contemplative genius, the culture, and brilliance that has emerged from liminal spaces to resist and transcend oppression. Holmes (2017) describes jazz as just such a contemplative turn, "For in the midst of unthinkable rhythmic and tonal combinations, we also hear the impossible being brought within our reach. When Miles Davis blows the cacophony that can barely be contained by the word *song*, we come closest to the unimaginable, the potential of the future, and the source of our being" (p. 188).

Reference List

Akómoláfé, B. (2015, August 17). Decolonizing Ourselves. *Báyò Akómoláfé website.* https://www.bayoakomolafe.net/post/decolonizing-ourselves

Anzaldúa, G. (2012). *Borderlands/La Frontera: The new mestiza* (4th ed.). Aunt Lute Books.

Holmes, B. A. (2017). *Joy unspeakable: Contemplative practices of the black church* (2nd ed.). Fortress Press.

Lavelle, B., Vigna, A., Walsh, Z., & Porter, E. (2021). Relationshift: The CourageRISE model for building relational cultures of practice. *The Arrow Journal*, 8(1), 130–152. https://arrow-journal.org/relationshift-the-couragerise-model-for-building-relational-cultures-of-practice/

Paul, A. M. (2021). *The extended mind: The power of thinking outside the brain*. Mariner Books.

Rendón, L. (2021) Sentipensante Pedagogy. *Laura Rendón website*. https://www.laurarendon.net/sentipensante-pedagogy/

Scott-Clayton, J., & Li, J. (2016, October 20). *Black-white disparity in student loan debt more than triples after graduation*. Brookings Institution. https://www.brookings.edu/articles/black-white-disparity-in-student-loan-debt-more-than-triples-after-graduation/

PART II
Conjuring Transformation
We Who—*Know*—Know

David W. Robinson-Morris

What does it mean to conjure? What does it mean to transform? How can we *be* differently, so that we can *know* and *do* differently? As a Black American, I—like others who know the texture of injustice and the weight of oppression—understand what it means to conjure, to make manifest, to call forth from the depths of your spirit in concert with all that is seen, unseen, old, new, and yet to come with all beings in ecological kinship—transformation. This conjured transformation does not necessarily connote an altered ontic or material reality but does require an ontological and spiritual metanoia—a conversion—right where one stands and in the midst of one's proverbial storm when all hell seems to be breaking loose.

Monica Son, Robin Raven Prichard, Candice Salyers, Virginia Diaz Mendoza, and Emmanuelle Khoury—the authors of this section assist us in coming home to ourselves as they illuminate the meditative wisdom and rituals they utilize to create embodied liberation and justice consciousness within the often-restrictive confines of higher education institutions. In my close reading of their respective chapters, the authors join in an ancient and vital tradition of energy shifters and evokers of the possible—conjurers—who help us to perceive the imperceptible, to unhide the hiddenness, and move us from bondage of whatever weighs us down to embodied liberation.

Reading and rereading the words of the authors in this section, I just happen to have music playing as background noise to ground my thoughts. Not coincidentally, because we who *know* know that all coincidences are synchronistic winks and hidden yet unconcealed messages, I breathe in the melodic voice of India Arie situated above the deep boom of a single drum singing, *Born for this Mission*, a song that I now play each morning as I commune with myself, whatever gods maybe, and my people on the other side.

I invite you to locate and play the song. Sit. Breathe. Listen.

As a southern born, Black American, these words and the words of this section's authors provoke me to enter into the recesses of my imagination to summon phantasmagorias of my people, my Ancestors who survived the horror of the Middle Passage, the brutality of enslavement, the terror of the post-Reconstruction South, the abuse of Jim Crow, and the ongoing enactment of anti-Blackness in the very country they were abducted to and forced to build—and yet they found the spaciousness to still love, laugh, relish in hushed joy, and fashion lives overflowing with milk and honey. As a Black man, a free and liberated Black person in the 21st century, I am forced to ask: how in the hell did they survive? How might we survive?

In the quiet of my heart, they respond:

We understood what the "other" could not know—the hidden wholeness, the beat of the cosmic drum matching the beat of our heart in rhyme and meter, the call to witness light that takes shape and darkness that moves; we knew the chains we wore were nothing in comparison to the chained and trembling hearts of those who thought they denied us of our humanity. We know that truth does not wither, and water is not always wet.

We survived because we saw you, we conjured you from the depths of our imagination and wrapped you in the strength of our faith. There were days that were beyond difficulty, where death would have been a balm, but we carried on and so you must as well.

Go inward, go deep, and use everything you have and must to practice survival, to practice resistance, to enjoy hope and hopefully practice joy, to live fully—use everything because everything will be required of you to topple oppressive systems, battle injustice, and most importantly—to remain whole, well, and full while doing so ethically and creatively. Call on Us, we will hasten to help you.

Child, you mustn't just survive; you must thrive! We practiced a prophetic hope, we laughed and sang when we could, and we understood that love should be luscious, and joy should be savored and never ever be made a crumb.

Dance. Sing. Pray. Cry. Think. Love. Imagine. Resist. Persist. Do what you must, but do not look away. You were born for this mission.

Looking at our present moment squarely and unflinching in the eyes, we must conjure; we must call forth the unrealized potentialities and cosmo-ecological energies that some of us have been disciplined to ignore through our overreliance on the mind, on rationality—the Cartesian curse.

The contributors in this section assist us in the transformative journey of coming home to ourselves to gather intuitive and ecological wisdom through practice and ritual to manifest liberation and justice in spite of oppressive systems and institutions that lack the ability to recognize our individual and collective full humanity. As conjuring contemplatives, the contributors evoke unique understandings of wholeness utilizing contemplative approaches to movement, power, envisioning, beholding, consciousness awareness, and disruption.

As you read this section and experience each author's offering, I ask you to pause at the end of each paragraph. Listen to your body; feel how it responds and where the words call you to grasp and/or release, to laugh or to cry; where their experiences rouse a verbal response of affirmation or denial.

I ask you to read with the intention of releasing, regaining, reimagining, and remembering—you were born for this mission.

May you be well.
May the 10,000 be your constant guides.
May you always walk upright.

8
REVEALING HEALING, WHOLENESS, AND POWER

Sitting Zazen

Monika L. Son

> *Leaning into truth*
> *I am both light and dark; one.*
> *Present with it all.*

In 2017, I attended the Association for Contemplative Mind in Higher Education conference.[1] My presentation shared leadership practices I used with my faculty and staff at the time that focused on building compassion, critical love, support, and vulnerability. By then, I had been a Zen practitioner for a few years and often turned to contemplative practice in my leadership roles and in the classroom. Among the most resourcing of my contemplative practices has been meditation. When I became Chair and guided the department through the pandemic, sitting meditation (zazen) was an everyday practice I shared with others too. Zazen has been a foundation for healing and awareness in my life. It has enabled me to find the courage and strength to include all my lived experiences, including the ones that have caused grief, rage, and powerlessness. In the depths of these strong emotions, I have surfaced painful inquiry around internalized oppression, particularly the narratives I hold around who I am and what is possible in my life. It also allowed me to see the many ways I too can replicate oppression, power, and privilege if I remained ignorant to my own pain. Zazen has supported an internal transformation of coming into my own power and agency, a key to deep healing and embodiment.

Zazen: Why This Practice for Me?

Life is my practice.
The cushion is where I rest.
Where I see the truth.

Zazen is a Japanese word for seated meditation Although instructions for seated meditation may vary across Buddhist traditions, I will be specifically discussing zazen from the Soto Zen tradition. In Soto Zen, the instruction for sitting is quite simple.[2]

My busy stressful life brought me to practice. The end of my late twenties found me working full time as a lecturer and a full-time doctoral student. In addition, I was married, a parent of two boys under the age of three, and a caregiver for my aunt who was living with Alzheimer's. After eight long years of doctoral study, I earned my Ph.D. The last few years were the most challenging. One afternoon, while I was preparing to present at a conference, my husband picked up our boys from nursery school. The school had called because his mother did not come to pick up the children. When my husband opened the door to our home, he found his mother unconscious, in a pool of her own blood. More sickness soon followed.[3]

We had a Buddhist ceremony for my mother-in-law. I recall the monk leading the service took one look at me and said, "you look terrible, you should come to my meditation class." In those days, my body craved stillness. Like a much-needed oxygen mask, those first few weeks of practice saved my life. My nervous system began to slowly build a habit of slowing down and resting. I could connect with a level of peace and rest deep within my bones. It took weeks, but I learned to settle my body/mind through continuously inviting myself to come back to my breath.

During this time, identity, race, and ethnicity were my main professional research interests. On a theoretical level, I understood that the social construction of identity permeated all the ways in which stories of who and what we are take shape. As a developmental psychologist, I had this deep curiosity to study the self. Was it possible to know a self that was "untouched or unharmed" by systemic oppression? I chose academic settings as a micro-system to engage with this inquiry. I was curious about how young people understood and practiced agency in institutional contexts. My research demonstrated that narratives of marginalization and not belonging were pervasive (Son, 2013). And yet, a deep will to transcend others' projections remained untouched. Their experiences resonated with a place I was beginning to tap into inside of me. I had a hunch that I was touching a universal experience that developmental theory could not explain.

Simultaneously, my career was in deep transition. I stepped into leadership roles in both faculty and administrative spaces. I took a seat at the table but my attempts to engage the college community with inquiry around power, privilege, and oppression led to burnout, moral distress, and outrage.[4] As a first-time Chair, nominated to lead the Council of Chairs, I received an alarming email to congratulate me that included a patronizing "did it make sense for an assistant professor with a humble publication record?," remark. Some of my colleagues offered to support me, short of taking on any leadership responsibility themselves. In perpetual offense mode, I often left those meetings depleted, rageful, and ungrounded. During this time, my overall health declined.[5] Counseling was helpful, yet it was in zazen that transformative healing opened for me.

Healing: Accompanying Body/Mind

Drain, cut, dry yourself.
Thoughts get in the way.
Too exhausting, breathe.

Zazen is returning to the body. In sitting, I would gather my awareness, rest into my breath, and feel my body. Feeling into my body, I would feel tightness and constraint in my throat and chest. "What is that?" I would ask myself. Stay with it; come back to the breath. The zazen instruction is to not push discomfort away or be consumed by it. One returns to one's breath. Through returning to breath, I learned to regulate my nervous system to a place that was neither reactive nor numbing, but quietly growing into somatic capacity. Cognitive and neuroscience research demonstrates that meditation practice supports the development of somatic capacity by cultivating a nervous system response of regulation (Baker, 2021; Menakem, 2019 Van Der Kolk, 2015). As one practices this level of mind/body regulation, there is more capacity to discern the reality of our experience and how we attach meaning to that experience.

Mental Narratives and How We Attach Meaning

In daisans[6] with my first Zen teacher, Sunim, he shared that zazen was a process of studying myself, an inquiry into who I knew myself to be. He instructed that whenever I was able to "catch" the stories that arose, I should ask myself: "what is this? Is it true? where is it coming from?" Some of those stories were as follows: "if you cry, people will see you are weak," "you can't be weak, you're a woman of color, don't expose your pain, you are giving them power over you," and "it doesn't matter how hard you work, you're never gonna have what other people have, you were born to struggle." I began to develop what Buddhist teacher Lama Rod Owens (2020), refers to as a deep intimacy with my own suffering" (Williams et al., 2016 p. 67).

In their book, *Radical Dharma*, the authors explore the paradigms of race within the context of American Buddhist communities and the mental suffering experienced by black-bodied members. In sitting and touching into my stories, I could feel the tension in my belly, not being able to fully distend in the inhale or fully expand in the exhale. For me, this constriction is related to power – the sense of my own capacity to be in choice. I sensed a helplessness that ran deep, as if connected to so many beings. It was bigger than me, and I wondered how many others felt this way.

One of the greatest insights I received from zazen is that the mental suffering of oppression is real and not just in my mind. As I became more disciplined in my zazen, I grew to discern better that what was being projected onto me was not just about me; I was part of an oppressed collective. In other words, the messages I had internalized were not unique to me, but part of a collective story many of us deemed as "other" share.

In my sits I often found my mind creating to-do lists of more responsibilities and then resenting those responsibilities. Some of these habits were not necessarily harmful. For example, creating more responsibilities for myself supported professional growth and competence and visibility in my career. However, since I was also resenting these responsibilities, it helped me see that the habit of performance was not about career goals. Underneath an internalized habit to perform was a constant need to prove my worth. I had a deep fear of remaining invisible and stagnant, of no one ever knowing who I was or what I could achieve. These habits are not mine alone, but a product of living in systems of dominance, supremacy, and extraction, that teach us to exalt visibility, status, and achievement.

Zazen allows me to open myself to everything, even suffering. Zazen is about turning toward our own suffering so that we can better serve the suffering of the world. The more I allow myself to truly experience my own pain, the more I can authentically accompany the pain of others. Through zazen, I move from a mental understanding to an embodied knowing of what it means to walk in the world in a Black body. Moving in an embodied way draws me to the Black community and to beloveds in a way that helps me reconnect with joy, pride, and belonging, not just pain. I become increasingly able to hold my complex lineages and ancestry in a way that includes all that I am. I am learning to be whole.

Wholeness: Waking up to All of Me

Ser entero (To Be Whole)
No se necesita mas (One does not need more)
Solo unirme. (Only join myself.)

"Us vs them"

One of the greatest harms I have experienced and witnessed in academic spaces is the devaluing and exclusion of who and what is different. My work in the academy was an intersection of faculty, advisor, counselor, and administrator. The workload required me to meet with students for 80% of the week. Advising and counseling students requires an engaged presence, and it was challenging to simultaneously meet the teaching and scholarship requirements for tenure and promotion. I craved more spaciousness to tend to scholarship like many of my colleagues at my institution, but I was torn about what it would cost the students. The mission of the program and department was to serve students who traditionally would not have access or opportunity to attend college. The students I served were often the most marginalized at the institution. To honor their experiences required a sustained level of advocacy and organizing (Son et al., 2022). It was a classic "us versus them" setup; a story of exclusion, of separation; *these* students. *These* come with all these problems: attrition, academic probation, need for resources. One of the gifts of this role was that it forced me to bring to center what it means to be at the margins; to always include the real-world contexts of what it means to be of systemically marginalized communities. For folks who hold privilege, including me, the real-world contexts are often challenging to witness as they may elicit guilt or shame. In my leadership roles, I spoke often of the realities of systemic poverty, violence, and lack of access to basic needs that contribute to students' ability to succeed in school and the inability of those who serve them to significantly remove the impact of those factors. Meeting spaces were tense and ridden with conflict; the discomfort of not being able to control external factors was unbearable, as was the threat to institutional power and its gatekeeping mechanisms to control for success. In other words, success often equates to keeping *these* students out. Systems of oppression convince us that "othering" controls for threat, or loss of power. White supremacy, patriarchy, colonization are strong systemic paradigms because they continue to maintain the illusion of an other – "us vs them." Othering "asserts disconnection; and demands domination" and extraction from the whole (Morgan, 2022, p. 43). Returning to wholeness is challenging when we blindly believe the illusion of separation these paradigms impose. Surfacing our othering habits and remembering our interconnectedness is necessary for our collective liberation. Practicing in this way allows us to better bear witness and be in choice of how to act. When we are in choice and can embody our agency, we are transforming our relationship to power.

Inner Power: Letting Be

I've got the power.
It's getting kinda hectic.
Move, walk, sit, breathe, be.

I recently explained a double bind[7] to a friend. In both choices, the tightening of my belly rose in my chest, and a sense of suffocation in my throat. From a systemic perspective, to be invested in justice is to highlight that double binds are often presented to people like me. It was not the first time I was met with double binds and likely not the last. Thus, my interest here was not in how to change the double bind, but in my response to the feeling of constriction and my own power within to transform that feeling to meet my decision from a place of spaciousness and flow. Upon witnessing my distress, my friend asked me the following: "Is it being in your own power that feels uncomfortable or unfamiliar? Are you afraid of what living in it will be like?" Her inquiry immediately awakened me to where I often find myself stuck in these double binds. What do I need to come to terms with to be in my power? How does my practice resource me in these moments?

A Deeper Look into Power

I have been weary of people and institutions with power. My reservation stems from living in a BIWOC body in a culture that is cloaked and deeply conditioned by white supremacy and patriarchy. My trepidation became enforced in the world of academia, particularly while serving as a Chair. In the years I served, the council of chairs was predominantly straight, cis, and white male. Hoarding power, or feeling threatened when their agent identities were questioned, was a common occurrence. In these spaces, which mirror the collective embodiment of our relationship to power, it often felt like those who did not hold the power had to fight to take it back. While fighting back is necessary in undoing systems of oppression, when it becomes the default we often bypass the deeper level of work required to sustain true transformation. Power develops from an awareness of our own suffering that cultivates an attentiveness to the suffering of others. Experiencing power is not about being empowered, not about feeling on top of the world; it is about being *of* the world. Power is belonging. I belong to the world and so do you. I do not hide or try to force; I take up the space that is inherently mine, as is for all beings. To take up space with intention, I practice spaciousness in my zazen.

Practicing Spaciousness

I am a light-skinned cis Dominican woman of Black ancestry, daughter of immigrants, born from a lineage of colonization, slavery, misogyny, and patriarchy. There are many histories, narratives, and traumas that thread across those social locations. Trauma scholars have noted that harm by race-based micro-aggressions causes embodied responses that lead us to react in habitual ways that may seem like personality or culture (Menakem, 2019). This finding resonates with how people like me may engage with the world. The social and cultural projections placed on female, Black bodies deem where we belong in the world and what seems possible. What does it look like to engage with the world from perspectives or shapes that place limits on the body?[8] Research on the impact of trauma also supports the use of embodied practices to support an internal shift/realignment of responding from a place of choice (expansion), not reactivity (constriction). In sitting meditation, where was I limiting myself? Could I inhale more deeply into the belly, could I extend my exhale a bit longer? Could I relax the gripping in my psoas or right shoulder, to dissipate more energy into other parts of my body? And how could I practice this kind of spaciousness in my life? To embody spaciousness, I accompany seated practice with more physical somatic practice; a long walk, a yin yoga class, a practice with my jo staff.[9] I often think of my mind/body as a system, where all parts are in relationship to each other, impacting the capacity for the whole being to meet the world. The spaciousness within my body moves into my thoughts and energy. I can see where the points of my stories and thoughts lead to constriction; where others' perception of my race, ethnicity, gender, or immigrant identity limit my capacity to imagine possibility. I can let those stories be because I recognize that they are not all of me. To let be *is* belonging. To connect with a felt sense of belonging is liberatory. Letting be is powerful. But, letting be is not about magic or superpowers; it is about confronting the reality of loss and impermanence.

My life has prepared me well for this reality.[10] To recognize that everything will change, that we all will succumb to loss, including our own sickness and death, is an incredible assurance. Through the sickness and death of dear beloveds, I learned to live with impermanence; the reality that I had no control about how and when I would lose everything. While I may experience a powerlessness to this fundamental truth, I am not a helpless victim to it. The teaching of zazen is simple: come back to the breath, come back to this moment, through trusting that the next breath will follow. In letting be, I neither follow the pain, nor hold onto it. In letting be, I include everything, the broken heartedness and the wholeness, the point at which we become "other" and where we "other." We other one another; we other the parts of ourselves we cannot tolerate; we fall into a cycle of individual and collective separation. How can we change the world when we disown it? How can we embrace love and be in relationship with the world if we are holding onto pain? In her talk to the first Black Buddhist gathering at Spirit Rock, Alice Walker illustrates this sentiment through the following story:

> Suppose someone shot you with an arrow right in the heart. Would you spend your time screaming at the archer? Or even trying to locate him? Or would you try to pull the arrow out of your heart. White Racism, that is to say envy, covetousness and greed (incredible sloth and laziness as in the cases of enslaving others to do your work for you), Is the arrow that has pierced our collective hearts. For centuries we have tried to get the white archer to see where the arrow has landed. [The teaching of letting go] says Enough. Screaming at the archer is a sure way to remain attached to our suffering. A better way is to learn, through meditation, through study and practice, a way to free yourself from the pain of being shot, no matter who the archer might be.
>
> (p. 197)

Too many arrows
How can I make the pain stop?
Zazen serves the world.

Practice: Everyday Zazen

Rest in your seat; feel your feet on the ground as they rise up to meet you. Sense into the support of your back. Strong back, open, relaxed front. Breathe deep into the belly. Inhale and exhale. Notice physical sensations, sounds, or thoughts. Keeping eyes slightly open, return to the breath each time your attention goes elsewhere. Recall your intention to practice. Allow it to permeate your body. Bring to mind a being that is suffering. Keep returning to the breath. Close with a dedication to end suffering.

Notes

1 The conference was titled *Radicalizing Contemplative Education: Compassion, Intersectionality and Justice in Challenging Times.*
2 Described at the end of this chapter, as adapted from Upaya Zen Center. See also https://www.upaya.org/zen/
3 My mom was diagnosed with Alzheimer's, and I became a full-time caregiver for my father, who suffers from chronic illness and traumatic brain injury.
4 According to Roshi Joan Halifax, moral distress occurs when "we are aware of a moral problem and we determine a remedy, but are unable to act, because of internal or external constraint" (Halifax, 2018, p. 101). Moral outrage

is "an external expression of indignation toward others who have violated social norms" (p. 101). Roshi Joan's work focuses primarily on the context of clinicians in the healthcare system, and in end-of-life.
5 I suffered from anxiety, fatigue, immune system weakness, digestive surgery, and skeletal muscular injuries.
6 Daisans are interviews or one on one check-ins between Zen teachers and practitioners.
7 A double bind is a sense that no choice is a good choice. There are many aspects of life in which a double bind can occur (personal, work, moral, systemic), but perceptually we feel constricted, cut off to possibility.
8 Shape is a term used by many somatic teachers/therapists/scholars to describe how we hold or position our bodies in response to activation, stress, and pain. It includes tracking the emotions and narratives that accompany the shape, as well as how the shape impacts your worldview.
9 A jo staff is a long wooden staff used in the martial art of Aikido. In my training in embodied leadership with Rusia Mohiuddin and Rev angel Kyodo Williams, the jo was used to elicit our conditioned shaping and to create embodied shifts within the body (TakemusuAikidoNL, 2009)
10 My parents and in-laws, immigrants from other countries, came to the United States in search of a better life. My in-laws, who worked six, sometimes seven, days a week, were forced to retire in their late fifties because they were laid off. They died suddenly due to illness by the time they reached the ages of 62 and 65. My father, who went back to school to earn an already received MD (medical doctor degree) in the Dominican Republic, worked odd jobs and was off the books as a physician's assistant, until he suffered a devastating car accident that left him disabled for life. He was about to complete his first year as a psychiatrist on Rikers Island. My mother, who enjoyed physical health for most of her life, was diagnosed with Alzheimer's in her early seventies that degenerated her mind and body quite rapidly. She lived for a time in that state and transitioned in her early 80s from complications of COVID.

Reference List

Baker, W. B. (2021). *The wakeful body: Somatic mindfulness as a path to freedom*. Shambhala Publications.
Morgan, C. (2022). *The heart of who we are: Realizing freedom together*. Sounds True.
Chari, A., & Singh, A. (2021). Embodying Your Curriculum. https://www.embodyingyourcurriculum.com
Halifax, J. (2018). *Standing at the edge: Finding freedom where fear and courage meet*. Flatiron Books.
Hanh, T. N. (2008). *The heart of Buddha's teaching*. Random House.
Menakem, R. (2019). *My grandmother's hands: Racialized trauma and the pathway to mending our hearts and bodies*. Central Recovery Press.
Morgan, C. (2022). *The heart of who we are*. Sounds True.
Owens, L. R. (2020). *Love and rage: The path of liberation through anger*. North Atlantic Books.
Son, M. L. (2013). *Pathways of activity: Lessons from Dominican college students*. City University of New York.
Son, M. L., Diaz-Mendoza, V., Alford, S., King-Toler, E., Cuesta, G., & Hayman, L. (2022). Echoing: A practice of liberation through transformative education. *Journal of Contemplative Inquiry, 9*(1), 21.

TakemusuAikidoNL. (2009, May 11). *Aikido Instruction; 13 jo kata* [Video]. Youtube. https://youtu.be/j5f1-UwwtMg?si=csruesG-IHhWHv1b

Van der Kolk, B. A. (2015). *The body keeps the score: Brain, mind, and body in the healing of trauma*. Penguin Books.

Williams, R. a. K., Owens, L. R., & Syedullah, J. (2016). *Radical Dharma: Talking Race, Love, and Liberation*. North Atlantic Books.

9
FROM BODY OPPRESSION TO BODY SOVEREIGNTY THROUGH CONTACT IMPROVISATION

Robin Raven Prichard

Overture: Half as Far Away as the Nearest Star

The light from the closest star
Is four years away.
I can't remember the light from four years ago:
can you?

A book is at least half as far away
As the nearest star,
And always a rambling message
from the past.

A poem is as close as the sun.
Seven minutes away,
It is a more immediate response
To our body's tremblings.

A dance is as close as the moon.
Light refracted off the body's wisdom,
It is a sudden crash,
A bewildering collision
1.3 seconds away.

Or,
a dance is the light refracted from your eyes.
Taking only microseconds
And requiring only the barest of light.

Many people – particularly those who do not dance much – celebrate dance as freedom, as if moving in various ways allows one to escape into a utopia in which the constrictions of society disappear. Those who dance professionally or train seriously, however, rarely equate dance with freedom; they know that oppression occurs as much through the body as any other site of culture and that the body can be constrained, repressed, and manipulated through the medium of dance.

It is also true, however, that dance and movement can be ways to access bodily contemplation, conscious embodiment, and liberation. But for the first two decades of my life, nothing was further from my experience. I took dance lessons originally for fun and eventually as serious training for a career. I loved the big, bold physicality, but I did not work with my body; I worked against it. My body was sometimes a distant friend and often an enemy, but never was it "me." I worked to fit it into the given molds, to imitate shapes and energies, and I evaluated my body based on visual criteria applied from outside the movement and exterior to myself. I tried with a desperate love to become the non-subject that contemporary dance required. Moreover, my Native American ancestry and culture, although occasionally fetishized, was usually "wrong" for dance, and so I strove to become the White, mostly object, never-quite-subject that my dance education demanded.

It was not until leaving my undergraduate conservatory that I was able to begin healing the damaging mind/body, subject/object, White/non-White split that served as the foundation of my dance training. I started to explore what it meant to be a subject moving, a sovereign bodymind in relation to others. The movement form Contact Improvisation (CI) was fundamental to my transformation. Now as I teach CI in higher education, I continue to appreciate how transformative this practice can be. It changes students' bodyminds and physical practices and opens possibilities for richer movement and deeper artistry. But the true transformation happens when students value their subjectivity, connect to movement as the "thinking" of the body, and allow themselves to treasure the bodymind as integral to being. Most importantly, the practice of CI helps to develop body sovereignty and oppose body oppression, leading to more just relationships – interpersonally, within the university, and within society.

In this chapter, I outline the concept of body sovereignty as I use it, providing contrast to other available concepts such as consent-based and autonomy-based concepts of the body. I argue that body sovereignty is needed to battle body oppression and to de-colonize power relationships both within bodies and between bodies. I show how CI transformed my relationship to myself, allowed me to develop my subjectivity while moving, and offered possibilities for battling body oppression. I then discuss how CI guides my teaching in fostering body sovereignty and how universities might transform by considering their constituents as bodymind sovereign entities.

Body oppression is not about negativity or negative feelings – it is about control and power over others. It cannot be countered with bouts of positivity, nor with gaining power/control over oneself. Overcoming body oppression requires nothing less than a rethinking and regauging of the way power and control work on bodies, including one's own bodymind, others, and society as a whole.

I use the term bodymind as an intervention into language that concretizes the division of mind and body. Bodymind refers to an individual in their wholeness as both a body and a mind without division into two separate entities (Cohen, 1993); it challenges the Cartesian dualism that separates the body from the mind. Bodymind intends to signify an individual in their wholeness. It is not intended to become an object, even when language demands it conform to an object as a form of grammar.

Body Sovereignty

The body sovereignty concept I propose originates in Native American philosophies and lifeways. It encompasses the idea that an individual is unequivocally in full determination of their body, with full authority. To hold body sovereignty is to be absent of body submission, subjugation, external threats, or coercion, and to be free of implicit and explicit violence (Ace, 2021). It includes the ability to advocate for one's needs and desires and the authority to seek fulfillment of them. Rather than a concept of ownership, which perpetuates the commodification of bodies and measurements of use-value, body sovereignty is a relationship of guardianship (Gillon, 2020). Power is not "over" our bodies; rather, body sovereignty indicates that full authority and the ability to express it resides within an individual.

With body sovereignty, each individual makes choices for themselves and does not impede on the sovereignty of others. This incorporates the critical elements of consent: choices should be freely made, informed, reversible, and specific to each context. It is not synonymous with autonomy, which many body-positive and consent-based rhetorics emphasize. As James Kloppenberg asserts, unrestrained autonomy can become an excuse for cruelty (Kloppenberg, 2017). It has been a justification for slavery, rape, and many kinds of body oppressions. Thus, I suggest that models that rely solely on autonomy are based too much on a rights-driven culture that worries about individual rights to the detriment of other people in society. Body sovereignty balances autonomy with reciprocity, which recognizes that people are bound to act reciprocally in their communities and to others (Prichard, 2023).

Reciprocity recognizes that we are anchored together – that we survive or fail together – and that one's sovereignty is interconnected to the sovereignty of all. Body sovereignty identifies that not all people's sovereignty has been equally respected or recognized and that those who have historically been denied sovereignty – people of color, women, children, and the disabled – are more vulnerable to having their bodily boundaries ignored and transgressed. It also acknowledges that a threat to one person's sovereignty is a threat to all. Thus, body sovereignty works to secure sovereignty for all, particularly the historically vulnerable.

Body sovereignty's attention to systemic oppression is one crucial difference from most models of body positivity or body autonomy. Body positivity and autonomy movements put the onus onto the individual to solve the problem for herself: if she feels bad about herself, it is her job to enact a personal solution to her personal problem. Bodily positivity and autonomy movements create individual solutions for systemic issues, encouraging (mostly) women to see themselves as stymied by internal impediments and personal defects. Body sovereignty recognizes the systemic oppression faced by particular groups and does not encourage these groups to turn inward to face internal demons, but rather to identify this as oppression and fight it as a problem of power and control.

Because the model of body sovereignty originates in Indigenous thought, it is crucial to note the unique ways that the concept operates in Indigenous communities that are still fighting for both land and body sovereignty (Barker, 2006). Dispossession of land sovereignty and body sovereignty occurred together in colonialism, and they continue to occur together today (Estes, 2019). Violence against the land is inextricably linked to violence against Indigenous bodies, and thus, Indigenous sovereignty over lands is inseparable from sovereignty over Indigenous bodies (Estes, 2019; Simpson, 2016).

The fight for body and land sovereignty endures in contemporary movements such as Missing and Murdered Indigenous Women, Idle No More, and #NDAPL (Estes, 2019). With land valenced as "female," the violation of land becomes a metonym for the violation of women (Barker, 2006). Indigenous women suffer disproportionately large rates of gendered violence with little response from the U.S. Department of Justice (Urban Indian Health Institute, 2018). Researcher Annita Lucchesi estimates that 25,000 native women and girls have gone missing or murdered since the beginning of the 20th century (Lucchesi, 2019). The constant violence against the land is tied to the epidemic of violence against women and girls, as violence follows extractive mining, timber, and water operations and their temporary "man camps" of workers. Meanwhile, peaceful Indigenous protests of environmental injustice have incurred increased criminalization and military-style violence (Howard et al., 2018). The labeling of environmental protestors as terrorists allows protestors to be treated as a state of exception in which their rights – and their body sovereignty – can be breached in the name of national security. Thus, those who fight for Indigenous land sovereignty find their own body sovereignty at risk.

Native American body sovereignty extends to all beings, including plants and animals, land formations, and bodies of water. The end point of body sovereignty is that the self-determination of all beings is recognized and respected, challenging colonial ideas of power, environmental abuse, the transactional value of other beings and land, and the heroics of conquering.

Body Sovereignty Toward Decoloniality

There are conceptions of body sovereignty that differ from what I propose, and these are generally disconnected from Indigenous thought. Many models of consent and some body sovereignty models stress a person's autonomy; some suggest that body sovereignty is to be beholden to no one but yourself. Others stress the idea of power "over" one's body. All of these reinforce and recreate ideas of colonial power, individuality, and hierarchy and thus do not lead to transformational change.

Having power over one's body creates a microcosm of colonial relations within an individual, positioning some parts of an individual against other parts of themselves. It reinforces a mind/body dichotomy in which a person associates the self with the mind ("mind over matter") that then oppresses the body. Even when aiming to have friendly relations with the body, the concept of "power over" creates a relationship with oneself that will serve as a model for relationships with others. For instance, my early dance training taught me to use power over my body and to withhold care until "it" did what "I" wanted, and to create transactions in which my body would get care/rest/nourishment after it satisfied my demands. Once this dichotomous, hierarchical, transactional, and domineering relationship is established within oneself, it will naturally be a model for relations with others. One cannot use a model of power over oneself to eliminate the desire individuals have for power over another. Utilizing a model that creates an intrapersonal relationship with oneself that can be translated into relationships with others is paramount in reforming asymmetrical power relations and agencies. Decolonial relationships begin intrapersonally, as I discovered through dancing CI.

What Is Contact Improvisation (CI)?

CI sprang from the late 1960s – early 1970s milieu of experimental modern dance, which strove, among other things, to give autonomy to choreographers. With CI, its creator Steve Paxton returned decision-making to dancers. He wanted movers to be "emancipated without confining or restricting others" (Paxton, 2003). Predominantly a duet form, CI began as an experiment into the physical possibilities between two bodies.

CI orients movers toward the sense of touch. This can be the lightest of touches or fully weighted catching and throwing. CI is based on becoming sensitive to the sensation of bodies, listening through the body, and being responsive to the moment. As an egalitarian movement form, it now exists on six continents in a plethora of practices and diverse situations. CI explores movement as an interconnected practice where bodyminds connect to each other, their environment, and the surrounding cultures/communities. Its possibilities lie not in one mover's choices or another's but in a third entity between the two movers: the dance. Each dancer has autonomy and neither is the follower nor leader; rather, they embody a third element in which listening and responding create a dance that exists both within and apart from the bodies. Ideally, neither person is in control of – or at the mercy of – the dance. In its most fully realized form, the dance exists in both autonomy and reciprocity.

Describing CI is a bit like the parable of the blind men describing the elephant – it holds various meanings for different practitioners. Some use CI contemplatively; some use it in therapeutic situations, some utilize it as a performance form, and others participate in weekly jams as a social event. CI has become part of university dance training and is often taught as a supplementary course in dance major, non-major, and general population programs. Often, it supplements modern technique, as CI has become part of the skills that contemporary dancers are expected to know. For me, CI's potential in higher education is in its ability to change states of awareness and to develop body sovereignty, altering how students relate to themselves, their bodyminds, and others.

Changing the Relationship with One's Own Body

CI changed my relationship with my own body by bringing me out of my visual default – a way of being in the world that dominates our Western culture. I was conditioned to use vision as the paramount experience for judging myself and others, and for learning and reflecting on dance. This encouraged me to treat myself as an object rather than a subject. Removing the visual codes I depended on took away my main way of processing, evaluating, and judging movement, my body, and aesthetic experiences and required me to find other criteria by which to gauge my experiences. Focusing on physical touch, the weight of another person or object reoriented my awareness. It allowed me to ask what I physically desired from a movement experience. Orienting my bodymind toward pleasure, in which no other person could provide an answer or direction, I built a relationship with myself.

Treating myself as a subject with body sovereignty encouraged me to build relational connections and mutual bonds, rather than transactional connections that demanded and withheld. In teaching and learning, we often consider working together as building mutual, relational, and reciprocal skills, but cooperation can be – and often is – transactional. People can choose to work together so that they both get what they want; e.g., A's on a group assignment, promotion, accolades. CI showed me that when outcomes are unknown, when roles remain constantly shifting, when perception and experimentation are the only goals, relations are more likely to develop than transactions. We are likely to see our partner as a subject rather than an object either standing in the way of, or a pathway to, what we want.

Universities and Body Sovereignty

My early dance training ended up being valuable for the educational institution I work for. Without conscious realization, I became solely the measurement of my bodily productivity: monetized, capitalized, and reduced to what I produced for the institution. My university wanted to keep parts of me and discard the rest, and it counted on me not to notice. I became a series of transactions; no longer a person or a subject.

How might our universities be different if all constituents were regarded as body sovereign entities? Even more radically, how would universities transform if they took a body first approach – one that asked what the body needed, rather than denying its existence from the onset?

A body sovereignty model suggests that when a university respects the autonomous subjectivity of every person, it creates relations rather than transactions. Students, faculty, donors, and neighbors can then become deeply invested in the co-creation of a university, rather than serving as a means to an end. In creating relationships, an institution must give up forcing control onto others, manipulating others for their own benefit, or parceling out the parts of their faculty/staff/students based on use-value. This in itself would create life-giving spaces in which liberation is possible.

One integral element of CI is listening through multiple systems as a mover's most important skill. Without listening to your partner's movement, the atmosphere in the room, or the external environment, a person cannot move with integrity toward the moment or their partner. Others are constantly expressing their sovereignty; if they are not, it is our job, as teachers, administrators, and institutions to help them. CI teaches us that listening makes us mindful of ourselves and others and facilitates a deep striving for co-created, non-hierarchical systems. Listening is crucial for creating spaces in which healing can occur.

The body sovereignty model shows us that institutions with integrity can only exist when every person's sovereignty is acknowledged and respected, when autonomy is balanced by reciprocity, and when power and control over cease to be the goals. The concept of body sovereignty within universities would transform relationships at every level from transactional to relational decisions about people. It would necessitate treating all constituents, particularly those at the lower end of the hierarchy, like subjects rather than unruly objects who need to be controlled. And it would reform the intimate relationship between faculty and student, when coercive methods so fundamental to the university, such as grades, advancements, and other regulatory methods, are eliminated in favor of non-coercive ones.

Dance and movement are not guaranteed to be contemplative or transformative, and they can easily contribute as much to body oppression as bodily liberation. Yet when we consciously engage our bodyminds in the fullness of being, we create opportunities to counter body oppression, create sites for healing, and strengthen our interconnectedness. We create opportunities to foster body sovereignty in which each person is both consciously autonomous and reciprocally connected and in which each individual can fully inhabit the world in a responsible and life-giving manner.

Practice: Rolling Point of Contact

This exercise explores how to sequentially follow the point of contact with your partner, attuning you to touch. This exercise can be done with one or both partners sitting in a chair or on the floor. It can also be done with a wall or floor surface if no partner is available or as a warm-up.

Begin with wrists: facing your partner, place your wrist onto your partner's wrist. Slowly begin to roll your wrists/arms so that the point of contact between you and your partner rolls to different points on your bodies. Let it roll up your arms, to your shoulders, through the edges of your fingertips – follow the rolling point wherever the movement takes it. You and your partner will not be symmetrical: for example, your partner's point of contact might be their shoulders while yours is your fingertips, or you might have a forearm to a forehead.... Let the activity of rolling decide where you go. You do not have to remain standing; you may end up kneeling, lying down, or bending backward; go only where you are comfortable and allow your partner to do the same. Be conscious of how you are touching your partner – how much pressure, how much demand, or permission you assert, when you are consciously leading or following. Stay with the rolling and try to avoid **slides** and **skips**.

A **slide** is when one person's point of contact stays the same but the other slides along the body to a new point. For instance, if I am shoulder to shoulder with my partner and I move along my partner's body so that I am now elbow to shoulder, I have slid along their body. A **skip** is when the point of contact moves to a new part of the body without rolling sequentially. For example, if I am head to head with my partner, then suddenly I am shoulder to shoulder with them without having rolled through the skull, neck, and upper back, we have skipped. When skips and slides happen, note them quietly so that both you and your partner begin to become aware of when they happen.

Stay with the activity for 2–3 minutes. Afterward, talk to your partner about your experience and any sensations you noticed. Repeat the activity beginning forehead to forehead. Try shin to shin. Experiment with starting with different body parts than your partner. To culminate, try having a rolling point of contact "dance" where you and your partner let the rolling point take you into larger movement and more choices. Experiment with sharing more and less weight. Experiment with having much larger points of contact (for example, the entire surface of the back) and much smaller points (the end of a fingertip). Let this end "dance" be an experiment where you hold the idea of rolling point loosely in your bodymind and see where it takes you.

Reference List

Ace, H. (2021). *Treaties: The symbiotic connection between land and body sovereignty; An exploration into re-presencing Indigenous epistemologies to re-story Sovereignty.* [Masters Thesis]. University of Manitoba.

Barker, J. (2006). Gender, sovereignty, and the discourse of rights in native women's activism. *Meridians: Feminism, Race, Transnationalism, 7*(1), 127–161. https://doi.org/10.2979/MER.2006.7.1.127.

Cohen, B. B. (1993). *Sensing, feeling, and action.* Contact Editions.

Estes, N. (2019). *Our history is our future.* Verso Books.

Gillon, A. (2020). Body sovereignty and Te Matatini: Thoughts from a kaimātakitaki. *MAI Journal, 9*(2), 173–178. https://doi.org/10.20507/MAIJournal.2020.9.2.8.

Howard, S., et al. (2018). Indigenous resistance to the Dakota access pipeline criminalization of dissent and suppression of protest. *The University of Arizona Rogers College of Law,* 16 Mar. 2018. https://law.arizona.edu/sites/default/files/Indigenous%20Resistance%20to%20the%20Dakota%20Access%20Pipeline%20Criminalization%20of%20Dissent%20and%20Suppression%20of%20Protest.

Kloppenberg, J. T. (2017). *Toward democracy: The struggle for self-rule in European and American thought.* Oxford University Press.

Lucchesi, A. H. (2019). "Indigenous trauma is not a frontier: Breaking free from colonial economies of trauma & responding to trafficking, disappearances, and deaths of indigenous women and girls". *American Indian Culture and Research Journal, 43*(3), 55–67. https://doi.org/10.17953/aicrj.43.3.lucchesi.

Paxton, S. (2003). Drafting interior techniques. In A. C. Albright, & D. Gere (Eds.), *Taken by surprise: A dance improvisation reader* (pp. 175–184). Wesleyan University Press.

Prichard, R. R. (2023). Performing arts education for democracies: Are we cultivating citizens or docile laborers? In K. Schupp (Ed.), *Futures of performance: The responsibilities of performing arts in higher education* (pp. 241–255). Routledge. https://doi.org/10.4324/9781003316107-22

Simpson, A. (2016). The state is a man: Theresa Spence, Loretta Saunders and the gender of settler sovereignty. *Theory & Event 19*(4).

Urban Indian Health Institute. 2018. *Missing and murdered women and girls*. Report. www.uihi.org/wp-content/uploads/2018/11/Missing-and-Murdered-Indigenous-Women-and-Girls-Report.pdf.

10

FROM PRACTICE TO PURPOSE

Contemplative Dance as a Method for Moving through Resistance

Candice Salyers

Kneeling on the plush red carpet of a Los Angeles mosque, I immersed myself in simultaneous solitary and community contemplation. During this weekly jum'ah prayer service, the imam redirected our attention from the mechanics of our practices to the purpose behind them. He calmly asked the congregation, "If our practices aren't helping us become better people, then why are we doing them?" Although determining what constitutes "better" may rely on individual perspectives, the ways in which our practices transform us can have reverberations in the world beyond our separate selves, including within our universities. I carried this question with me from California to my new teaching position at a university in Mississippi. Perhaps because Mississippi magnifies the difficult history and complex beauty of human nature, I have found it to be a significant site for exploring what it can mean for my contemplative practices to help me become a better person—and how that "better" can contribute to a more humane university community.

Although contemplative practices are frequently promoted as a solution for the stresses of everyday life, their larger transformative potential for individuals and social structures does not necessarily result in instantaneous bliss. The journey through contemplative practices to a "better" self rarely comes without struggle. In fact, my practices are often where I encounter resistance to change within myself as well as the tools to move beyond it. Writing about his use of such practices in the classroom, Paul Wapner (2016) points out, "The forms of uneasiness that can accompany the use of contemplative practices *themselves* provide pedagogical value" (p. 82). Such uneasiness has been instructive for me as both a practitioner and a

DOI: 10.4324/9781003416777-12

teacher. As a Muslim, my contemplative practices and the uneasiness that sometimes accompanies them teach me to look beyond the surface appearance of a situation (and my initial reaction to it) in order to learn from each experience in life. My practices as a dancer help me bring those lessons into embodied understandings and tangible forms that can be shared within secular university settings.

When I was a university student myself, my experience of dance shifted from a focus on its outer mechanics to understanding the power of its contemplative purpose, especially in working with Liz Lerman. Dance movement can be a mindful practice of embodied change within oneself as well as in the world, and Lerman's insights have inspired my performance and pedagogy for the past 20 years. Her belief that "we can use artistic process to help us understand and negotiate issues in our lives" (Lerman, 2014, p. 248) formed the foundation of her professional inter-generational company known for creating dances in unlikely places and with people who had never considered themselves to be dancers. While her impact on higher education spanned the U.S. as her company toured and later as she accepted positions at Harvard and Arizona State University, it was her invitation to "turn discomfort into inquiry" (Lerman, 2014, p. 6) that became a pivot point in my artistic life and teaching. Her quiet tone always made me lean closer to hear the wisdom in her words, even as we were focusing on the articulation of our feet in a modern dance technique class. Mirroring her movement, I would drag the outside edge of my foot across the floor, noticing how the physical friction revealed an embodied intelligence. Her insistence that "Resistance is information" (Lerman, 1999) turned the friction of experience into a mantra for looking through the practice itself to the pedagogical potential of every moment.

As a young teacher, I repeated that phrase silently to myself during class as it became a cornerstone of my contemplative pedagogy and my approach to becoming a "better" person. Lauren Fritzsche (2022) describes that students' resistance can pose a significant challenge to integrating antioppressive and contemplative pedagogies into higher education. Such resistance "encompasses verbal and embodied reactions in which students are skeptical and/or hostile toward classroom experiences" (Fritzsche, 2022, p. 171). These behaviors can impact not only an individual student's learning but also the entire classroom environment, so it has been vital for me to understand, respond to, and help transform their resistance rather than simply reacting to or punishing it. For example, when a student rolled his eyes during class, I knew I wanted to compassionately care for what was happening inside him on a deeper level rather than react in anger to the behavior itself. By recognizing that his outer resistance was covering over an inner insecurity, I could adjust my explanation of an exercise to create an environment in which he felt safe to fully participate, and I felt more capable of guiding him and the whole group with kindness.

Initially I tried to work around my students' resistance with my own actions as a teacher. Then, I began teaching students to recognize it in themselves. Acknowledging that resistance can appear in many forms that we might describe as "anger," "frustration," "boredom," "fatigue," "hopelessness," and other affective states, I encouraged students to explore what self-knowledge they could discover behind their emotional reactions. When students were frustrated by an article we read, I led them through contemplative exercises to help them uncover what valuable insights about themselves lay behind their initial anger at the author. As students felt disappointed by the feedback they received on their performances, I invited them to make space for their feelings while also looking beyond that emotional moment to what beliefs they were holding that allowed someone else's words to overshadow their own embodied experiences. I developed a series of contemplative movement improvisations that could help them physically identify resistance as well as experiment with a variety of responses to it. I reminded them that if they could understand it on a bodily level, they have demonstrated the capacity to find options for freeing themselves from getting stuck in resistance in other areas of their lives. As Wapner asserts, contemplative practices "introduce a type of wildness into the classroom where people can feel their edges and learn themselves into new understandings and, by extension, ways of being in the world" (Wapner, 2016, p. 82). Practicing embodied approaches to moving beyond resistance as dancers has supported my students in understanding the value and purpose of moving beyond resistance in their lives outside of class.

In Mississippi, I have been inspired to connect contemplative practices from classes to a larger sense of purpose in our campus community as a whole. Although at first glance contemplative dance practices may seem to be impractical ways to address some of the difficulties facing our campus, my students and I have found that our presence can inspire a sense of embodied compassion within a diverse community. Such embodied compassion can be particularly significant when confronting issues of food insecurity. Mississippi routinely ranks as the hungriest state in the nation with food insecurity impacting 22–40% of the total population (Move for Hunger, 2018), and the problem can be exacerbated on college campuses. As Langston Moore, Communication Director for the Mississippi-based College and University Anti-Hunger Alliance acknowledges, "Just in the Jackson Public Schools alone, 100 percent of students qualify for free and reduced lunch. When they go away to college, those needs don't stop" (Ciurczak, 2019). Yet hunger itself is only one component of the problem. Although food insecurity directly impacts so many people, and by extension, systemic food injustice impacts the entire state, perceptions of hunger can perpetuate stereotypes about who is hungry and why they are hungry such that among college students, "receiving food aid is often seen as socially unacceptable, creating stigma, shame, and embarrassment for recipients" (Peterson et al., 2022, p. 141). In Mississippi, such stigma impacts not only those needing assistance but also the state's public policies as it has some of the most stringent requirements to qualify for support. Joint research conducted by the national organization New America and the Mississippi-based Springboard to Opportunities reveals that "Mississippi puts up more barriers to receiving public assistance than nearly any other state" (Wolfe, 2017, para 1). The report concludes that the idea that "poverty is solely to blame on individual behavior" (Wolfe, 2017, para 9) underlies both barriers to accessing support and the limited amount of support available. Whether in the form of governmental aid or direct support between individuals, resistance to giving and receiving food assistance is heartbreaking to witness on our campus.

In order to help address food insecurity, my students and I designed a dance performance to raise funding for our campus food pantry. Although this performance was intended to be a tangible action in the fight against hunger on campus, we also realized our efforts might not create a meaningful shift in the other problem associated with this issue—the resistance to offering and receiving support. Because contemplative practices have the ability to move us intellectually, imaginatively, emotionally, physically, spiritually, and communally, we turned to these practices to expand the performance beyond a fundraising effort. Integrating contemplative experiences for both the dancers and the audience foregrounded what I understand the essential purpose of movement practices to be; that is, transformation.

Our movement practices during rehearsals led to the creation of the performance itself but also gave dancers the opportunity to explore their own beliefs and experiences related to food insecurity. Because these student dancers would lead the audience through contemplative practices during the performance, our rehearsals served as an important time to consider these issues through internally focused exercises. As Valin Jordan proposes, "The change sought on our campus communities requires those who are charged with leading efforts of change to do a lot of internal work in order to effectively support those they serve" (Jordan, 2020, p. 39). My students and I each developed individual contemplative dance sequences within a shared palette of movement tasks. First, we explored moving from a passive to an active stance by physically progressing from a supine position to a standing position over an extended period. The slow pace of the movement provided us with time to quietly question the ways we want to take a more active role in transforming food insecurity on campus, while the embodied transitions we each chose on our journey to standing gave us physical opportunities to reflect on developing the internal strength and confidence to empower those actions. Once arriving at a standing position, our second task required us to face our resistance. We each considered an existing belief that created resistance to or prevented us from taking action. If a dancer chose to let go of what they determined to be an unhelpful belief, they turned to the left, and if choosing to establish a new supportive idea, they revolved to the right. Our third movement task involved creating two gestures—one that signified giving and one that denoted receiving. The simultaneous presence of giving and receiving was an embodied reminder of the balance between them and the fact that we all do both.

The performance then opened this contemplative process for audiences. Through its demonstration of physical change, dance can offer transformative experiences for individuals as well as a communal body. States of performance also conjure a public contemplative atmosphere through the shared focus, attention, and presence they inspire. Using dance's ability to foster these contemplative experiences, the 35 student dancers and I spent eight hours performing our sequences in order to grant our campus community time and space to examine perspectives on food insecurity. Having been influenced as an artist and teacher by both Paulo Freire's *Pedagogy of the Oppressed* (Freire, 1968) and Augusto Boal's subsequent *Theatre of the Oppressed* (Boal & McBride, 1974), I have long appreciated how the practice of forum theater invites the spectator to step into an empowered role as actor and change the story as it unfolds. Although we did not ask audience members to step into the role of performer, we invited them to walk through the dance itself as the performance created an immersive environment filling the room that dancers and audience inhabited together. Each audience member's own physical movement and chosen positionality in relation to the dance shaped what they perceived and how they understood the "story." By extension, this physical experience proposed that our different positions in the world also impact the ways we perceive food insecurity.

In our performance, we moved slowly and continuously through positions that merge ease, difficulty, beauty, and distortion. We offered audiences a period of suspended time inside the performance event to slow down and to allow the shapes our bodies moved through to evoke images and associations within their own imaginations. Interestingly, all of this movement was accomplished by using resistance—allowing friction to slow and propel motion within our bodies and through the performance space. During the performance, we provided audience members with a reflective exercise as a means of intentionally bridging the meditative movement and contemplative thought. Emerging from Islamic practices that encourage practitioners to contemplate how an outer form can reveal an inner understanding, this creative exercise led audience members through a series of questions to allow them to discover the ways in which what they each uniquely perceived in the dance from their position in the room could translate into an insight about themselves and their lives. What moment or movement did they remember the dancers doing within the performance? What word would they use to describe the particular flavor of that movement or resistance? Where is that quality of movement or resistance currently appearing in their lives? How is that quality of movement or resistance present in them? Once these discoveries were made and experienced as a gift of insight, they could then be applied to help viewers further explore their beliefs in relation to food insecurity. We invited viewers to use these public contemplative practices for the purpose of gaining knowledge about themselves and also engaging with one another on common ground—considering food insecurity with thoughtfulness and care rather than shame and separation.

The performances and subsequent practices were not didactic messages telling audiences what to think. Instead, they offered people dignity through the opportunity to reflect on their lives, examine their ideas, and consider moving beyond their resistance into new insights about themselves and their responsibilities within the campus community. Unlike Boal, we did not ask audience members to dance, but we still encouraged them to become active subjects during the performance event by using the dance they witnessed and the focused environment it fostered to experience their own contemplative journey. Our campus audience is composed of people holding many different perspectives on food insecurity, and our dancing served as an invitation for all of us—those of us experiencing food insecurity, those of us believing stereotypes about others, and those of us judging those who don't want to provide assistance—to recognize the resistance within ourselves as well as the insights and potential for transformation it can reveal.

While it dominates contemporary political conversations in this state, resistance to feeding people is not new or only present in Mississippi. I am reminded of the longevity of this issue every morning as I read from the Qur'an's chapter Ya Siin (يس) that originated more than one thousand years ago: "And when it is said to them, 'Spend [on others] out of what Allah has provided you for sustenance', those who are intent on covering over [Truth] say to those who believe, 'Shall we feed someone who, if Allah wished, He could have fed? You are in nothing but clear error'" (The Tajwidi Qur'an, 2003, p. 707). While I may often feel isolated in my Islamic practices at a public university in Mississippi, it has become important to me to share the ways Islamic principles impact my perspective on what "better" looks like for me as an individual and contributor to my campus community. At the heart of Islam is the understanding that you have not reached a state of faith until you want for someone else what you want for yourself. This faith is not merely an abstract wish for all people to be cared for but instead requires tangible action in the world as hadith proposes, "Whosoever of you sees an evil, let him change it with his hand; and if he is not able to do so, then [let him change it] with his tongue; and if he is not able to do so, then with his heart—and that is the weakest of faith" (Ibn Sharaf An-Nawawi, 2021, p. 100). The practices of Islam support inner transformation—the struggle against one's ego desires so that one can actively stand up for justice and compassion in the outside world. For me, willingness to engage in this struggle with my own forms of resistance constitutes a way of becoming "better" that I am seeking as an individual, as well as a purpose for sharing contemplative dance practices with my students and our whole campus community.

Practice: A Dance with Resistance

Take a comfortable position in a space open enough to allow you the freedom to move. Relax your eyes and mind and allow yourself to turn your awareness to your body. Notice a place of resistance within your body. That resistance might be showing up as tightness, fatigue, pain, collapse, or another quality that requests your attention.

First, allow yourself just to notice that location in your body and the resistance. There is no need to change it—just allow it to be seen and acknowledged.

As you feel ready, allow yourself to explore that place of resistance further. If you let the place of resistance lead you, how do you move your body? Spend a few moments letting the resistance drive your movement within your body and through the space of the room.

Next, allow the resistance to be as it is and to occupy the space in your body where it is located, but to no longer lead your movement. Allow yourself to notice the resistance and move *around* it.

Then, surround the place of resistance in your body with extra tenderness. Observe how this affects your movement.

Now, try moving very gently *through* the place of resistance.

Finally, imagine putting the resistance down and experiment with the feeling of moving without it.

What did you discover as you explored your resistance and options for moving in, with, without, and through it?

Next, identify a need in yourself or others. What type of emotional or intellectual resistance do you experience in the face of this need? Repeat this movement exercise with the awareness of that emotional resistance. What do you discover about yourself in this process? What insights do you gain about the resistance itself? What approaches do you now have to meet that need?

Reference List

Boal, A., & McBride, C. A. (1974). *Theatre of the oppressed*. Theatre Communications Group.

Ciurczak, E. (2019, March 20). *Hungry for more than an education: College students use food pantries, trying to survive*. Hattiesburg American. https://www.hattiesburgamerican.com/story/news/local/2019/03/20/anti-hunger-alliance-mississippi-group-college-hunger-campus-food-pantries/3091393002/

Freire, P. (1968). *Pedagogia del oprimido*. Siglo XXI Editores.

Fritzsche, L. (2022). Integrating contemplative pedagogy and anti-oppressive pedagogy in geography in higher education classrooms. *Journal of Geography in Higher Education*, 46(2), 167–184. https://doi.org/10.1080/03098265.2021.1946766

Ibn Sharaf An-Nawawi, Y. (2021). *40 Hadith of Imam An-Nawawi*. (J. Dywan & U. Mohamed, Trans.). Independently Published.

Jordan, V. S. (2020). yoga for social justice: Developing anti-oppressive change through yoga. *The Journal of Contemplative Inquiry*, 7(1), 39.

Lerman, L. (1999). *Modern dance technique class*. Liz Lerman Dance Exchange.

Lerman, L. (2014). *Hiking the horizontal: Field notes from a choreographer*. Wesleyan University Press.

Move for Hunger. (2018, August 8). *Why is Mississippi the Hungriest State in the Nation?* https://moveforhunger.org/why-is-mississippi-the-hungriest-state-in-the-nation

Peterson, N., Freidus, A., & Tereshenko, D. (2022). Why college students don't access resources for food insecurity: Stigma and perceptions of need. *Annals of Anthropological Practice*, 46(2), 141. https://doi.org/10.1111/napa.12190

The Tajwidi Qur'an. (A. Nooruddeen Durkee, Trans.). (2003). An-Noor Educational Foundation.

Wapner, P. (2016). Contemplative environmental studies: Pedagogy for self and planet. *The Journal of Contemplative Inquiry*, 3(1), 67–83.

Wolfe, A. (2017, November 15). *Mississippi's public assistance 'most meager, least accessible' in the nation, report says*. Mississippi Clarion Ledger. https://www.clarionledger.com/story/news/politics/2017/11/15/mississippis-public-assistance-most-meager-least-accessible-nation-report-says/864628001/

11
CREATIVE ENVISIONING

A Contemplative Practice That Promotes Healing, Personal Growth, and Professional Development

Virginia Diaz-Mendoza

Introduction

I am Virginia, daughter of Jose Diaz and Nereida Fernandez, immigrants from the Dominican Republic; I am granddaughter of Braudelina Rodriguez, Ramon Fernandez, Anselma Batista, and Miguel Diaz; I am mother of Lauren Capellan and Louis Diaz and grandmother of Logan Diaz and Luna Branzuela. I am a first-generation college graduate and a member of the BIPOC academic community at the City University of New York.

When thinking about how I show up in the world, I wonder what words I would use to tell my story and if words could tell the whole story. Probably not. When I first began the process of self-discovery, it was purely an intellectual process where inquiry was void of a deep excavation of the self, curious reflection, and true understanding. I read daily meditations and extracted information I believed was valuable. I journaled about the reading and then continued with my day. It was easy for me to engage in this extractive process because of my academic background. In 2020, during the global health pandemic, I completed my doctorate training; using words in a theoretical way helped me to avoid the pain and anguish I was feeling. My father had been diagnosed with Alzheimer's years ago and was now in the late stages of the disease. He was silent most of the time and eventually lost his ability to speak. This was devastating for me because I loved being in dialogue with him about our shared history, values, and interests. Although my father could not speak, he was able to communicate affection, joy, and contentment throughout his entire illness. I, on the other hand, found it difficult to use words to communicate my feelings. I was losing a man I had known and loved my entire life. I intellectualized everything including my father's illness, the overwhelming despair I felt, and the grief that consumed me.

After years of intellectualizing my healing and personal development, it had become second nature. This was not the deep work I needed to do now, so I decided to engage in the process of healing and development in a very different way. I began to apply Lectio Divina, a form of contemplative reading used by Catholics, during my daily morning reading of divinely inspired texts (Painter, 2011). *Lectio* is the act of slow, attentive reading with the purpose of noticing what stands out, *Meditatio* is deep reflection on the reading, *Oratio* is silent prayer, and *Contemplatio* is rest in the presence of the Divine. This four-step process is followed by action, usually a conversion of the mind or spirit. While I found the practice of Lectio Divina useful, the process still felt extractive and not generative for me. *Lectio Visio*, a related contemplative activity often practiced while viewing religious art, involves attentively noticing what stands out from visual images, engaging in deep inquiry, meditating on what meaning the images have for the viewer, and seeking guidance in prayer. Engaging in this practice slowly led me away from the intellect toward a creative process of reflection, inspiration, and guidance. I wondered what would unfold if I used the process of visualization to deeply understand myself. More importantly, I wondered how visualization could aid me in feeling the depth of my sorrow and despair so that I could slowly find comfort and joy and feel more whole.

What Is Creative Envisioning?

Creative Envisioning is a meditative practice where you can be in silence and encounter your authentic self while engaging the imagination. Living in a noise-polluted world has turned silence into a luxury. However, Creative Envisioning has helped me to experience a deep flow that drowns out the noise. In her book *Interior Castle*, St. Teresa of Avila, a Catholic mystic, describes a form of contemplative prayer where she imagines herself moving through a castle to encounter her whole self and ultimately experience ecstatic consciousness (Teresa and Peers, 1961). Reminiscent of Ignatian Spirituality, Creative Envisioning involves contemplative prayer, discernment, and dynamic involvement in service and mission (Fleming, 2008). While Creative Envisioning is not new and has a long history, my intention here is to share how I have engaged in the practice and what has resulted from using imagination, inspiration, and divine guidance to experience wholeness and conceive future possibilities.

During my father's long battle with Alzheimer's and subsequent transition, I struggled with words to describe my thoughts, feelings, and emotions. I sat with him in silence for hours and sought comfort in his presence. Slowly turning the pages of my favorite magazines, I saw images that were complex, interesting, and involved. I was drawn to beautiful images of people, places, and things. This mindless activity became a mindful practice, full of mysterious anticipation. Accessing my intuition, I patiently waited for inspiration during the Creative Envisioning process and selected images that resonated with my feelings and emotions. I carefully cut them out of the magazines and slowly positioned them on a blank page forming a collage. Each week, I created a collage of images that illustrated my deepest sentiments, absent the intellectualizing I had learned to rely upon within the academy. For two years, instead of a written journal, I kept a visual journal. This visual story evolved over time as I asked: What transformation of mind or heart are these images inviting me to consider? The visual journal allowed me the flexibility I needed to understand the story that was developing: a story of sorrow, despair, endings, and new beginnings. Words were inadequate and unnecessary.

Adapted from scenario planning, a technique used in government, business, social organizing, and movement building, I outlined the following steps to use while practicing Creative Envisioning. This list is not exhaustive and possibly incomplete. However, it is useful in helping us to begin to imagine desired futures.

1 Decide on what will guide or inspire you during the Creative Envisioning practice. Select a comfortable space where you feel safe to engage in the practice, where the lighting is ideal. Play soft, inviting music if that helps inspire your imagination to soar.
2 In your mind's eye, map out different types of visions and include as much visual information as possible. Find images that represent your desires and create a collage.
3 Set the scope of the vision.

   a Are the desired changes big or small?
   b What should be accomplished first, next, and last?

4 Assess how the vision will impact others.

   a Who is impacted by the vision? How are they impacted?
   b Who can assist in making this vision a reality? How can they assist?

5 Brainstorm trends and driving forces that can influence your vision.

   a How is the vision impacted by current trends?

6 Assess uncertainties and possibilities.

   a What is a realistic timeline for the desired vision to be accomplished?

7 Assess all possible outcomes.

   a What goals, hopes, and dreams do you truly desire?

8 Identify needs.

   a What do you need to make your vision a reality?

9 Do a quantitative analysis of needs.

   a How much? How many? How long?

10 Identify decisions and action.

   a Rank the different visions and prioritize what is most important now.

Creative Envisioning as a Spiritual Practice

In her highly recognized book *The Artist's Way: A Spiritual Path to Higher Creativity*, Julia Cameron (2016) states, "we undertake certain spiritual exercises to achieve alignment with the creative energy of the universe" (p. 3). The author contends that we can partner with the Great Creator to experience creative flow, generative expansiveness, and desired changes. The creative process is an invitation and as such can be refused, but at what cost? The cost is really a missed opportunity to encounter your most authentic self. For me, Creative Envisioning has been a catalyst toward self-exploration, self-acceptance, and a search for meaning and purpose. In this offering, I reflect on the following:

- How has Creative Envisioning impacted me personally?
- How has Creative Envisioning impacted my work?
- What can emerge from Creative Envisioning for myself and others?

Through Creative Envisioning, I have noticed personal longings such as my deep desire to experience health, balance, peace, and pleasure. I found strength to understand death and dying, courage to face my father's impending transition, and the ability to effectively prepare for his departure. In addition, there were hopes that my work in the academy could expand to have a wider reach and more transformative impact. Table 11.1 outlines some of the goals, practices, and desired outcomes that showed up through my engagement in Creative Envisioning. This is not a proscriptive list. Rather, it is a reflection of my personal experience with Creative Envisioning. Your list will be unique to you.

TABLE 11.1 Observations of Personal Experience Using Creative Envisioning

Goals	Practices	Outcomes
Healthy mind body soul	Embodied practices	Increased intimacy and pleasure
Energy, peace, pleasure	Being present/here and now	Reduced self-defeating thoughts
Joy and comfort		
Intimacy	Meditation	
Personal growth	Deep breathing	Decreased technology use
Self-love and confidence	Moments of silence	Connection with nature
Aging gracefully	Gentle loving-kindness	Exploring research interests
Authenticity	Self-care	
Flexibility	Satisfy my needs	Increased flexibility
Wealth/wealth management	Deep reflection	Pride of place
	Self-discovery/curiosity	Understanding my calling
Healthy work/life balance	Travel and exploration	Experiencing contentment
	Time in nature	Increased productivity
Professional development	Nurturing relationships	Moving beyond fear
Fulfillment and satisfaction	Creative collaborations	Expanded possibilities
	Artistic expression	Discovering my power
Positive impact on youth	Learning about myself	Co-creating knowledge
Mission-driven work	Learning about others	Understanding my place in the world
Belonging/community	Morning ritual	
Community care	Creating healthy spaces	Experiencing flow
Ancestral healing		Deep satisfaction
Healthy relationships		

How Has Creative Envisioning Impacted Me Personally?

Creative Envisioning has prompted me to slow down, be silent, and explore the desires I have for myself, others, and the world. This practice made it possible for me to engage in the expression of my gifts and talents while exploring my wholeness. I moved from using only my intellect toward a more creative practice of imagining possible futures. All creation begins this way: travel by land, sea, air, and space, as well as ideas about justice, freedom, and change. Certainly, all innovation and technological advancements are born from the creative mind and become reality through sustained effort. In *Creative Visualization*, Shakti Gawain (1978) invites readers to imagine themselves being, doing, or having their most desired outcomes. The author believes three elements are necessary for effective creative visualization: desire, belief, and acceptance. The process of Creative Envisioning is an opportunity to explore and accept our deepest desires while believing that they can become reality through conscious effort.

Creative Envisioning has impacted my personal life and professional work in several interesting ways. This practice has helped me to remember an important part of my identity that I ignored for years, the creative visual artist in me. I also recognize this practice as a gift from my ancestors. Aside from his many talents, my maternal grandfather was a photographer and his wife, my grandmother, was a clairvoyant visionary. I believe Creative Envisioning marries these gifts and talents in a way that has been instrumental to my personal and professional development. I feel more integrated now that I regularly engage in Creative Envisioning.

How Has Creative Envisioning Impacted My Work and My Community?

Working in higher education for over 20 years, I have observed how the intellect overshadows other ways of knowing, particularly the emotional, spiritual, and imaginative. Creative Envisioning encourages wholeness through the inclusion of our various ways of knowing and being. In higher education, Creative Envisioning can enhance the experiences of both students and faculty alike. Michelle Chatman, co-editor of this volume and professor at the University of the District of Columbia, uses vision boards as a contemplative exercise with undergraduate students. Chatman states, "The assignment is ... a wonderful way to teach students the power of setting intentions and visualizing positive futures for themselves" (Chatman, 2019, p. 35). Similarly, I have offered students the opportunity to engage in Creative Envisioning and encouraged them to imagine their most desired future outcomes. Creative Envisioning prompts students to engage in meaningful dialog about what they want and need from leaders including faculty members and administrators at the institution.

In addition to using Creative Envisioning with students, I have also shared the practice with colleagues. During a professional development workshop at the end of a very challenging semester the year Donald Trump was elected president of the United States, I used Creative Envisioning to help faculty members envision ideal states of well-being in four distinct areas: spiritual, mental, physical, and emotional dimensions. This exercise centered the Medicine Wheel, an indigenous healing framework that focuses on emotions, the mind, body, and spirit. During the workshop, I provided participants with the materials needed to create a vision board and led them through the process. Many of the vision boards created included images that represented healthy ways of being and actions to achieve wellness. In the conversation that followed, faculty shared actions that they intended to take to achieve desired wellness goals including healthy eating, meditation, visits to the spa, taking vacations, going to the theatre, or just taking a long drive. Faculty members who engaged in the practice reported feeling less stressed and more hopeful. Many kept their vision boards in their offices as reminders of the importance of self-care and leisure. They were able to see images that brought them a sense of calm and joy throughout their workday. During these precarious times, it is important to hold space for feelings of discomfort, uncertainty, and helplessness while also providing opportunities to create counternarratives about wellness, joy, peace, and pleasure. Furthermore, this work enables students and faculty to imagine possibilities for personal and institutional transformation.

What Can Emerge from Engaging in Creative Envisioning?

In their book *Rehearsals for Living*, Robyn Maynard and Leanne Betasamosake Simpson state, "Our communities are already post-apocalyptic experts and can best imagine worlds beyond our current realities, but in order to imagine, some of us have to first survive" (Maynard & Betasamosake Simpson, 2021, p. 44). This constant pursuit of survival makes it difficult (but not impossible) to engage in Creative Envisioning. Creative Envisioning prompts us to ask, what kind of future do I deeply desire and how can I make that possibility a reality? The practice of Creative Envisioning is meaningful for several reasons. Creative Envisioning gives us the opportunity to look beyond terrible conditions such as the climate crisis, natural disasters, and our recent experience of a global health pandemic. In "*Envisioning a Future that Works for All: Characteristics of the Visioning Process*," Daniel Christian Wahl (2017) writes,

> It is important to understand that in the process of creating a vision for a sustainable community, society, culture and civilization we should not be restricted by what may be perceived right now as insurmountable obstacles to achieving that vision. The initial formulation of a vision has to be idealistic, creative, poetic, aesthetic, ethical, intuitive and imaginative.

Working with others on Creative Envisioning, I have witnessed resistance to creatively dreaming of a better world. J. Peter Scoblic (2020) highlights how challenging this can be in *Learning from the Future: How to Make Robust Strategy in Times of Deep Uncertainty*. The author invites us to move beyond ordinary conceptions of time and space: past, present, and future. This can be quite liberating because it allows us to engage the imagination in more exciting and expansive ways. Engaging in this way brings us back to a time where our imagination was limitless and we could come up with the most incredible ways of being, doing, and having whatever we imagined. Scoblic (2020) proposes the institutionalization of imagination and argues, "one-off exercises are not enough: Leaders must institutionalize that process, building a dynamic link between thinking about the future and taking action in the present." To that end, institutional leaders and their teams can participate in this transformative activity together and initiate both personal and organizational change.

Conclusion

The practice of Creative Envisioning makes room for expansively imagining our futures and pathways to reaching our most desired outcomes. Creative Envisioning can positively contribute to healing, personal growth, and professional development. Using this practice, I have experienced comfort and joy during the most challenging times of my life. Furthermore, I have utilized Creative Envisioning as both an effective pedagogical practice and constructive professional development strategy given its positive influence on my students and the faculty in my department. Some may believe Creative Envisioning is idealistic, and they may be skeptical about its effectiveness. I close with an invitation to readers to slow down enough to get in touch with their wholeness and experiment with Creative Envisioning in the pursuit of healing, personal growth, professional development, and transformative organizational change.

Practice: Creative Envisioning

Gather the materials you will need to create your Vision Board (a collage of images and pictures that represent the vision you are hoping to create). You will need a few of your favorite magazines, scissors, glue, and poster board or other cardstock.

Decide on what will guide or inspire you during the Creative Envisioning practice. Select a comfortable space where you feel safe to engage in the practice and where lighting is ideal, and consider playing your favorite music.

Slowly look through the magazines. Notice the images you are most drawn to and cut out those pictures or words that capture the essence of your vision. These might be representations of things you desire or images that capture the ideal you are envisioning. Include phrases that have meaning to you.

Arrange your pictures on the poster board and begin to glue the pictures onto your Vision Board in a way that feels right for you. Continue adding to your Vision Board until you feel it is complete.

Once you've completed your Vision Board, take time to look at each image and contemplate the meaning each image has. Look at the entire Vision Board. What story does your Vision Board reveal?

Find a place to put your Vision Board where you can look at it often. Reflect on the following:

Scope of the vision

- Are the desired changes big or small?
- What should be accomplished first, next, and last?

Impact on others

- Who is impacted by the vision? How are they impacted?
- Who can assist in making the vision a reality? How can they assist?

Trends and driving forces

- How is the vision impacted by current trends?

Uncertainties and possibilities

- What is a realistic timeline for the desired vision to be accomplished?

Desired outcomes

- What goals, hopes, and dreams do you truly desire?

Identify needs

- What do you need to make your vision a reality?

Quantitative analysis of needs

- How much? How many? How long?

Decisions and action

- Rank the different visions and prioritize what is most important now. What steps will you take now?

Reference List

Cameron, J. (2016). *The artist's way: A spiritual path to higher creativity 25th anniversary edition.* Penguin Random House.

Chatman, M. C. (2019). Advancing Black youth justice and healing through contemplative practices and African spiritual wisdom. *The Journal of Contemplative Inquiry, 6*(1), 27–46. https://www.researchgate.net/publication/338701328_Advancing_Black_Youth_Justice_and_Healing_through_Contemplative_Practices_and_African_Spiritual_Wisdom

Fleming, D. L. (2008). *What is Ignatian spirituality?* Loyola Press.

Gawain, S. (1978). *Creative visualization.* Bantam Books. https://www.luc.edu/media/celts/Ignatian%20Critical%20Reflection.pdf

Maynard, R., & Betasamosake Simpson, L. (2021). *Rehearsals for living.* Haymarket Books.

Painter, C. (2011). *Lectio Divina - the sacred art: Transforming words and images into heart-centered prayer.* Skylight Paths Publishing.

Wahl, D. C. (2017, April 28). Envisioning a future that works for all: Characteristics of the visioning. *Medium.* https://medium.com/age-of-awareness/envisioning-a-future-that-works-for-all-characteristics-of-the-visioning-process-ab02332a63ce

Scoblic, J. P. (2020, July-August). Learning from the future: How to make robust strategy in times of deep uncertainty. *Harvard Business Review.* https://hbr.org/2020/07/learning-from-the-future

Teresa, O. A., & Peers, E. A.. (1961). *Interior castle* (Translated and edited by E. Allison Peers, from the critical ed. of P. Silverio de Santa Teresa.). Doubleday.

12

ON BEING (A) CONTEMPLATIVE IN HIGHER EDUCATION

'Moving' through Familiar and Unfamiliar Spaces

Emmanuelle Khoury

> *I recognize the Kanien'kehá: ka nation as custodians of the lands and waters on which this essay was developed and written. Tiohtiá:ke/Montréal is historically known as a gathering place for many First Nations. Today, a diverse Indigenous population, as well as other peoples, reside here.*

My main aim in teaching, supervising, and mentoring is to transmit a social work identity rooted in the critical and reflective imperative of the profession and of the socio-historical and socio-political systems and contexts in which we live. The anti-oppressive perspective in social work prioritizes interrogating and interrupting power dynamics in human relationships, with a specific focus on the inequalities embedded in social processes. This work can be artful, specifically as social workers develop an awareness of self, others, and the world, and they begin to integrate theory, diverse knowledges, contextual elements, and personal lived experience. This is what I call 'seeing one's constellation' – looking into the night sky and trying to take it all in by making connections, finding familiar shapes in the stars. Each of us can create our own constellation in this way, in which each star represents a part of ourselves and the world around us. As a social work educator, once I can 'see' these connections, then I can become artful in my practice of navigating the social space of academia by developing praxis; that is, connecting to my whole, true self, through connecting with theory, ideas, knowledges, and practice wisdom, and adapting to unique environments and situations within which I am interacting. In this essay, I discuss the ways that contemplative practices such as interconnection

DOI: 10.4324/9781003416777-14

visualizations and movement practices are sustaining and vital for radical resistance in academic settings.

My Journey towards a Contemplative Life: Navigating the Night Sky

How does it feel to imagine a singular star in the night sky? What comes up in your mind, in your body when picturing one shining pin drop on a black canvas? Can you imagine moving from one star to the next, tracing a constellation, a connected network of stars?

In an undergraduate and graduate social work practice seminar that I teach, I invite students to think about becoming a social worker and to consider their future professional self as a star in the night sky. I invite them to imagine that star shining bright, twinkling against the dark, blank backdrop of space. Many students share that it feels cold, lonely, and frightening. Some share physical sensations like a tightness in their stomach. Others express feelings of awe and might. I then ask my students to imagine other parts of themselves that make up who they are and who they will be as professionals, as individuals, and as citizens. I encourage them to visualize adding a star to the night sky for each part of themselves. Perhaps there is a star that represents a history of lived experience with forced migration, mental health problems, or foster care; a star that shines for one's interests and hobbies; other stars that represent family, friend, and work relationships, or past professional experiences including academic training, research, and accumulated professional knowledge. And so on. I then guide students in imagining themselves 'connecting' all their stars, and together we discuss these constellations – a group of related things – that they have drawn. We also talk about the dark, empty backdrop of space, and what else surrounds their constellations. Students observe that other constellations surround theirs and sometimes they can draw imaginary lines to connect them. Each student's vision of their constellation and the matter that fills the emptiness is slightly different.

When I pay enough attention to the dark night sky and to the constellations, I am better able to see how they are connected to each other, and how each celestial object shifts, moves, and influences the visualization. The capacity to 'draw' one's constellation and, through critical reflexivity, redraw it as new stars, space clouds, meteors, and asteroids become known is deeply tied to intuition, to that capacity to know, access, and 'see' the familiar dark night sky and one's ever-evolving place in it. For me, it is an exercise I regularly return to as I evolve and transform as a social worker, researcher, professor, and person.

My identity has been largely shaped by the experience of identity negotiation. This is a common experience amongst those who have immigrated

(Benet-Martínez & Haritatos, 2005), although it is also acutely singular. My parents came from Argentina and Lebanon, and I moved permanently to Canada with them at the age of seven. Navigating very different cultural spaces as I encountered new environments was a familiar process. At an early age, I recognized how the ease with which I navigated the Canadian cultural space was not shared by my parents, especially my father who was a brown(er) man from the Levant. Despite his fluency in several languages, including French and English, it seemed more difficult for him to interweave aspects of Canadian and Lebanese cultures into his everyday life. I believe this was partially due to the 'othering' he experienced when he arrived in North America. His body, his accent, his gestures took up space in a very different way from my mother's (white) body. I wonder about the tensions my father must have learned to hold, navigating culturally privileged spaces while seeking to hold onto crucial life-giving parts of himself such as the movements, speech patterns, cognitions, emotions-in-interaction shared with his ancestors. These experiences with my father contributed to my curiosity about the ways we are allowed to take up space, the spaces we have access to and can inhabit, and the ways in which we allow others to take up space vis à vis our position of power. I reflect on the ways my father and I hold these tensions differently, though we both do so with radical inventiveness, harnessing the limitlessness of space and the stars in the sky. In holding these tensions, we actively push the boundaries of space, creating new areas with others *to be*.

I began mindfulness and meditation practice during my graduate studies when I didn't think I had any energy, power, or joy left in me to navigate the turbulent and confusing ocean of academia. As the first woman in my family to obtain an undergraduate diploma and the first person to enter graduate school, I quickly realized I was traversing strange waters without a compass. In many ways, my early practice helped me recognize that my physical and emotional exhaustion was related to the ways in which academia is constructed. I slowly reconnected with myself to find my power as I contemplated impermanence, returned to intentionality, and began to understand the interconnectedness and interdependence of all beings. My contemplative life sustains the work I do in higher education by grounding me in loving-kindness (Brach, 2003). This has helped me embrace uncertainty and fear of change so that I can continue learning and moving towards compassion, love, and understanding. In interacting with my students and my colleagues, I see that many of them need to heal, as I too continue to heal. Some are healing from trauma and the impact of intersecting structures of oppression; many are affected by the capitalist, neoliberal system that relegates them to a number, grade, or performance, rather than fostering their body, mind, and heart growth.

As I completed my doctoral work in 2018 with three children, a supportive partner, and a part-time social work job on top of adjunct professor work, I felt my body asking me to slow down and return to creativity. However, in the throes of worrying about contributing financially to my family, proving that my doctoral studies were worthwhile, and wanting to teach and continue my research, I initially ignored the calls to creativity. It wasn't until I was at a near breaking-point, both physically and emotionally, that I returned to the arts. As a child, I spent countless hours observing insects, marvelling over the sensory experience of fresh mud, and paying attention to the colours and lines of photographs and paintings that my father created. This is neither surprising nor unique; as Tobin Hart states, 'Children – young children especially – are natural contemplatives' (Hart, 2004, p. 37). The challenge for me has been in connecting with my creativity (e.g. through dreaming, imagining, and exploring), and giving myself permission to carve out space for it in my adult life. I recognize that this experience is not uncommon for those of us living in a Western, neoliberal society; through schooling, post-secondary training, and higher education, we inherit norms of busyness and disconnection (from self and others) as acceptable responses to pressures for productivity, individualism, and a narrow definition of success.

I enrolled in a creative writing class and was reminded that creativity is vital in identity construction, self-awareness, connections and community, and meaning making. That creative space reconnected me to my meditation practice. In short, by writing for no reason other than to write, to experience the joy of words, the shape they make in my mind, the sound they make in my soul, I was reminded how to pause and to notice when I am not present. Since then, all forms of writing – journaling, poetry, short stories – have been by my side as I endeavour to gain a sense of who I am and how I want to *show up*. It is through valuing creativity in all its forms, delivered via creative assignments and exercises, that I believe social work students can better develop core social work skills including self-awareness, compassion, conflict resolution, active listening, and most importantly, the ability to critically assess social structures, policies, and practices.

Drawing the Lines of the Constellation: Becoming a Contemplative in Higher Education

My contemplative life is driven by my profound desire to understand and connect with myself, others, and the world around me. As the daughter of immigrants from the Global South, I struggled to understand my identity as a child. I don't speak the language of my ancestors (Spanish, Arabic, and Catalan), although I do connect with their traditions and cultural practices.

For me, a contemplative life means showing up in my classroom and in my research work with humility, curiosity, and compassion. Contemplative practices help me to see the constellations and the night sky: that is, to see others, myself, and the interlocking systems of oppression and systems of hope in which we are all operating. Contemplative practices help to draw the lines between the stars, to make visible the constellations: social justice and oppressive relations; dualistic discourses and lived experiences; cognitive understandings, 'heart' understandings, and emotions; bodily sensations and somatic knowledge. I have discovered that contemplative practice and pedagogy, in their call for a rapprochement between what is learned and the learner, create an opportunity for clearer night skies.

I am now entering my fourth year as an assistant professor of social work at my institution. I believe that caring about students, staff, and personnel well-being is transformative and can change social conditions within the university setting. However, this care is also entangled in a capitalist system of labour. Sustaining life-affirming, liberatory spaces in the university setting has been possible, in part, through the dedication of several mindful professors and students, as well as through the support of our department. For example, we have organized drop-in support for students experiencing microaggressions or discrimination in the classroom, and in 2022, I co-launched an initiative to develop digital tools and workshops to foster inclusion and rapprochement of students of diverse identities. The project uses the structure of community, with a critical perspective, and the tools found in contemplative practices to integrate mindfulness, meditation, movement, and art into workshops on identity, diversity, and anti-oppressive practices. Mindful practices combined with social justice values can teach students tools for well-being, deep understanding of racial, economic, environment, and gender justice, and what it means to explore differences with curiosity and compassion (Gaard & Ergüner-Tekinalp, 2022). These initiatives come from students and professors who are committed to transforming higher education institutions. They are borne out of a belief that higher education is a place for learning, and also for becoming. It is this community and fellowship with others that has nourished my capacity to continue in this difficult work of transforming our university space and remaining available for creative opportunities in my classroom and in my life.

There is also an internal sustenance that I draw from contemplative practice anchored in loving-kindness and compassion that is fundamental in my pursuit of wholeness. bell hooks' work on love (2001) first showed me that love starts with knowing and being with oneself. This is the refuge that meditation, nature, neighbourhood walks, and present-moment awareness offer me. Before self-compassion (Neff, 2021) became a topic of research and part of our North American lexicon, hooks talked about self-loving and how important it is to be able to offer love to others. How is this related to my ongoing journey as a contemplative pedagogue? In order to be fully present for my students, to center their needs and learning, I need to create spaces for me to engage in self-loving. I have found that self-compassion meditations, as well as the radical act of saying 'no' to societal expectations of busyness and stress, have been necessary components of my personal development and my capacity to intentionally choose to contribute to creating structures that support my well-being and in turn, student well-being.

Mindful Movement – Interrogating How Our Bodies Take up Space

My own mindfulness practice is inspired by many contemplative practitioners who make explicit the mind–body–heart connection in living and learning (Barbezat & Bush, 2014; Batada, 2018; Berila, 2015). Embodiment is key to negotiating complex social work encounters. For example, Harry Ferguson's (2018) research shows that social work home visits are an embodied practice in which all the senses and emotions come into play and movement is central. However, in traditional university settings and social work training, the embodied social worker is not centred and so I learned how to be a reflexive social worker through writing and discussion. Though beneficial, these exercises do keep us in a cognitive, 'head' space. As I continue to evolve as a teacher, I find myself needing to move into an affective and embodied body and soul space so that I can sustain the work that I want to do and support my colleagues and students in the amazing work that they do.

In my senior year of high school, I chose Drama as my optional course. Our performing arts teacher had us practice Tai chi before rehearsals, and although I did not continue with that specific practice, the benefits of Tai chi's slow, intentional movements and of being aware of the muscles of the body have stayed with me. Movement practices aim to integrate the mind and the heart with the body. Movement, and the awareness of our motions, is also necessary to experience and learn about the space around us, its possibilities, and its limits.

As a social worker, I was obliged to enter people's homes, sometimes without their permission, to explore and investigate their feelings, thoughts, and actions. I now enter the university halls and the university classroom. I often ask myself – how do I navigate this space? How *am* I navigating this space? How do I move differently than the people around me? Do I move in diverse ways depending on my environment, on my capacities, on my physical and emotional well-being? Understanding my own movements and the motions of others has been crucial in dealing with my own body in space. Social workers are always constructing their practice in a situated way, in interaction with their given environment. I have rediscovered mindful movement as a way to slow down, pause, and return to intentionality and access the full lived experience of the body (Tangenberg & Kemp, 2002). This has been vital for me in developing an openness to the feeling of discomfort in the complex social encounters we experience, and in integrating a phenomenology of my social identity and the way I 'take up' space and the way 'others' might be 'taking up' space. Social work, and the care work that is inherent in the human relations field, has a mobile character; working with people demands making human contact with them. Caring for people requires interaction. This means that it is crucial to become aware of how one's body, emotions, words, and energy inhabit the professional and personal spaces in which social workers labor. After all, movement and interactions are 'acted out, performed and lived from below' (Jenson, 2013, p. 5). Remaining anchored in a social justice approach requires a conscientious letting go of conceptions of social workers as 'expert' and of client outcomes as performance indicators. It requires a re-conception of social workers as 'guest'; a temporary guest in the life of a person, group, or community wherein the social worker recognizes that they are a visitor, a transient that is respectful, adaptable, humble, considerate. By foregrounding movement, it becomes possible to learn to be aware of one's movements, why they are being enacted, and how they impact intersubjective interactions. Entering into a space with care and love means being accountable, compassionate, trustworthy, committed, honest, and communicative. It is the constant practice of integrating new knowledge into the fold of the uniqueness of our own self as a social worker along with the singularity of the experience of the individual, family, group, or community that we are working with. This is the art of social work.

Conclusion

My journey to understanding the vital role of embodied social work practice opened my heart to the possibility of using mindful movement to build upon discussions, reflections, and exercises around identity construction. The goal of this practice is to ground one's attention in the body to increase mindful presence, which in turn can cultivate capacities associated with mindfulness such as attention, curiosity, self-awareness, and compassion.

The movement practice presented below is inspired by a mindful movement practice that I encountered early on in my contemplative journey toward wholeness (Barbezat & Bush, 2014). It is a practice that can be done in your home, outside, at the park, sitting in a chair if that is comfortable, or standing beside it. It is adaptable to all mobilities and comfort levels. It can focus on movement of one part of the body, or the whole body. This practice supports increased awareness of not only the experience of the body as a social work practitioner (embodied practice) but also recognition of that body as a site of power and a site of intersecting oppression and privilege. Furthermore, it attunes the social worker to the client body in the space of interaction and connection. In other words, it helps us to chart our own constellations.

Practice: Social Work in Motion: Negotiating Space and Place

Sit, stand, or lie still, if possible. Keep your hands either at your side or in your lap.

Feel the sensations of sitting, standing, or lying down. Deep breath.

Notice the point of contact with whatever you are sitting, standing, or lying on.

Is there pressure and tension in your muscles and tendons? Deep breath.

Feel into your hands at your side or resting on your knees. Pay attention to your shoulders. Are they high, close to your ears? Pull them down.

Are there any sensations in your lower back, your hips, or your tailbone – each has a different part to play for each person.

Now that you have become aware of your body, keeping your eyes closed or lowered, see if you can sense the person closest to you. Take a deep breath as you sink into an awareness of where you are, and of those around you.

What feeling or word does this sensation of bodily awareness evoke?

Shift your attention to your body's movements. This can be adapted to attend to parts of the body or the whole body. There is no one right way to move.

If possible, focus on the lower part of your body, from the hips downward.

Notice how your feet connect to the floor, how your thighs and back connect to the seat or the floor. Be aware of your legs, hips, thighs, legs, knees, calves, feet, and toes. Remember that all sensations, including no sensations, are ok.

Intentionally lift your right foot and put it back down on the floor. Think about all the ways your body supported you while you did that, the tendons, muscles, and nerves. Lift your left foot and put it back down. Have the sensations changed?

Alternate lifting each foot, keeping your attention on the sensations. You can lift your legs or feet at different rates and in different ways. The aim is to move consciously.

You can gently, and in the time and in the way that is appropriate for you, stop moving.

Now bring awareness to your upper body. Notice how your back connects to the chair or floor, how your shoulders, arms, and hands are placed. Is there tension? Observe any sensations you might feel without changing them.

Bring your attention to your arms and hands. Deep breath.

Can you also become aware of the space around you? Is anyone or anything near you?

Intentionally begin to stretch out your arms to the side, if possible. You can alternatively extend your fingers or your chin. Notice how far you are comfortable stretching out into the space around you.

Deep breath and let your arms relax on your lap or at your side.

How do you imagine others taking up this space? What thoughts, sensations, or feelings are coming up?

Take a few breaths at your natural rhythm.

As this practice comes to an end, when you are ready, open your eyes and return to the room.

Reference List

Barbezat, D. P., & Bush, M. (2014). *Contemplative practices in higher education: Powerful methods to transform teaching and learning.* Jossey-Bass.

Batada, A. (2018). Utilizing contemplative practices with undergraduate students in a community-engaged course on health disparities. *Pedagogy in Health Promotion, 4*(1), 71–76. https://doi.org/10.1177/2373379917697992

Benet-Martínez, V., & Haritatos, J. (2005). Bicultural identity integration (BII): Components and psychosocial antecedents. *Journal of Personality, 73*(4), 1015–1050. https://doi.org/10.1111/j.1467-6494.2005.00337.x

Berila, B. (2015). *Integrating mindfulness into anti-oppression pedagogy.* Routledge.

Brach, T. (2003). *Radical acceptance: Embracing your life with the heart of a buddha.* Bantam Books.

École de Travail Social. (2020). *Comité antiraciste et inclusif de l'École de travail social de l'UdeM (CAÉTSUM).* https://travail-social.umontreal.ca/ressources-services/comite-antiraciste-et-inclusif-de-lecole-de-travail-social-de-ludem-caetsum/

Ferguson, H. (2018). Making home visits: Creativity and the embodied practices of home visiting in social work and child protection. *Qualitative Social Work, 17*(1), 65–80. https://doi.org/10.1177/1473325016656751

Gaard, G., & Ergüner-Tekinalp, B. (2022). Introduction to contemplative practices and anti-oppressive pedagogies for higher education. In Gaard, G. & Ergüner-Tekinlap, B. (Eds), *Contemplative practices and anti-oppressive pedagogies for higher education: Bridging the disciplines* (pp. 3–16). Routledge. https://doi.org/10.4324/9781003201854-2

Hart, T. (2004). Opening the contemplative mind in the classroom. *Journal of Transformative Education, 2*(1), 28–46. https://doi.org/10.1177/1541344603259311

hooks, b (2001). *All about love.* HarperCollins.

Jenson, O. (2013). *Staging mobilities.* Routledge.

Neff, K. (2021). *Fierce self-compassion: How women can harness kindness to speak up, claim their power, and thrive.* Harper Wave.

Tangenberg, K. M., & Kemp, S. (2002). Embodied practice: Claiming the body's experience, agency, and knowledge for social work. *Social Work, 47*(1), 9–18. https://doi.org/10.1093/sw/47.1.9

13

CONJURING TRANSFORMATION

The Magic Is in the Process

Maria Hamilton Abegunde

Conjure||Conjuring

To create, influence, or call up through invocation, spell, or ritual. Supernatural practice that leads to healing for self and community, or to do harm as a way to protect. To do and use rootwork to heal and to protect oneself against violence. Learn more about conjuring traditions in *Black Magic: Religion and the African American Conjuring Tradition* (Chireau, 2006) by Yvonne P. Chireau.

When we think of conjuring practices and traditions, what comes to mind for some are Hollywood movies or Shakespearian plays in which a woman is standing over a cauldron or body, stirring herbs and using implements to call up something to do harm and wreak havoc.

However, in African American and African-descended traditions, to conjure or to engage in conjuring is a way to heal one's self and community. Before conjuring can begin, one must gather themselves and all the required materials to plan the rituals that will ensure a proper outcome. In other words, one must have a cool head, clear mind, open heart, and willing body to do the work necessary to heal the spirit and bring it back into alignment with one's divine purpose.

Central to conjuring work are breath, stillness, movement, inquiry, listening, and action. What we see in the movies is the last part – action – sometimes with brief references to preparation. But, as a healer, priest, full-spectrum doula (prenatal to death), and contemplative practices adherent for nearly forty years, I know that what you do not see is the birthing process: the hours of finding herbs, making your own implements and instruments, praying or meditating, dancing and movement, and cultivating relationships with others. What manifests from conjuring is not automatic. The working of the "magic" takes years of personal growth and training.

"Conjuring Transformation" pulls back the veil of contemplative work to gently guide us through intimate processes. Read separately, these essays offer us an opportunity to understand how each contributor found their way to wholeness. Read together, and in the order the editors have arranged, they offer us an intersecting, multi-dimensional way to move along our own paths. As a ritualist and poet, I immediately began looking for inter/connections that would help me map out a way through and forward.

As someone in the academy, I have had to activate contemplative practices, African-centered rituals, and knowledge that make these practices visible in ways that others can take what they need and leave what they don't. These essays do the same and help us think about how contemplative practices can help us remember that healing and transforming ourselves and institutions are to be done, as the Yoruba say, bit by bit, and not always alone.

As with all things, we begin with/in ourselves, we begin with breath, we begin with stillness. In other words, we begin with what scares us most: touching, as Monika Son writes, the stories we have told ourselves.

Possibilities and Limitations

If we dwell in possibilities, there are no limitations. Yes, institutions and those within them will try to limit our desires and practices for transformation based on their own narratives. It is important that each of these essays share stories about how each author uses contemplative practices to resist and refuse those limitations.

The possibilities in the essays reside in their invitation for each of us to do the work of freeing ourselves: to become still enough to listen to the voices that guide us, and to move (literally) and breathe to release what separates us from our bodies, minds, and spirits. After sitting with, touching of, and becoming intimate with our own very real suffering (Monika Son), Robin Raven Prichard invites us to consider what it means to make choices from this place of knowing our own bodies in relationship to and with others. This is an invitation to make choices to be in community in ways that are often the antithesis to the isolation of higher education.

Practices as Service of Self and Systems

The thing about sitting with one's self in stillness and moving through what you find there, and then choosing for one's whole self to be in relationship with community differently, is that it will invite you to question everything. As Candice

Salyers points out: "The journey to a better self rarely comes without struggle..." From my own practices and teaching, I know that the struggle begins when we resist any and all information that challenges who we believe we are.

The authors offer practices that challenge us – selves and systems – to dare to be still and quiet enough to allow the questions about what we desire and need most to arise in us. Then, they invite us to ask the questions out loud, of ourselves, others, and the spaces we inhabit. In this way, we know – as Son writes – that our suffering and dis-ease – are real. When we speak out loud, we also learn that we are not alone in our desires for more.

It is not enough for us to stop there. We must dare ourselves and our institutions to respond to the questions without placing limitations on the responses, or reframing them because they make us uncomfortable. This type of constraining action kills dreams and the dreamer.

Virginia Diaz-Mendoza writes that Creative Envisioning made it possible for them to slow down to acknowledge their deep desires for "...health, balance, peace, and pleasure..." In so doing, they were able to know what was authentic for them and, I would argue, to practice the "body sovereignty" (Prichard) needed for wholeness. This can be scary and can sometimes lead to us realizing that we must separate from our institutions as we leave behind parts of ourselves that no longer serve us. However, it can also lead us to deepening our commitment to our scholarship, study, teaching, and mentoring.

Service to the institution begins with service to self; this means that we do not become the sacrificial bodies for advancing institutions that may remember us, and who will replace us when we die from our commitment to [fill in the blank]. We all have something we can write in that space.

Service to self and institution means knowing what our capacities and boundaries are, and recognizing when these change and why. By creating processes that allow us to choose how we move in the world, to be honest about what we resist and reclaim, and to be in relationship with those who support our well-being, we can reimagine and create paths toward wholeness without seeking domination or supremacy.

Most of all, when we commit to this type of process, we are able to recognize when we, ourselves, do not have enough air or breathe, or space to move, or places from which we can gather what we need for healing processes and supporting communities. These essays offer practices to balance us and, just possibly, lead us to harmony.

Cultivating Wholeness and Transforming Institutions of Higher Education to Advance Wholeness

To engage contemplative practices as paths to wholeness, much like engaging with my primary discipline of Black Studies, means that one is intersectional and community-centered, and that one questions intentions and methodologies and who they/we serve.

Khoury ends this section with a series of questions that lead us back to Son and Zazen, and that are worth repeating: "– how do I navigate this space? How *am* I navigating this space? How do I move differently than the people around me? Do I move in diverse ways depending on my environment, on my capacities, on my physical and emotional well-being?"

When these questions arise, we can return to sitting, quiet, silence, community, breath, movement. And, when we are in community and in our institutions, these questions can serve as a guide to check in with ourselves: Are we being true to the self that wants to emerge, and to our desires and needs to be whole? What does it mean to be whole? Are we in a reciprocal relationship with that self? Our communities? Are we seeking body sovereignty instead of oppression?

What are we willing to do to be free of the struggle, and to stay free? How does our freedom help others? The answers are neither magic nor blowing in the wind. The answers lie in practices that conjure the life you want through your preparations and choices that alter how to be alive.

May you find peace on the path to wholeness.

Reference List

Chireau, Y. (2006). *Black magic: Religion and the African American conjuring tradition*. University of California Press.

A Pause.

14
COOL LIKE JAZZ

A Loving Dialogue on the Multiplicity of Black Manhood

Bradford C. Grant and Michelle C. Chatman

A Note from Michelle

Brad Grant is a dear contemplative colleague, elder, and friend. We've lectured, practiced, and served together on the board of the Center for Contemplative Mind in Society. We typically meet for an end-of-year check-in at a Black-owned coffee shop on historic Georgia Avenue in Washington, DC, across from the campus of Howard University, where Brad works as Professor and Acting Chair of the Architecture Department, and where I completed my first year as a college student. We begin our chat at Sankofa Books and Cafe, which houses a resplendent collection of books and videos by and about people of African descent. We talk over Ethiopian coffee and lentil sambusas, pausing frequently to greet artist and activist friends who come into the café. Their warm exchanges are like unexpected zawadi, gifts that come days after the Kwanzaa festivities have ended.

Our being together, smiling through words, laughing, and leaning in toward each other as we talk feels like jazz – exciting, playful, layered, expansive, reflective, and intimate – all at once. It is a coming home of sorts, a way of being seen, a contemplative practice in and of itself.

As the café becomes busier with the approaching lunch hour, we migrate over to Howard's campus. It is early January and students have not returned yet. In the soft quiet of Brad's office with cool sunlight streaming through the window, surrounded by books, sketches, and wall hangings, we dive into a delightful exchange on contemplation as a conduit for deepening love and uplifting justice.

DOI: 10.4324/9781003416777-17

Black and Buddhist Resonance

MC: Hi, Brad. Thanks for chatting with me today. Let's start with you sharing how you got into contemplative practices. What are your early experiences with contemplation or meditation?

BG: My journey with contemplative practice started very young because my late father, Reverend George Grant, Jr., was a Baptist minister, so I was steeped in the religious tradition of a Black Baptist church. On Sunday mornings in the Bay Area where I grew up, there was a Buddhist broadcast that came on the radio. Now, my family is listening to the gospel every Sunday morning downstairs as they're getting ready for church. But I was in my room listening to a Buddhist kind of broadcast. (laughter)

MC: Oh, really! And how old were you?

BG: I was about 12 or 13, middle school age going into high school.

Then I'd go to church and listen to the minister, and over time I realize there is this kind of connection between the two based on love. And I was like, wow, this is very interesting; the Black tradition and the Buddhist tradition have this connection. I became intrigued with Eastern philosophy, which ignited my interest in meditation, mindfulness, and contemplative practices. Then, in high school, as an athlete, I played basketball as a minor athlete. There was lots of evidence on how mindfulness and contemplative practice can help you excel in sports and rest your mind, and I bought into that and found that was very helpful for me. I would do deep breathing and mindfulness before a game and found it useful.

I've always been drawn to art, and I've integrated this passion into my approach to observing the world. Drawing, for me, is a contemplative practice – a process of sitting, observing, and depicting either an imagined or real world through art, and this aspect of contemplation really allows me to engage more deeply with my surroundings. Beholding, in particular, has been a significant aspect of my practice. It's about seeing others in the world with the kind of attention and perception that mindfulness encourages. This has been especially impactful for me as a Black man, shaping the way I view and interact with the world around me.

MC: How did you come to CMind and begin using contemplative approaches in your teaching?

BG: I first heard about the Center for Contemplative Mind in Society (CMind) through the fellowship while teaching at Hampton University. I saw a flier for this Contemplative Teaching Fellowship program they had so I applied and was selected. At the time, I was working on a project in a Black neighborhood that lacked greenery. We planted trees there with students and residents, and we celebrated their growth with a kind of tree libation ceremony. At the time, I didn't see it as contemplative practice, but the fellowship helped me make those connections. After that, I became much more involved with CMind and our wonderful, diverse community of practitioners and scholars through the Association [for Contemplative Mind in Higher Education]. The language of contemplative pedagogy legitimized my teaching methods to the institution and brought me into a supportive community.

MC: How do you use contemplative approaches now to help your students, particularly Black males, cultivate the ability to see themselves and the world more broadly?

BG: Michelle, fundamentally, I've always been inspired by the wisdom of bell hooks, who said that our teaching should be about liberation, to help our students expand their consciousness and fight oppression (hooks, 1989).

With that, I approach contemplative pedagogy as a direct way to expand consciousness and awaken students to their future role as enlightened professionals with social agency as citizens for a better world. I utilize contemplative practices initially to help them have a better internal understanding of themselves and then, from there, to talk about how we can look at the world in another way and eventually transform the world.

One of the interesting practices I have students do is take out a sketchbook and draw a tree, automobile, or any subject. Like a scooter! I had students draw scooters that you see littered around the city; just draw what you see. Many students have a hard time drawing what they see. Generally, they draw what they know. I know a scooter has two wheels, so I'm going to draw two wheels, but if you're sitting at a certain angle looking at the scooter, you may not see two wheels. Even if you know there are two wheels, you don't see two wheels. If you're assigned to draw what you see, then you shouldn't show me two wheels. For several students, this is a difficult task. They may say to themselves I know there are two wheels, but I only see one wheel there so would I draw one wheel or two? So I have to reiterate the importance of drawing only what they see. This hearkens back to mindfulness and contemplativeness as being more aware and perceptive of your environment or being. So, this helps to sharpen at least the visual awareness of students or individuals practicing that understanding of the world.

MC: Do you also have them draw themselves? How do you make the exercise more interior or self-focused?

BG: Yes, I do, in fact! For their self-awareness, I have students draw themselves. Part of the exercise involves what I call writing a "This I Believe" statement. This comes from an old NPR show where people from all walks of life would write and share essays on their deeply held beliefs. So for my students, as they're drawing themselves, the exercise adjacent to that is to write out what they believe about themselves. Sometimes they write about spiritual or religious beliefs. Some students have very pragmatic and practical beliefs they share about themselves. The other requirement is that they draw themselves upside down.

MC: Upside down!

BG: Yes, as a means of connecting to the right side, the creative side of their brain. There's a tendency for us to draw ourselves in the best light possible to make ourselves as beautiful or as handsome as possible because we want to take away any flaws. If you draw yourself upside down, there is less scrutiny. You have to take your time because you aren't used to seeing yourself that way. I find that it inspires a tendency [for students] to be more accepting of how they look in the moment and say, no, I'm not trying to eliminate the flaws; I'm just drawing myself in a different way as part of this exercise. Students experience a high degree of success with this assignment. [Brad shows me some of their stunning drawings]. In turn, that excites and motivates them. This goes back to creating self-worth and self-understanding.

MC: And what does contemplative practice look like for you?

BG: I carry a sketchbook everywhere I go and I draw trees, people, buildings, and almost anything that catches my eye. But I also resort to music, specifically jazz. It really propels me to reflect on our cultural attributes and resilience. I listen to jazz often, while washing the dishes, cleaning the house, or doing menial tasks. I also enjoy jazz while having dinner with my wife or with company. Its multimodal stimuli – being with people I care about, eating food I like with jazz music in the background!

MC: Sounds like a perfect combination!

BG: It really is! And if there's a nice piece playing, I'll stop chewing (laughter)! So I can savor the music and take it all in.

MC: Do you have a favorite jazz artist!

BG: I have 50 favorite artists! (chuckle) It's always hard to choose, but J.J. Johnson, a jazz trombonist, has a composition written by Miles Davis called *Neo* that I really like. It's just one of my favorites.

MC: And why is it one of your favorites?

BG: It's because of my brother! He [Theodore Grant] was a DJ back in the Bay area. He had a jazz show and that piece, *Neo* by J.J. Johnson, was his theme music. He's the one that turned me on to jazz! So I was excited because MY brother had a show and "his own" theme music (laughter)!

MC: So every time you listen to *Neo* is like honoring your brother?

BG: Yeah, yeah, I guess it is a kind of honoring of my brother. And our relationship.

Black Men, Meditation, and The Illusion of Togetherness

MC: Our former CMind Executive Director, David, says that oftentimes Black men come to internalize an external narrative about who we are, who we can be, and what we mustn't do. Do you agree with that?

BG: I agree absolutely! I believe it's absolutely true. There are popular views of Black men as having a certain kind of prowess or physical superiority, running faster and jumping higher. And at the same time, Black men are also seen as perpetrators of violence and are victimized by violence. These stereotypic characteristics of Black men are wrong and incredibly damaging. They come from living in a society with a fictionalized view of Black men as brute, dangerous, unintellectual, and less than humane.

I've always been concerned about the lack of diversity, especially Black men, in the contemplative community. It's a vibrant community with all kinds of folks, but not a lot of Black men. It seems to attract more Black women and women in general. I think the Black male experience and conceptualization of masculinity doesn't quite connect with this idea of mindfulness and contemplative practices. There seems to be some hesitancy or some difficulties with this idea of Black men meditating, or being quiet and introspective, which I think is part of the problem. I have always wanted to do more exploration of this.

I can recall as a young man, maybe college age, this idea of *coolness* as a Black man as being important. It was very important to be perceived as cool or particularly skilled and savvy in something like singing [crooning] or dancing, or sports, things that people more readily associate with Black manhood. Meditating wasn't one of those things. Being cool as a meditator didn't quite work; not back then and not now! Unfortunately, even today, it is perceived as something that only White people do; an attribute of whiteness.

> I often see Black men so reluctant to go deeper than the superficial, and maybe that is tied to [needing to display an] appearance of togetherness. This idea of going beyond the superficial is helped by the attentiveness of contemplative practices.

MC: Where have you seen Black men going deeper? Do you see it in your classes?

BG: Here at Howard, there is a large Black male population. I don't see it with students in a more public setting. If you take a student to a more private setting, there is a chance to get beyond the superficial or the kind of public persona. Generally, in public space, I see the same attributes, where Black men want to be cool or popular. In a more private setting, you're likely to get different personae. I have done workshops, meditation workshops, and mindful workshops where students will tend to shed that.

MC: And what is it that you sense that Black men are shedding in your offering of mindful and contemplative practices?

BG: I think they're shedding the facade about Black masculinity that says you have to always appear strong and together; that you can't be vulnerable. I've actually seen Black male students [in my class] who were suppressing their sexual identity end up feeling empowered, or feeling safe enough, comfortable enough to come out. This is a big deal because even with the advances we've made around inclusion and the progression of attitudes; generally, I think HBCUs are fairly conservative in our social views around sexual identity. So it can feel really unsafe for a Black male to come out in an environment where attitudes may not be so welcoming.

MC: Do you think contemplative practices help Black men restore and resist these stereotypes and the legacy of racism?

BG: Well, I think contemplative practices can help by encouraging you to pay attention to your inner self so you can begin to identify and sift out who you really are. [You can] begin to interrogate the lies and uncover the stories. You find the space to ask, "Who am I really and what are my true attributes and abilities?"

MC: In what other ways do you think contemplative practices can benefit Black men?

BG: I think it allows for at least the questioning or the critique of what Black manhood might mean. It allows for an opening of a broader understanding of who you are in a broader sense. Conversely, contemplative practices can support us in being more compassionate and aware of our judgment toward others.

MC: Speaking of Black men, what about your son [Asa Moore Wynn-Grant]? What does contemplation look like for him? Does he meditate? How do you share contemplative practices with your son?

BG: As far as my son, we mostly connect by just being ourselves and being in nature. He doesn't meditate in a pronounced way like I do. One day we were out walking, and he's an attorney, so he has the ability to pose really deep and interesting questions and debate. And we were talking about the realization of God. Is there a God? Is God real? And we just had this really close attentive time talking and that's how we often bond.

Contemplation for Activism and Healing

MC: Brad, You're a pretty calm, stoic kind of guy. How does your contemplative demeanor support you in being an agitator for justice?

BG: Well, I'm old now so that's just the way I show up! (laughter)

BG: Being an advocate for justice and change through my contemplative practices of drawing, I guess, hearkens back to supplying me with the necessary mental and emotional armament to engage in that kind of change. So it's a way of fortifying me to engage in the world. I look at myself often as a reporter or storyteller but my stories are visual stories.

MC: How has that supported your self-acceptance, self-awareness, and self-love, particularly as a Black man in a white man-dominated field?

BG: It's a way of protecting you from some of the spears of oppression that we can face in a real and healthy way; the daily cuts. The little spears [insults and microaggressions], not the big spears, but the many spears you receive. Having a place of understanding yourself and paying attention to that and having a keener understanding of the motivation of some of these spears, to discern what they're about [is helpful]. I find myself engaging with contemplative practice as a way to access forgiveness. So, instead of hostile retaliation, there may be love and forgiveness, as appropriate for the circumstance. This has been helpful to me when I've had to sit back and meditate on things that have happened to me.

I find the contemplative mindset has a lot of healing qualities by allowing me to access a deeper sense of myself, and connecting with other people in a way that is fair and loving. I think contemplative practice is probably a little bit of a buffer from oppression.

MC: A sort of healing.

BG: Yes, a healing that we desperately need in many communities.

MC: And what impactful contemplative teachers and mentors have helped you adopt his perspective?

BG: Howard Thurman is someone I highly respect and look up to today as a teacher. Reading his materials and following some of his ideologies has been very impactful for me.

MC: Can you say why?

BG: Oh, because he is a Black man who has a broadened view of himself and the world and how we should interact in the world. I like the way he encompasses others in his ideology. He was so accepting and comforting to incorporate others into his worldview, his thoughts, and how he treats others. He was so thoughtful in his presentations and his delivery. I love that about Howard Thurman. He taught here at Howard for a while, and there is a nice stained glass window of him over at the chapel. And he founded the first interdenominational spiritual center in San Francisco, in my hometown. It is very "Bay Area" of him to have started that (laughter). I also enjoy Dr. Bernard Richardson, Dean of our Divinity School. I like his intellect, his kind attributes as a theological scholar. His intellect is spot on and I enjoy that about him. And I have to say that our community, our CMIND community, has been among my greatest teachers.

MC: This has been delightful, thank you Brad.

BG: Always a pleasure, Michelle. I enjoyed the conversation.

Practice: This I Believe: A Self-Portrait Practice

Use a selfie as your model for drawing a self-portrait.

Draw exactly what you see, not what you think should be there.

This exercise is about seeing yourself more deeply, not achieving perfection.

Reflect on your beliefs about yourself as you draw, noticing your thoughts without judgment.

Return your attention to your breath and drawing if you get distracted by busy thoughts. You can work on this over several sessions.

After completing the drawing, write about your deeply held beliefs about yourself.

Share with a friend or family member if you'd like.

FIGURE 14.1 Bradford Grant, Drawing

Reference List

hooks, b. (1989). *Talking back: Thinking feminist, thinking black*. Between the Lines.

PART III
Rhizomatic Awakenings
New Plateaus: Rhizomes, Connection, Ruptures, and Lines of Flight

David W. Robinson-Morris

During graduate school, a group of friends, a beloved professor, and I engaged in a close weekly reading and study of Deleuze and Guattari's, *A Thousand Plateaus: Capitalism and Schizophrenia* (1987). I will not bore you with all that we discovered together that year, but I will highlight the importance of the rhizome in assisting us with understanding the fluidity and interconnectedness of subjectivity, of being and becoming, of the multiple and various ways we might be able to conceive of ourselves and the world—and the various ways it might be remade through the connection and rupture of various assemblages.

Rhizome. The rhizome is a generative concept. Colman (2005) asserts

> Rhizomatic writing, being, and/or becoming is not simply a process that assimilates things, rather it is a milieu of perpetual transformation. The relational milieu that the rhizome creates gives form to evolutionary environments where relations alter the course of how flows and collective desire develop. There is no stabilising function produced by the rhizomatic medium; there is no creation of a whole out of virtual and dispersed parts. Rather, through the rhizome, points form assemblages, multiple journey systems associate into possibly disconnected or broken topologies; in turn, such assemblages and typologies change, divide, and multiply through disparate and complex encounters and gestures. The rhizome is a powerful way of thinking without recourse to analogy or binary constructions. To think in terms of the rhizome is to reveal the multiple ways that you might approach any thought, activity, or a

concept – what you always bring with you are the many and various ways of entering any body, of assembling thought and action through the world. (p. 235)

A rhizome "has no beginning or end, it is always in the middle, between things, interbeing, intermezzo" (Deleuze & Guattari, 1987, p. 25). A rhizome is a plateau, beginning at middle never reaching end; it is a line of flight always already in the process of transformation, deformation, awakening, and dormancy. The rhizome counters the image of arborescence; it lacks roots and it is not planted. The rhizome is a Derridean event: a ruptural surprise that occurs as a multiplicity. Multiplicities have "neither subject nor object, only determinates, magnitudes, and dimensions that cannot increase in number without the multiplicity changing in nature" (Deleuze & Guattari, 1987, p. 8). This change in nature is what Deleuze and Guattari (1987) term a body without organs (BwO). Of course, this is not a literal body without organs, but the "impermanence—interpenetration—insubstantiality" of being (O'Sullivan, 2014, p. 258). As I have written elsewhere (Robinson-Morris, 2016), becoming a BwO is a liberation not from the body, but from subjectivity—an escape from the black hole into the light of a new stratum, new being, evolved becoming, and new understandings of the hidden wholeness of all things at various flows and intensities.

A rhizomatic awakening is a collective assemblage of creative, ontological, and epistemological emergence with the ability to metamorphose into anything, cross any threshold, and shape-shift into a new you—a new us and a better we, together.

Contributors Jeffers-Coly, Ahmed, Chari, Thompson, Mosemghvdlishvili, and Boring, invite us to enter onto their respective plateaus of awakening. With great courage and deep love, each author provides a space of vulnerability, truth-telling, Spirit-engaging, and a glimpse into their own (r)evolutionary becoming to, perhaps, assist the reader in catalyzing their own rhizomatic awakening.

Phyllis Jeffers-Coly illuminates us for how existing on the margin in the academy materialized for her as a physical ailment. To cope with the epistemic violence of higher education, Jeffers-Coly began to engage in contemplative practice by bearing witness to the polite brutality of being relegated to the margins. She looked to the organic intellectualism of Maroon communities and to her own ancestors for guidance, wisdom, and the strength to surrender to Spirit—to allow hush hollows of healing to emerge and re-emerge so that she could release what no longer served her.

Ahmed, Chari, and Thompson construct a contemplative and pedagogical "body without organs" (BwO). Teaching from a multiracial feminist perspective, these authors crafted a pedagogy of power by rising back into the body; that is, they re-membered themselves to the physical body to reckon with the layers of trauma and violence that bodily dissociation allows when we privilege the mind—a major issue for most of us who reside in or live adjacent to the academy.

Ahmed, Chari, and Thompson recognize that the body joined together in harmony with the mind provides "potent space that contains layers of memory and historical experience that we can begin to access when we deepen our relationship with sensation and embodiment." Extending their practices into the virtual space, the authors construct a body without organs—or rather enter into a continual process of becoming within a system that it cannot break from in its entirety, yet yearns to escape. A body without organs requires that we "sense the field" or be attuned to the world in ways that are destratified, deterritorialized, and decoded. Thus allowing us to see, feel, know, be, and think beyond ourselves—imaginatory liberation for ontic transformation.

Lela Mosemghvdlishvili reminds us of the invitation that each interruption offers us to see more clearly, feel more deeply, decide more decisively, and befriend the very energy that threatens to topple us over or take us down. What might it mean to "dance barefoot in the university"? What might it feel like to practice an openness so radical—within the confines of the institution—that your willingness to see and be seen causes a ripple effect of compassion, humanity, and generous becoming? How might feeding your demons actually save your soul?

Finally, Boring invites us into her life of raising and living with a child with autism. Boring illuminates for us the joyful, fun, mundane, and difficult moments of caring for her son, Aaron. She explains how she came to place her experience of walking alongside Aaron in service to her work with students. The author assembled the ruptures, outgrowths, and spiraling questions into a new methodology of becoming, growing, and being with oneself and others.

As you read this section, I invite you to feel the words and allow each author's energy and intention to flow from the pages through your hands, beyond your eyes, past your mind, and into the reaches of your soul. I invite you to call on your Ancestors—those of blood and spirit who are benevolent—to serve as your guides as you read, contemplate, and meditate on the words in this section. Utilize the practices of each chapter and, finally, ask yourself: What new lines of flight, what new life-giving nodes are budding? Where am I being called and how am I being called to show up? Listen and prepare yourself for the surprises of new plateaus.

May you be well.
May you be liberated.
May you be free and know it.

Reference List

Colman, F. J. (2005). Rhizome. In A. Parr, Ed., *The deleuze dictionary*. Columbia University Press.

Deleuze, G., & Guattari, F. (1987). *A thousand plateaus: Capitalism and schizophrenia*. University of Minnesota Press.

O'Sullivan, S. (2014). A life between the finite and the infinite: Remarks on Deleuze, Badiou and Western Buddhism. *Deleuze Studies*, *8*(2), 265–279. https://doi.org/10.3366/dls.2014.0145.

Robinson-Morris, D. (2016). From Arborescence to Rhizome: West (Finally) Meets East at the Intersection of the Buddhist and Deleuzian Subject. Presentation at American Educational Research Association (AERA), April 8-12.

15

SHOWING UP AUDACIOUS AND BAD ASS FROM THE EDGES AND ON THE MARGINS LIKE MY ANCESTORS

Phyllis M. Jeffers-Coly

I exist on the edges. On the margins. Perhaps, as an HBCU-educated, working-class Black woman from North Carolina who is committed to healing and restoration work that exclusively and unapologetically centers Black people, I will always function there. Like, in my wildest imaginings, when I feel audacious and bad ass, I figure myself to be a maroon tucked in the mountains or in the Dismal Swamp that straddles what is current day North Carolina and Virginia. Waiting. For those who want to be free. Understanding fully that the maroons were "audacious, self-confident, autonomous, sometimes self-sufficient, always self-governing; their very existence was a repudiation of the basic tenets of slavery" (NYU Press, para. 2, summarizing Diouf, 2014). A powerful notion of a heritage that for me and many other Black folks challenges dominant narratives. Allowing us to see our ancestors, familial and collective, as resilient, resourceful, and resistant. A notion that affirms the value of my husband and I holding space for Black folks to find sanctuary and to deepen their capacity for healing, restoration, and liberation. Lofty, I guess. Maybe.

But, nonetheless, I think that as a former hip-hop generation student leader and HBCU administrator who began my career teaching at a community college, I will always be on the outside looking in. From the mountain on my best days. Or on the edges of the swamp or lush hush harbor in the woods. Or in real time from the balcony overlooking our outdoor café terrace where we feed our guests. On the edges. On the margins. Of higher education. Of the Academy. Because, if we are being honest, HBCUs and community colleges have never ever garnered the same respect as other institutions even though they often tend to be the places where Black folks like me can flourish and feel safe, secure with a sense of belonging.[1]

Because, if we are being honest and engaging in the contemplative practice of bearing witness, the Academy functions as a codified and contested space that typically reveres the Ph.D. and the Ed.D. over lived experience, wisdom, and other ways of knowing. A space that relies on epistemic violence (Shahid, 2018) tied to negating what people like me know while continuing to insist on canons, credentials, and conventions that have historically and consistently ignored, negated, and questioned the intelligence of my ancestors and my still-living elders.

And, while this contested space has fed my creativity and intellectual curiosity, the Academy is, as expressed in the CMind webinar *Healing Higher Education: Racial Reckoning, Racial Justice* (2022), in need of deep racial healing. True indeed. To be sure. For me, the Academy is a space that I now recognize as a place where I engaged in high-effort coping that was the result of race-based stress and trauma. Manifested physically as red, painfully itchy psoriasis patches all over my body from the moment I left North Carolina to attend graduate school. Coexisting with intermittent bouts of shame, self-loathing, low self-esteem, anxiety, and depression that Parker (2020) and Menakem (2017) told us in their groundbreaking works are tied to racial trauma. Long before I knew that *The Body Keeps the Score* (Van der Kolk, 2014) or understood that all of that striving, big stepping[2] and high-effort coping would leave me exhausted, broke down, and burnt out. And, eventually finding myself collapsed on the floor and cracked wide open.

A collapse that reflects how higher ed did me harm and continues to harm and injure Black folks even when they, like me, show up bad ass and audacious on behalf of Black folks. Even at HBCUs serving the first-generation, Pell-eligible students so that they felt safe and secure and a deep sense of belonging.

Now, fast forward, finally off the floor, I continue to operate on the edges of it, higher ed, as a bad ass and audacious Black woman who created a space, a sanctuary that offers Black folks a hush harbor, like the ones my ancestors knew in the woods and swamps. A sacred healing place geographically far away from the places where they were wounded by anti-Black racism. Audacious (or crazy) enough to believe that my commitment to Black liberation and healing could exist. Audaciously centering Blackness and celebrating SOUL as ways to foster racial healing for Black folks wounded, harmed, and injured by race-based stress and trauma. Audacious enough to believe in the healing that they seek can be found on a pilgrimage they never thought they could or should make. Paying homage to their ancestors who in some way resisted and who were certainly resilient. Leaving and releasing their own pain that they have often not fully understood or acknowledged. In the halls of the *Maison des Esclaves* on Goree Island. Or in the turbulent waves of Mami Wata. Or tucked away in a remote farming village where our connection to nature and spirit still flourishes. In a place that feels immediately like home. Where their souls and SOUL are fed. Where they realize that they are, evoking Nigerian Afrobeats artist Burna Boy, African Giants. Where they nap on couches and no one calls the campus police on them. Giggling out loud in boats bobbing as dolphins swim close by. And playing the dozens during games of Uno. And cutting hair in the middle of the night. And letting down their guard, getting out of their heads and surrendering long enough to learn dance steps and drum rhythms in a place from where our ancestors were taken. Where they receive warm reassuring hugs from me, Ta Ta Phyllis aka Sweet Potato, and deeply loving wisdom of Ton Ton Eddy aka Professor Onion Sauce. At no direct cost to them.

Our heritage and healing experiences integrate SOUL (culture) and contemplative practices in ways that allow us to "create a space to receive others where they feel loved, they feel cared for, they feel nurtured – a space for peace – for freedom – for clarity."[3] Diasporic Soul, which we founded in 2016, allows us to introduce Black people to their heritage and history in ways that deepen their capacity for healing and restoration. So that they can be well, resilient, and engage, as need be, in resistance. We are clear that we are in fact holding a deeply sacred and communal space with humility, compassion, courage, and love where Black folks can deepen their *svādhyāya* in a place where "contemplation is a destination as well as a practice" (Holmes, 2017, pp. 11–12). On a pilgrimage to a hush harbor in Senegal, West Africa.

Which, to be clear, is an absolutely audacious notion as higher ed still seems to be failing Black people amidst the pernicious anti-Black backlash that is playing out nationwide.

To sustain my capacity to be bad ass and audacious like my ancestors, to hold this space, the hush harbor, I engage in a range of contemplative and spiritual practices. Including yoga, which I understand to be far more than asana-based movement practice. My yoga practice is harnessed by *tapas* (devotion), *svādhyāya* (self-study), and *ishvara pranidhana* (surrender to the divine) as well as restorative asana and nidra that integrate communion with nature and engaging in rituals tied to my ancestors. This is how I stay well enough to continue to serve others.

So, from the margins, on the edges, in the swamp and in the hills tucked away and among trees with the spirit of my ancestors, my ongoing contemplative and spiritual practice is meant for me to stay grounded, rooted, and centered. And to continue healing the wounds tied to race-based stress and trauma and the samskaras that I continue to work on as a working-class

Black girl from North Carolina. Healing that Alice Walker (1997) reminds us in *Anything We Love Can Be Saved* means putting the energy, heart, and courage back into my body with my own culture. And SOUL is the culture Walker speaks of, which, according to scholar-practitioner Dr. Sharon Harrell (2018), is "the transformative healing resource that reflects the cultural sensibilities of the African diaspora" (pp. 1–3). An understanding that reflects Malidoma Somé's (1998) assertion in the *Healing Wisdom of Africa* that our healing as folks of African descent require spirit, community, and ritual. A sentiment that Barbara Holmes (2017) affirms in her work *Joy Unspeakable: Contemplative Practices of the Black Church* when she insists on the significance of communal and mystical spirituality and faith practices that have and can continue to sustain us individually and collectively.

In *Radiant Rest: Yoga Nidra for Deep Relaxation and Awakened Clarity*, Tracee Stanley (2021) offers us yoga nidra to support our capacity to be well, to remain rooted and grounded. And, to restore our connections to all that is divine, including our ancestors. Early in the text, she encourages her readers to create a nidra nest – a protective sacred space that includes our mat, blocks, blankets, bolsters, and eye pillows. Reflecting too what I see as her connection to SOUL, Stanley encourages us to invite our ancestors into the space to support our nidra practice. Ancestors, of course, who mean us well. Ancestors who might themselves find some healing by joining us as we find rest and feed our sense of self-worth. Ancestors who might whisper to us when we fully surrender and open up to spirit. Giving us guidance and reassurance that they can only share with us when we make room for them in this way – being still. On our mat, in our nest, which we might understand to be our version of a hush harbor, a safe and sacred space we might imagine in the woods, the forest, tucked in the hills or in the dense, dark, reassuring swamp. Knowing that we will not be found, disturbed or taken back. A place where we can surrender, let down our guard, and connect to spirit, our breath, and our own power. And, let go of the pretense, prestige, and positions that we have all become so tethered to. Able to fully experience a connection with our ancestors and their capacity to help us heal. But, only if we too are able to rest in the sweet way that Stanley and others like Parker, Hershey, and I invite us to on our mats, in our nests, on our bolsters, connected to our bodies and our breath. Like the maroons beckoning their enslaved sisters and brothers to steal away.

My nest, my refuge, my sacred place where I feel safe, secure, and supported by spirit is at my ancestral altar. I come to it knowing that "[w]e work for the ancestors and they send us messages. As much as we think about them, they think about us" (Constant in Mitter, 2023, para. 31). I come to my ancestral altar understanding that I am a descendent of folks who initially continued their indigenous belief systems in ways that continue in fact to co-exist with Christianity and Islam. Further, I come to my ancestral altar, my yoga mat, and my nidra nest understanding that ritual expression offers us access to what we know in yoga as *samadhi* or the bliss state; it opens us up to playful energies and blurs the boundaries between the ordinary and the extraordinary. It offers me the opportunity to be transformed and the ability to "traverse the limits of time and space" (Holmes, 2017, p. 30). And the opportunity to experience healing and restoration. Well-being and liberation.

As I outline in *We Got Soul, We Can Heal* (2022), I began my altar when I learned that my maternal grandmother was passing away in 2018. Now, today, my altar has expanded to consist of a church pew that Eddy and I bought on the roadside near our home. An altar that for me ties me to the faith traditions and contemplative practices of my ancestors. My L-shaped church pew ancestral altar holds a range of items that invite and welcome my ancestors. It is where my ancestors and I meet daily. When I visit each morning with water and cups of hot tea and coffee. And, on some mornings fresh flowers. Or a glass of *ngalakh*, the fermented millet drink of the Serere, for Eddy's grandmother Laityr Kumba in particular. And, for Easter with bissap-dyed Easter eggs for my grandparents. And, sometimes a handful of cashews or black-eyed peas. And, sweet thangs that melt in your mouth when we get a chance to visit a bakery in Dakar. Fruits too – mango, watermelon, papaya, oranges, and soursop. Oh, yes, when I feel like we really need their support and guidance, I burn nag champa sticks and light candles – white or red. Or offer them a plate of food like *thiebbu guinar*, which we make for Eddy's father when we annually celebrate him in September with prayers and by feeding members of our extended family and community.

In addition to the consistent offerings that communicate our attention and gratitude, our ancestral altar is filled with a range of heirlooms and souvenirs that connect us to our ancestors. Including my grandmother's cake box, a ceramic cardinal, and remnants of a bird nest. And bookmarks she made, including the one that appeared on my desk in Senegal the day she passed. As well as photos of both sets of my grandparents and Eddy's father. And other items that have changed and shifted as I have expanded and deepened my ritual of engaging our ancestors, and finding stillness on my mat and in my nest directly in front of our altar.[4]

Now, let me be clear here, my ancestors have shown up for me in Senegal. More than once. In very clear ways and more subtle ones. Yes, there is the aforementioned bookmark on my desk the day my grandmother passed away. An item I had not seen in the two years prior since we arrived in 2016. And, prior to that, there is my grandfather who passed in January 2008, showing up unexpectedly in January 2017 in my office. This looked like my grandfather's eulogy that I had not even imagined I had brought with me to Senegal, sitting on my desk at the time of year when my grandfather passed away. I did not take it out and sit it there. I truly did not even think I had packed it with my files that got shipped to Senegal. My grandmother, as I explain in "When Grandma Comes to Visit (Jeffers-Coly, 2022a & b) shows up over and over again in the form of brown seeds in white whispy whirls that float around the house (even though every window is closed), and on the balcony and terrace of our café. And, at times, in the U.S. and in a little village in the La Charente region of France this summer. Always warm, playful at times, and reassuring. Saying to me, "I am here, I love you and you will be alright."

And, at least twice in Charleston where I had traveled for the Association for the Study of African American Life and History conference in September 2019. I cannot be absolutely sure who the ancestor or ancestors were, but I sensed very clearly that they needed me to recognize them, and our ties to the port city where I imagine we may have arrived on boats to join the masses of African people who built America for free. As an odd detour off the rural highway after the GPS seemed to miss putting us on the interstate between Durham and Charleston. An interstate that my long-time South Carolina-native friend knew quite well. And as small brown prickly barbs sticking on my pants at my ankles after meeting a fully domesticated cat on the street in Charleston after eating at one of the last remaining family-owned soul food joints on the edges of its gentrified "historic" district.

Recognizing my ancestors speaking to me in this way is me practicing *ishvara pranidhana*. When whispy whirly white encased seeds float by. And brown prickly barbs delivered by a "random" cat stick to the bottom of my pants. And, when bookmarks and eulogies appear out of nowhere on my desk in another country. These moments are when I am open to spirit and I am able to "let go of the attachment to the mind as [my] sole authority" (Parker, 2020, p. 158). These are mystical moments where I truly feel and sense my ancestors. These moments of what Daniel Fore (2017) refers to as spontaneous communication with our ancestors that result in me surrendering to the divine energies around me and embracing my relationship with my grandparents and other ancestors. Practicing *ishvara pranidhana* means I am accepting rather than dismissing my ancestors showing up as mere coincidence. Moving to Senegal has allowed me to let down my guard and surrender to spirit in ways I never ever had in the U.S. In part because I have a daily ritual and other ways I engage them to say thank you and to honor them.

My practice at my altar connects me to spirit, including the existing energies of my ancestors. I feel their energy and support as clearly as I feel my breath moving and the weight of my aging body pressed against my bolster and lying on my mat as I connect to the earth below me.

Here, I encourage you to consider a practice that allows you to be open to the spirit of your ancestors. A practice that might allow you to deepen your own capacity to experience healing and restoration. And, how developing a ritual around an ancestral altar might allow you to feel grounded, rooted, and centered in ways that the academic culture far too often erodes and makes difficult. A generative practice that affirms your worth, value, and your enoughness particularly when the space you occupy most days does not.

For me, continuing to open up and surrender has also included reconsidering or inquiring about other ancestors. For example, there are my fathers' parents who I did not have the same connections to as I had with my mother's parents. My grandmother passed away when I was young. Addiction and notions of respectability I think got in the way of me having a close relationship with my grandfather. Yet, now I have made room for and begun to engage them at my ancestral altar. My racial healing work has allowed me to better understand and extend grace to them and forgive them, because I now recognize that they were in pain and hurting because they lived in Jim Crow America, facing white supremacy and the threat of white violence. I now respect them in part because I no longer conflate how much education a Black person has with their value and worth. Me included. While being able to simultaneously respect folks who pursue their education in ways allow them to extend themselves for the well-being of Black people without posturing and pretense. I now realize that my paternal grandparents are also supporting Eddy and I and our family. And that our love and attention is healing for them. I now accept that I have a responsibility to harness my courage and compassion to offer them the love, grace, acceptance, and forgiveness that they might need to heal.

For you, is there a way that you might reconsider how you see your ancestors or living elders that might serve your or their capacity to experience healing? You might consider reflecting on or doing a moral inventory of the ways that your sense of self is impacted by shame and self-loathing. Or on how you may have been taught to perceive Black folks. Or taught to hold on to notions of respectability and/or what constitutes excellence. A *svādhyāya* practice that is akin to taking the moral inventory called for in step four of Bill W's 12 steps (Alcoholics Anonymous, 1953) or putting your legs up the wall and shifting your perspective in ways that serve you and your ancestors.

Having a ritual practice that ties me to my ancestors and that is tied to having a sacred, personal place allows me to continue to heal and restore myself from the effects, long-term and more immediate, of race-based stress and trauma as a Black woman from the working-class South who exists on the edges and margins of higher ed. A space where I can release what no longer serves me. Where I can weep and wail out loud. Where spirit and yoga make me feel deeply supported. Allowing me to find stillness so that I can receive guidance and insights from my ancestors and other spiritual energies. So that I can remain grounded, rooted, and centered enough to continue to hold space for heritage and healing experiences for Black folks that celebrate Blackness and center SOUL. My ritual practice bolsters my capacity to be courageous and audacious and rebellious and bad ass as I continue to reach my hand out to Black folks – like Harriet in that large mural in Cambridge, Maryland[5] – inviting them home, inviting them to take a pilgrimage so they can experience healing and restoration. Warmly welcoming them home to a sacred hush harbor in Senegal and at the base of my ancestral altar.

Notes

1 Racial trauma impacts our sense of safety, security, and belonging as well as our sense of innate dignity and worth, which often has meant compromising one for the another in ways that have not served Black people.
2 A reference to the latest Kendrick Lamar album, *Mr. Morale and the Big Steppers* (2022).
3 Diasporic Soul Heritage & Healing Experience Participant. Student Development Practitioner. Post-Experience Debrief. October 2021.
4 A session of our *Stopping the Clock Grief Series* focuses on the importance of creating an ancestral altar that includes a video featuring Nana Lawson Bush giving guidance on how to create one. Opening to Spirit, https://diasporicsoul.com/2020/07/17/altar/
5 Mural by Michael Rosato (2019) at the Harriet Tubman Museum and Educational Center in Cambridge, Maryland.

Reference List

Alcoholics Anonymous. (1953). *Twelve steps and twelve traditions.* AA Grapevine Inc.
CMind. (2022, April 21). *Healing higher education: Racial reckoning, racial justice* [Webinar]. The Center for Contemplative Mind in Society (CMind). Unpublished.
Diouf, S. A. (2014). *Slavery's exiles: The story of the American maroons.* NYU Press.
Fore, D. (2017). *Ancestral medicine: Rituals for personal and family healing.* Bear and Company.
Harrell, S. (2018). Soulfulness as an orientation to contemplative practice: Culture, liberation and mindful awareness. *The Journal of Contemplative Inquiry, 5*(1), 9–40.
Holmes, B. (2017). *Joy unspeakable: Contemplative practices of the black church.* Fortress Press.
Jeffers-Coly, P. (2020). Opening to spirit: Creating an ancestral altar. Diasporic Soul. https://diasporicsoul.com/2020/07/17/altar/
Jeffers-Coly, P. (2022a). *We got soul, we can heal: Overcoming racial trauma through leadership, community and resilience.* Toplight Books.

Jeffers-Coly, P. (2022b). When grandma comes to visit: Exploring how communion with our ancestors & nature deepens our capacity for healing, restoration, resilience, and resistance. *Journal of Contemplative Inquiry, 9*(1), 76–90.

Menakem, R. (2017). *My Grandmother's hands: Racialized trauma and the pathway to healing our hearts and bodies.* Central Recovery Press.

Mitter, S. (2023, January 25). An artist who blends secular and sacred (with sequins). *The New York Times.* https://www.nytimes.com/2023/01/25/arts/design/myrlande-constant-haiti-vodou.html

Opening to Spirit: Creating an Ancestral Altar. (2020, July 17). *Diasporic soul.* https://diasporicsoul.com/2020/07/17/altar/

Parker, G. (2020). *Restorative yoga for ethnic and race-based stress and trauma.* Singing Dragon.

Shahid, K. (2018). *Anti-black racism and epistemic violence.* Sentio.

Somé, M. (1998). *The healing wisdom of Africa.* Jeremy P. Tarcher.

Stanley, T. (2021). *Radiant rest: Yoga nidra for deep relaxation and awakened clarity.* Shambala.

Van der Kolk, B. (2014). *The body keeps the score: Brain, mind and body in the healing of trauma.* Penguin.

Walker, A. (1997). The sound of our own culture. In *Anything we love can be saved: A Writer's activism.* Random House.

16

OUR SKINS ARE MEMBRANES, NOT WALLS

A Multiracial Feminist Conversation

Zahra Ahmed, Anita Chari, and Becky Thompson

In 2021, three educators – one identified as African American, one as South Asian, and one as white – came together to discuss teaching during the COVID pandemic. We connected through our conversation exploring what it means to "teach with tenderness" in the face of the multiple and interlocking systems of oppression that we continue to experience. When we first began meeting online, what drew us together was our realization that multiracial feminism – a liberatory movement that centers the work of women of color as activists, theorists, and artists who are committed to undoing systems of oppression – was key to our work.

As the global uprisings mobilized in response to George Floyd's murder and the continuous state-sanctioned terrorism of Black people, our conversations intensified. We supported each other as we reckoned with our grief and rage. We discussed how the continued assaults on Black people in the US mirrors the devastating impact of COVID-19 on Black and Native communities. We also acknowledged the ways that higher education institutions expect us to deny part of who we are in order to be seen as serious academics. Finally, we shared the *yogas* (unions) and embodied practices that support us personally and in our teaching. Through our sharing of contemplative practices, our meetings became a healing space, a journey, and joy that moved beyond finishing this collaborative article.

In this essay, we discuss how we strive to deliberately connect our personal contemplative practices with our work to create more socially just systems and structures. Zahra Ahmed shares the synergy she found between contemplative and critical pedagogies and explains how she brought these two fields together. Anita Chari hones in on her practice of sensing the intercorporeal field, explaining how we can use it to expand our sense of connection with the things and people around us. Becky Thompson offers both insights and intriguing questions around how we can use Zoom technology for the common good in order to strengthen community rather than weakening it. Though we speak with different voices, we co-wrote this essay as a demonstration of our commitment to using the multiple crises impacting us as catalysts for moving forward in making fundamental, systemic change.

Crafting a Pedagogy of Power (Zahra Ahmed)

I did not realize it at the time, but I began meditating when I was about 15 years old. I would rise in the early morning, light a candle, and simply sit with it. Sometimes I would engage in conscious visualization and other times I would just allow myself to be. Sometimes I would play music that connected me with Spirit, and sometimes I would dance. I would also practice a kind of deep listening by intentionally being open to receive any messages or feelings that arose within me. I relied on a knowing that I am connected with forces much greater than me to help me get through tough times.

When I was 19 years old, my maternal grandmother, Mama Lil (short for Mama Elizabeth) suddenly passed away. Mama Lil had been my second mother; she had fed and clothed me since I was born. Some of my earliest and fondest memories were at her house in Southern California, either sitting with her on her front porch, sitting beside her as she played piano and sang, or sitting in her kitchen while she made us sassafras tea. I was away at college in Baton Rouge, Louisiana when she passed, and my parents being the stoics that they were, didn't feel it was necessary for me to fly home to grieve with the family. I tried to process her transition while I was 2000 miles away from everyone I loved, but needless to say, it was very difficult.

During this time, I attended a communal healing ceremony in the countryside of South Carolina. During the ceremony, we washed our faces with herb infused water, sat in a circle on the grass, and received blessings from an elder woman who reminded us of our responsibility to continue our cultural traditions. This ceremony touched me deeply and I began to search for ways to connect with and honor my ancestors. A friend of mine suggested I explore the ways that Ifa, a West African spiritual system, includes ancestor reverence as a foundational aspect of the religion. Through my exploration, I grew in my understanding of the ways I could connect with Mama Lil and all those who have gone before me. I built my ancestral altar, found photos and images of my ancestors, and developed my own rituals to strengthen my relationships with them. However, while I felt my search was leading me to become a more integrated human being on the one hand, I also began feeling increasing pressure in higher education spaces to compartmentalize my spiritual and professional selves.

As a student and a teacher, I have faced the expectation that I dissociate myself from my cultural context in order to be taken seriously. This expectation was usually part of what critical pedagogical scholars like Michael Apple calls the hidden curriculum of formal education, but sometimes it was communicated explicitly (Apple, 1971). For example, my graduate school professor told me I was "too close" to my research exploring how people of color can generate political power because I had a vested interest in my research findings. I saw then that the hidden curriculum was not hidden at all. As I matriculated through higher education, I realized that it offers many exciting possibilities, but it can also serve as a trap.

My response to this was to turn my analytical lens onto the educational institution itself to render what is invisible, visible. When I shifted my perspective, I realized that the same aspects of my identity that are marginalized through institutional white supremacy are actually my greatest sources of strength. I embrace multiple identities, including woman, mother, and unapologetically Black feminist teacher. While my identities help me create theoretical frameworks for living authentically in my worlds, I also allow space for growth. Therefore, rather than succumbing to self-alienation, I created a practice that empowered me to bring my full self into the higher education environment. I call this a pedagogy of power because it helps me create strong learning communities while challenging the multiple pandemics of systemic oppression found in academe and in our society.

Over the years, my contemplative practices have fused with my pedagogy. I continually find ways to fully represent who I am. I commune with my forebears, offering reverence for ancestors of the blood, the heart, and of my community. I have also integrated indigenous wisdom and Earth medicine by greeting the four directions each morning, doing walking meditation, and gardening. Just as the tree of contemplative practices illustrates a variety of possibilities, I use these practices as needed (The Center for Contemplative Mind in Society et al., n.d.).

Although I continue to work for institutional change, I have witnessed a hardening of oppressive systems. My practice helps me face the multiple pandemics of systemic injustice we face around race, gender, and sexuality, all of which were exacerbated by the COVID pandemic. I continue to grieve for the millions of lives lost to COVID while also remembering Tamir Rice, Sandra Bland, Ahmaud Arbery, Breonna Taylor, George Floyd, and so many others whose lives have been taken. This loss of life evokes a deep emotional response from me as a human being and I have also felt it among my students. So I teach them the practices of bearing witness and ancestor remembrance to create space for them to grieve even as they feel gratitude for the sacrifices made for them.

The synergy between these principles and practice reminds us that we do not have to disassociate or compartmentalize our academic and personal lives. Instead, we can explore what brings us joy and also find healthy ways to deal with trauma and pain. When my co-author Anita Chari led us through a grounding ritual called "sensing the field," it helped me remember that I am indeed connected with all that is. The somatic practice of intercorporeal perception allows me to be nourished by everything around me as well as those who have returned to Spirit before me.

On Intercorporeal Perception (Anita Chari)

As a South Asian feminist, political theorist, and somatic educator, I tremble in the face of the stacked crises we face in this new era of climate disasters, global fascisms, and daily acts of racialized police violence. The murder of George Floyd in 2020 and the waves of protest and consciousness that have risen against anti-Blackness in its midst continue to ignite in me a reflection about how the educational spaces I inhabit reproduce racialized and colonial violence, even as they provide us with tools to critique it. I am flooded with awareness that my own lifelong struggle with embodiment, which has also been an intellectual struggle, has always been racialized. In the midst of this brutality, it is a tiny relief that certain things can now be said.

I came to somatic work while I was in graduate school as I realized that the loss of one's body and disembodiment are often the price of intellectual legibility within academia. I had many experiences that forced me to reckon with my intellectual dissociation and to see it as a recapitulation of many other layers of trauma: the ancestral violence of colonialism, the shock that racism left upon my skin, and the relational betrayals I had experienced in my early history.

Dissociation became a portal for me, and the nectar of my creative vision emanated from my reckoning with it.

Weaving together the intellect with the body has led me to the work I do now–stitching together embodied experience with critical theory in academic, carceral, and healing spaces. My passion has been to bring somatic trauma-informed practices into these sites, working with the relational, contact-based practices of biodynamic craniosacral therapy, sensate practices, sound, and collective movement. These practices have allowed me to materialize my commitments to the intellectual and spiritual traditions that have shaped me: Black and postcolonial feminisms, Marxist theory, somatic trauma-informed practices, and Buddhist contemplative practices. I weave embodied practices into my work as a critical theorist and teacher, invoking what I call the *intercorporeal field* within the classroom space.

The intercorporeal field is a potent space that contains layers of memory and historical experience that we can begin to access when we deepen our relationship with sensation and embodiment. Sensing this field allows us to feel and practice within a space that is in some sense not yet individual, allowing us to have perceptual experiences that go beyond the boundaries of our individualized physical bodies. These practices require us to attend subtly to the specific locations of our bodies in physical and relational space. As many of us teach, work, and socialize within the confines of virtuality now more than ever before, attention to the intercorporeal field is especially important for creating generative learning communities. The field becomes a resource for us in our physical and virtual realities as we experiment with the ways that we can access different registers of contact. I remind my students that our skins are membranes, not walls, which means we have the capacity to access and feel the energy within and surrounding us. Even when we cannot feel the physical presence of the other, whether in person or on our screens, sensing the field brings another dimension of contact that emerges in new ways of being together across the vastness of time and space.

In May 2020, as the Black Lives Matter protests emerged, I walked around my Portland neighborhood searching for traces of the uprising. I saw graffiti on the sidewalk, signs of memorial and support tacked up on a building. I saw a picture of George Floyd, and his gentle eyes haunted me as I walked. Leaflets littered the streets across the lines of police tape. I actually preferred these traces to the images. The images are devastating. Images of a Black man lynched in broad daylight, bodies in protest, holding the line against the state and police violence. I also saw images of former President Donald Trump, images of hollow masculinity, mocking death, and spirituality. Finally, I saw images of us, in boxes and screens.

As an educator, I struggle to touch reality with my students, even as the layered catastrophes that we face bring a level of hyperreality to our lives. The art historian Barbara Stafford describes the hyperreal as a level of perception that is "intensified, and forced to become more than it was when it existed in the real world" (Bredekamp & Stafford, 2005). It describes, at a visual level, images that are both compressed and magnified. I asked how my students and I could relate to the image of George Floyd, which was at the same time everything beyond an image. I ask myself now how we can continue to respond to the vibrations in the streets of the protests ignited during that time of great political intensity. How can we bear witness to unfathomable events, rather than anesthetize ourselves from the pain of violence? How can we attune to the possibility in social movements with our vision and awareness, in our personal and public lives? And how can we do so when even "post-pandemic," we are having ever more conversations across virtual space, without the vibrations of voice and contact touching skins? As I grow with these questions, I am excited to know that the work we must do is a kind of self-undoing in the presence of history, race, sexuality, and capitalism, and the work of creating new capacities for sensing and connecting as we bear witness.

Practicing Liberation in Virtual Space (Becky Thompson)

When Zahra, Anita, and I began meeting to share our practices and support one another, I realized that, while we are quick to create healing spaces for other people (in prisons, in refugee camps, for our students, for vulnerable faculty, for children), we also need spaces for reflection and healing so we can keep doing that work. The twin troubles of COVID and state-sanctioned anti-Black violence have taught me like never before how we need to stay "loose in the knees" (flexible, willing to pivot in new directions) to respond during crises. When Anita led us in the practice of *sensing the field*, I became aware that my mind was extremely busy. I realized that mental busy-ness, if left unchecked, would make it hard to really listen to my colleagues. This was a humbling realization because mental presence is especially important for white women to nurture in relationships with women of color who historically and currently are talked over, talked about, and talked through – both within and outside of the academy. Anita's grounding exercise allowed me to find the kind of spaciousness I needed to listen deeply.

Another lesson that was particularly relevant for me was realizing virtual spaces as locations for expanding community. This is ironic because while the early months of COVID closed down so many communities, as students had to move back to childhood homes, as people could not meet collectively in a safe way, the essence of community seemed to hang on a very thin branch in a cold wind. I needed to think in expansive ways about what teaching with tenderness and from a student-centered perspective looked and felt like online. As my sociology, creative writing, and leadership classes at a private women's centered university in Boston met online, and as we tried to practice meditation and yoga through little tiny boxes, new versions of community started to arise. As students tried to find space in their apartments and houses to take our online class, I began to notice relatives, friends, and cats behind them, trying not to disturb them as they walked by. It occurred to me that our circle could expand if those in the background were invited to be part of our online community.

Of course, students should be the ultimate deciders of which of their family members, if any, should be invited into their educational community.

But as an educator, I was inspired by the realization that we could use Zoom culture to demonstrate that education does not have to happen in isolation from community. For example, there is a reason Barbara Smith, Audre Lorde, Leota Lone Dog, Cherríe Moraga, and others called the first publishing press by and for women of color "Kitchen Table Woman of Color Press." I brought these issues to my students and asked, "What if we understand learning as intergenerational? What does that change about how and why we approach our learning?"

Such an invitation counters notions of individualism and meritocracy that have often excluded the very people who have made that education possible. Many students I work with are the first generation in their families to go to college/university. Their relatives are the ones working two jobs, taking out a second mortgage, or selling blood, to be sure that their children can attend college. These same relatives were the ones trying to avoid being noticed during Zoom sessions. As students faced isolation and had few people to talk to about their studies, inviting relatives, roommates, and friends into online sessions expanded our community. It also allowed us to contemplate what community means, how boundaries are established, and how to prevent learning from becoming segregated by generation.

This historical moment gives us a chance to invite into the classroom ancestral knowledge, traces of memory that shape how we act in times of crisis. Yoga, meditation, free writing, and mindfulness all make space for us to not only invite our own bodies into the conversation (what we feel, sense, hear, yearn for), but also that electrical field (typically called the mind) that extends far beyond the body that allows us to think and feel in expansive ways. I asked myself and my students, "What if, as we teach/learn with Zoom, we understand the space between ourselves and those we talk to on the screen as sacred? What kind of energetic and sensation work could be done with this understanding?"

This is part of what Anita Chari is teaching us when she says that even when we are online, there is an intercorporeal energy field that can be named, experienced and worked with. She teaches us that this field carries historical memory and goes beyond the boundaries of the physical body. This energy field may be why the Opaskwayak Cree researcher Shawn Wilson recently shared that several Native elders had a similar dream where the earth was saying she wants to be brought to the Internet (Wilson, 2021). The earth wants to be seen and felt in multiple spaces, including online.

Once I realized that I could send Zoom links to anyone, the circle of community members who participated in my classes widened internationally. This had a positive impact on my mental health and well-being because I knew I was honoring an energy extending beyond myself. I remembered that, when I taught yoga in China and Thailand, it was simply assumed that mothers brought their children to class, that stretching and breathing together was communal, that yoga is an earth-based practice. This knowledge held all of us as we practiced together.

These experiences led me to ask, what if we see teaching as an earth-based practice, so that opening each class begins with people sharing what Native land they are on, where they are sitting, who is with them, and what they want to focus on today? What if those introductions also made space to talk about who is sick, who is still in jail, who is working in and outside of the home, and who the essential workers are in their lives that made going to school possible for them?

When George Floyd was publicly executed in 2020, those of us who were able to attend demonstrations to stop police brutality and to abolish the punishment industry brought our energy back to Zoom boxes. That energy is powerful. During one of our meetings, Zahra shared a quote from Winona LaDuke, "Power is not brute force and money, power is in your spirit. Power is in your soul. It is what your ancestors, your old people gave you. Power is in the earth. It is in your relationship to the earth" (Honor the Earth, para. 4). When George Floyd said, "mama, I am through" the earth heard his cries. Anyone listening heard him. The students I work with heard him and they needed to talk about it, write about it, demonstrate about it. Grounding rituals, free writing and yoga (even on Zoom) helped us stay connected as a community as we also invited people into the community who had been excluded from the Zoom box.

As my practice has evolved, I find myself yearning for collaborative ways of learning and loving. This has required me to think about who I invite to the table…not only those who are living, but those who we carry inside of us. As a white, antiracist queer woman and mother of three chosen children, as a yogi and a poet, I struggle to keep my body and mind calm when what I so often feel is sadness and rage. Community rituals of belonging help me move beyond stuck feelings toward a more expansive way of being. In Ross Gay's gorgeous book of essays, *The Book of Delights*, he makes the point that, even amidst police murders and environmental degradation, as human beings we have the right to nurture (and even multiply) joy (Gay, 2019). I center myself and my students through community rituals that seek to make somatic, intellectual, and psychological knowledge available for myself and my students as we take up the challenge of living full, questioning, and deep lives.

Conclusion

Many years ago, Bernice Johnson Reagon wrote an article on Black women and organizing where she explained that culture creates its own methodology. She asserted that embedded within the communities we are part of are the rituals we need to sustain ourselves (Reagon, 1982). As practitioners, scholars, and activist human beings, the three of us have created an evolving community by sharing practices that help us sustain ourselves and our students. Zahra's contemplative rituals help her feel connected with her predecessors. Anita's work with intercorporeal perception helps her realize somatic embodiment even in the face of historical and contemporary violence and trauma. Becky's practice uses technology to build community. Our methodologies stem from our cultural situatedness. Yet at the root, our practices are mutually reinforcing, allowing us to withstand the violence that is perpetuated through the white supremacist culture of the academy. We offer these reflections as a way of honoring ourselves while possibly helping other faculty who might draw on our experience to strengthen their own contemplative practices. Most importantly, we see this offering as part of our work to effect systemic change within our institutions and our society.

Practice: Sensing the Field

Find a comfortable place to sit where you can easily move between reading words on the page and sensing your body. Make sure you are sitting in a way that is relaxing for you. Begin to feel the sensations in your body. Notice where sensation is arising in your body and feel its texture. Notice the quality of sensation. Neutral sensation words that may help you include: cool, warm, tingly, fuzzy, fluid, hard, soft, constricted, pulsing.

Keeping your attention slow and fluid, allow your awareness to spread outward to your skin. At first you may sense discrete places on your skin; allow your attention to spread until you feel your skin as a whole. Take a moment to sense this membrane of your body, the permeable boundary between your individual body and the space outside of you. Then, allow your attention to move just outside of your skin. Keep your attention open, sense whatever impressions you may notice in the field just outside of your body.

As you become familiar with this practice, you might try maintaining this awareness for longer periods of time until it becomes habitual.

Reference List

Apple, M. W. (1971). The hidden curriculum and the nature of conflict. *Interchange*, 2(4), 27–40. https://doi.org/10.1007/BF02287080.
Bredekamp, H., & Stafford, B. M. (2005). One step beyond: Hyperrealism. *Tate Etc.*, 5, n.p. https://www.tate.org.uk/tate-etc/issue-5-autumn-2005/one-step-beyond
Gay, R. (2019). *The book of delights: Essays*. Algonquin Books.
Honor the Earth. (n.d.) Sacred ecology. https://sacredecology.com/blog/honor-the-earth
Reagon, B. J. (1982). My black mothers and sisters or on beginning a cultural autobiography. *Feminist Studies*, 8(1), 81–96. https://doi.org/10.2307/3177580.

The Center for Contemplative Mind in Society, Duerr, M., & Bergman, C. (n.d.). *The tree of contemplative practices – The center for contemplative mind in society.* The Center for Contemplative Mind in Society. Retrieved November 27, 2023, from https://www.contemplativemind.org/practices/tree

Wilson, S. (2021, February 25). *Can we digitize ceremony?* Ongomiizwin Research Indigenous Health Research Symposium, University of Manitoba. https://youtu.be/hiO-pxiWFMQ

17

DANCING BAREFOOT IN THE UNIVERSITY

From Burnout to Radical Presence

Lela Mosemghvdlishvili

Nadir: The Breakdown

Nadir is a word derived from Arabic and means the "opposite" of zenith, the lowest point in a situation. Nadir in my academic career and life dawned on me suddenly. I was sitting with a dear friend in a public library in Amsterdam. The day was ordinary, just another I had to get through. All would have gone unnoticed, but a friend's hand on my shoulder cut through the drift. "Lela, why are you crying?" I looked at my friend, startled, and noticed my vision blurred with tears in my eyes. "You cannot continue like this. You need to report sick," she said, looking straight into my eyes. As if finally given permission, tears started to roll down my face. I was so disembodied that even crying while working was not something I registered as alarming. With my friend's guidance, I wrote an email to my supervisors and formally reported sick. I was in the last year of my PhD project, conducting research, teaching a significant course load, and supervising MA students. With the pressure to publish and perform, to excel as a minority, I felt I had to work harder than others. Sending out that email marked a breaking point in my life. It was a recognition of the nadir, what I came to call "my mental breakdown." A chain of events followed: visits to the doctors, referral to a clinical psychologist and then a psychiatrist, diagnoses of burnout and severe depression, cognitive-behavioral therapy, regular visits to a mental health center, and an arduous path of recovery.

Between Healing and Living

I did not respond well to cognitive-behavioral therapy. Despite pressure from my doctor, I refused to start antidepressant medication. I had a deep-seated

DOI: 10.4324/9781003416777-21

fear of getting on the pills. I began to seek other modalities for healing: dance therapy, breathwork, mantra chanting, and various forms of meditation. In this process, I met the wisdom of master plants, sat through Ayahuasca ceremonies, and underwent Kambo cleanses. As I write now, recalling all the modalities I encountered, I feel privileged. Being an immigrant in an affluent Western country allowed me to access traditions from the most distant parts of the world. The wisdom and generosity of those I met on my path helped me reconnect with my body-mind and allowed me to feel again the interconnection of all life. After two years of medical leave, I could dance again, cook again, see a sunset and smile, hear someone laugh, and rejoice for their happiness. But returning to the workplace still seemed impossible. A gap was emerging between "normal life" and "healing spaces." For example, when I was in a retreat, I felt more connected with people than with co-travelers on public transport. My life was splitting in two. In sharing circles, I felt understood. Everyone was there to heal, exposing their vulnerabilities. However, outside those safe containers, the world seemed hostile and fake. The gap between *healing* and *living* was growing into an unbridgeable abyss. I started to entertain the idea of changing my profession, re-qualifying as a yoga teacher, and never going back to academia.

It was during this period that I encountered the Feeding Your Demons® (FYD) practice, which became a doorway to a path. In the beginning, I was seeking any healing modality as medicine, to 'cure' myself. Yet, encountering this practice made me realize the difference between medicine and a path. Medicine is needed when we are sick and need support, but a path is a direction we walk, regardless of falling ill or feeling well.

Paradigm Shift: Feeding Instead of Fighting

Lama Tsultrim Allione developed Feeding Your Demons® based on the teachings of 11th-century yogini Machig Labdron from Tibet. It is a therapeutic as well as a spiritual practice that integrates Western psychotherapeutic methods with the Buddhist view of the emptiness of self and all phenomena. It uses body scans, interoception, visualization, embodiment, and open awareness meditation to help a practitioner surface unconscious material, engage with it, and transform.

Demon, in this context, is any force that blocks our liberation. Lama Tsultrim explains it is any (inner or outer) force that prevents us from being free, happy, and at peace with ourselves; anything that drains us. Hence, the demon in this practice is not something out there, an evil force, but any part of us or our experience that we experience as negative. By trying to flee from these "demonic" parts of ourselves – these forces only become louder and more powerful. Through the Feeding Your Demons® practice, these most challenging parts of us and our experiences are acknowledged and integrated through compassion.

What makes FYD practice spiritual as opposed to only therapeutic is its contemplative (meditative) aspect, and the setting of an altruistic motivation. Before engaging with one's own demons, a practitioner sets an intention to do the practice for the benefit of all beings (known in the context of Buddhism as raising *bodhicitta*). After the feeding process, a practitioner dissolves all visualizations and rests in open awareness for a few seconds or an extended period. Such resting in an open, uncontrived, non-dual mental state is what Lama Tsultrim calls "gaps" between thoughts (Allione, 2008).

Benefits of the Contemplative Practice

Beyond the immediate benefits of alleviating negative emotions, Feeding Your Demons® loosened the idea of 'solid me' slowly, layer by layer. By repeatedly witnessing how the most unwanted 'demon' was a cry for help, a seeking for integration, it gradually dawned on me that at the core of both what I perceived as negative and as positive, lay the same living energy. The demons themselves were unresolved issues, which, if attended to with compassion, would transform into wisdom.

When I reread my practice log, which contains records of more than two hundred sessions, I see some patterns of 'when' and 'where' my demons would most frequently arise. It was in relation to my work (at the university), that I most regularly experienced my 'demons': irritation, anger, feelings of injustice, fear of failure, perfectionism, feeling either too good or not good enough, and so on. Working with these demons and transforming them did not mean denying the existence of unwholesome structures at my workplace. Rather, what these processes taught me was the impossibility of trying to change these structures without also doing deep personal work. Social struggle became shadow work and bridged the personal and professional, the individual and the collective.

"What if You Raise Bodhicitta Before You Write that Email?"

With continuous practice of Feeding Your Demons®, I completed my PhD and was offered an adjunct teaching position at the University of Amsterdam, which gave me a basic income, just enough to sustain my life with frugality. Still, spending time within the university building, interacting with colleagues and students was difficult. At the end of the day, I would feel my whole body drained, my eyes dry, and my shoulder blades numb and heavy. The most distant place from my contemplative practice, and my embodied being – was the university campus, its hallways, and classrooms.

"What if you raise bodhicitta before you send that work email as we do before the practice?" suggested Christiane, my partner in FYD processes, after hearing me discuss how, despite all the practice, working was still difficult. Her words pierced through, and as if a soap bubble dividing my *contemplative life* (with its formal practices on the cushion or sitting with trusted sangha members) and *the remaining life* (as in my work with supervisors, colleagues, and students) suddenly burst. Just like the breakdown I had had in the library years before, this phase marked another turning point in my life – a period when I came to see the interconnectedness of my personal quest for healing and the healing of the educational system which I was a part of through my profession. It dawned on me that there was no separation between work and path. My university work was a part of my spiritual and contemplative path, just like the formal sitting meditation was.

Something shifted in how I perceived and related to those I encountered, even in structured, highly performative spaces like universities. A "radical presence" – not only with students but also with colleagues – became possible (O'Reilly, 1998). Being aware of my struggles (fears, anger, longing to be successful, loved, liked, and so on) allowed me to see colleagues, supervisors, students, and subordinates without prejudice, simply as fellow sentient beings who also wanted to be happy and were caught up with fighting their own demons. Even more, a certain paradigm shift occurred in my worldview. Boundaries of in and out-group loosened, freeing me from the fear of being isolated and excluded, and the need to surround myself only with likeminded people.

Dancing Barefoot in the University

Over the past seven years, much has changed. If I were to distill what the most transformative effect of Feeding Your Demons practice was, it was the loosening of the idea of separations on various levels (between my feelings and outside events, between me and colleagues, between "us" and "them"). Additionally, the energy spent in fighting or fleeing from these demons seemed to have opened into creativity. Instead of expressing generalized criticism about how impersonal academic teaching is, I shifted my own teaching practice; I started openly integrating and speaking about contemplation, compassion, the need to slow down and recover first-person inquiry in learning.

My journey from nadir to radical openness – seeped and materialized into an elective seminar, *Bridging Self and Other through Mind and Dance*, that I developed at the PPLE college. PPLE (Politics, Psychology, Law, and Economics) is an interdisciplinary honors program under the Law faculty of the University of Amsterdam. In this course I introduced contemplative learning activities as the primary mode, substituting class debates with dialogue, and essays with movement improvisation. The assessment is completion-based, meaning there is no differentiation based on performance. Students are treated as whole, already complete, and capable of deep knowing. They are given only one text per week (which is drastically less than what they are used to). Instead of skimming, they are asked to engage in deep reading. Class discussions are different, too; instead of debating, they are encouraged to listen, to truly listen to each other and understand. Still, one of the most novel aspects is bringing embodiment, body-mind awareness, and movement into the university context. Students in this seminar have some classes in typical classrooms, and some in a dance studio on campus. Body-mind awareness, embodiment, and movement are used as pedagogical methods. For example, instead of presenting key concepts from the readings orally, they are invited to express them through non-discursive means. Abstract concepts such as 'self,' 'other,' 'alienation,' 'empathy,' 'interconnectedness,' and so on, are explored through their living bodies, in relation to space and each other.

This elective became one of the most highly evaluated courses among students. Still, the real (yet quiet) revolutionary power of contemplative pedagogy is that it stays with those who have experienced it. Even sometime after their graduation, a few have written to me, expressing how the course has been personally "the most meaningful" within their entire undergraduate education.

Rippling Out

In course evaluations, one of my students wrote, "There is something *human* about Lela's classes." Comparable comments, pointing to the 'different' teaching style, began seeping into my formal evaluations. Not long after, I was nominated by my program as an Education Research Fellow and invited to conduct research into teaching practices. The grant allowed me to research contemplative pedagogical practices and as an outcome, to create a professionalization course for lecturers at my university. In the course *Introduction to Contemplative Pedagogy,* I invite colleagues to slow down, turn their gaze inward, and reflect on how we embody pedagogy. In the beginning, I often hear resistance toward time-honoring pedagogy: "There is no time; we have so much to cover!" But as the course unfolds, not by teaching *about* but by demonstrating contemplative pedagogy – something shifts in my colleagues. This shift is an opening, a crack through which the inner intelligence of teachers starts to manifest.

At the end of the professionalization course, when the group has bonded, I share my aspiration to witness a university that recognizes students for who they already are and supports them in experiencing the wisdom of interconnectedness of all life before the acquisition of any skills and competencies. I share with colleagues that I dream of seeing universities where communal dance and singing are practiced, and where radical presence, playfulness, and compassion replace the undercurrent of competition, alienation, and fragmentation.

When the question arises about *how* to transform university teaching, my answer is that it is through turning the gaze inward, and going toward what we fear; it is not by fighting or engaging resentment, but rather by embodying radical presence and compassion. Radical compassion does not mean justifying structural inequalities or complying with unwholesome practices. No, it is an awareness with tender recognition that those we fight are no different from us. Looking back, I feel, the wisdom from Feeding Your Demons® practice is actually the experiential recognition of nonduality; that I am no different from those I perceive as 'other.' Acting from such ground is nourishing, heartwarming, healing, and deeply transformative.

Epilogue

"I have bad news for you," said the voice on the phone. "We did not select you for the postdoctoral position. The committee could not agree on your candidacy. Your work is very niche." As I put down my mobile phone, I felt a rush of tingling sensations under my skin like an ant nest suddenly exposed to the sunlight. Thoughts started rising in my mind and assembling into chains of disappointment: frustration with the interview outcome, insecurity with the income, and pressure to sustain my livelihood while paying sky-rocketing gas prices. These thoughts began getting uglier and angrier, and right before believing and identifying with them, I recognized my demon of insecurity forming right there. "Through practice, you will become able to directly see, recognize, and liberate your demons as they start forming," taught Lama Tsultrim. A rush of release flows over my body. I stand at the window. In this vast openness, clouds are passing in the sky. Being rejected from a postdoctoral position is not the end of the world; it's just another cloud passing.

Practice: Feeding Your Demons

This practice takes about thirty to forty minutes, and is typically guided by a facilitator in a one-to-one or group context. The setting requires two chairs (or cushions) to be placed opposite each other as the practitioner will have to switch places twice while embodying the Demon and then the Ally.

In this practice, a demon is a manifestation of inner conflict, or anything that hinders an individual and prevents them from being at peace. The Ally is a transformed form of the demon, which by being nurtured through compassion, turns into a source of resilience and wisdom.

Here I use one of my sessions recorded on March 31, 2021, to illustrate how the practice unfolds in five steps. That morning, my supervisor had given me critical feedback via email on the final chapter of my dissertation. As I read the feedback, discontent and anger rushed through me; I felt wrongly judged and so angry that it was impossible to work. I decided to do the practice focusing on the feeling of anger. I began by setting an altruistic motivation to do this practice for the benefit of all beings before moving through the steps.

Step 1: Finding the Demon in the Body

As I was thinking about the email and evoking the feeling of anger toward my supervisor, I started to scan my body to locate where I was feeling the demon most strongly. I discerned a tingling sensation throughout my body, noticing that it felt most strongly in my throat. According to the script, I started to describe the feeling of the demon inside my body.

What is its shape? It is round, like a plate.

What is its color? It's yellow.

What is its texture? It is a kind of dirty wax with all the impurities and hairs stuck into it.

What is its temperature like? It's warm, warmer than my body.

Step 2: Personifying the Demon

I intensify the sensation in my throat of a warm, wax-like plate, and when I feel it most strongly, I move it out of my body and visualize the demon as an animate being. I see a cartoon character of an evil stepmother in the shape of an old woman from Disney's version of Snow White. The cartoon character gradually becomes more life-like. She is all in rags, has no teeth, and is very dreadful to look at. Her body's surface seems sticky like a wax figure, and deteriorating. Despite feeling repulsion, I follow the script.

What is her character like? She is envious; she does not wish anyone good.

What emotional state is she in now? She is disengaged, avoiding eye contact. She expresses disgust toward me.

What is the look in the demon's eyes? I look into the Demon's eyes, and my whole body seizes. I feel a colony of ants rush down my limbs. The look in her eyes is so sad, so lonely, so sorrowful. Looking into her eyes shifts my attitude toward her. I start to feel for her. Repulsion turns into empathy.

Step 3: Becoming the Demon

The time to change seats and embody the demon comes. Without opening my eyes, I get up, turn, and sit on the opposite chair. I have to become the demon and feel how it is to be the demon.

How does it feel to be in the demon's body? Lonely. Sad. This feeling of sadness and loneliness is overpowering.

Embodying the demon, I answer three questions posed to the demon in this step. I speak as the old woman:

What I want is... to be young and strong. I want everything that I cannot have anymore.

What I really need is ...to relax, just relax, to release this tension.

When I get what I really need, I will feel... safe. I note the last answer (feeling safe), as it is what I will use as a nectar to nurture the demon.

I return to my original seat and see the demon as an old woman in rags with sad eyes in front of me. I prepare to feed the demon with the nectar that will satisfy its need for safety.

Step 4: Feeding the Demon and Meeting the Ally

I evoke the feeling of safety and when I feel it throughout my body, I dissolve into a nectar that has the quality of safety to nurture the demon. My body dissipates into golden-yellow snakes, which rush toward the demon. As they approach the demon, snakes transform into liquid nectar. The demon slowly absorbs the golden substance, first through her clothes, then through her skin, filling up her whole body. As the demon's body absorbs the nectar, it too becomes liquid and begins to melt. The colors change from golden to serene blue. Gradually, I see only light blue, like a vast ocean that merges with the sky. The demon is fully satisfied and dissolves into light blue space. In its place, another being emerges: the Ally.

A white crane rises out of the water. It has delicate feet and powerful, amazing wings, much bigger than a normal bird. It feels like a majestic creature, dignified and very present. It seems amused and playful, freely and gracefully dancing through the space.

Once I see the Ally and ask the required question on how it will help and support me, I switch chairs and take its seat. I open my arms, lengthen my neck, and become the majestic crane. I start speaking as the Ally:

I will help you by ... giving you confidence in such situations not to feel threatened.

I will protect you by ... reminding you that there is a non-separation even between you and those that you seem to fight or feel that you are against.

I pledge I will ... remind you that despite this inseparability, you can still act, you can still interfere, but only when you are calm, when you settle down your anger, when you are like a lake - then you can act, but not before, not while riding your waves of frustration.

You can access me by ... imagining me flying next to you.

I return to my original seat for the final time. I see the majestic crane again in front of me; I look into its eyes and let its energy pour into me. The energy of the Ally feels empowering. The Ally dissolves in turquoise light, which dissolves into me, integrating Ally's energy into every cell of my body. As my body expands, there is a spaciousness in each of my cells.

Step 5: Resting in Awareness

In the final step, I dissolve and rest in open awareness. There is a sense of resting in gaps between thoughts. Discursive thoughts appear soon, and I notice it is time to come back and open my eyes. However, throughout the day I maintain the feeling of the majestic white crane's energy in me and remember its wisdom.

After the practice, I reread my supervisor's feedback. Having sat with my demon and processed my anger, I was now able to discern helpful suggestions and revise my work.

Reference List

Allione, T. (2008). *Feeding your demons: Ancient wisdom for resolving inner conflict.* Little, Brown Spark.

O'Reilly, M. R. (1998). *Radical presence: Teaching as contemplative practice.* Heinemann.

18
ALONGSIDE AARON

Wendy Petersen-Boring

It's music night at Elphaba's House, and the energy is high. The roommates have picked the theme: Mariah Carey night. Neighbors, friends, and family stream in with potluck dishes and guitars. One roommate greets me at the door: "Did you know *Wicked* is being made into a movie?" Another is bouncing on a giant exercise ball in the kitchen. People hug and laugh. The karaoke begins, and soon the requests veer into crowd favorites: "Sweet Caroline – uh-uh-uh!" and "I can fly!" from *Peter Pan*. For a few hours on this otherwise ordinary weeknight, time seems suspended. Joy runs through our bodies under the disco ball.

Elphaba's House (named by the residents after the misunderstood witch in the musical *Wicked*) is a home for individuals living with intellectual and developmental disabilities (ID/DD). One of them is my 25-year-old son, Aaron. Walking alongside Aaron, attempting to see the world through his eyes, simply being present to him and with him, has widened the caverns of my soul in ways I could scarcely have imagined two decades ago. Being with him has shaped how I conceive of spiritual practices, what I teach, what I think about and choose to research, where I experience community, and how I connect with issues of justice and equity in my community.

Aaron lights up a room with his smile. His laughter is contagious. He loves swimming, walking, bouncing on his exercise ball to music, watching sports, and making smoothies. He needs support 24/7 – for dressing, eating, working, speaking, and outings. He cannot read, write, tie a shoe, zip a zipper, or use a fork. His individualized support plans identify "PDD NOS," "autism," "cognitive impairment," and "dyspraxia." They describe in detail how to respond when he resorts to aggression to communicate.

DOI: 10.4324/9781003416777-22

I am active in the disability justice movement in our community. He has no idea what that phrase means.

It would be easier if all it took was sustaining love for this child of mine who is now a man. That alone would be enough to warrant a book's worth of contemplative practice descriptions. Of course, it's not as simple as that – not loving Aaron, nor caring for my state (Oregon) with its history of racism and exclusion, nor caring for the planet with its crises of climate and extinction. Sustaining a gaze of love is foundational, necessary, and irreplaceable. But the questions that gaze provokes are more complex.

How do you hold space in your heart for the coexistence of love and pain, joy and grief, hope and despair? How do you hold on to the most expansive vision of what's possible for the future, while simultaneously working in the weeds of day-to-day problem solving and the mind-numbing, never-ending details of care? How do you cultivate joy and flourishing in the face of setbacks? How do you care for yourself, loved ones, and community in the face of a dysfunctional, underfunded, and unjust care system? How, in the midst of all of this, do you grow resilience, compassion, courage, and energy?

These questions have been my companions for over two decades. I have many stories to tell. Let me pick just two.

***

One day, when Aaron was about two years old, we were jumping on the bed together, giggling and falling down. At that time, I was deep in the Land of Diagnoses and Therapies – Floor Time Therapy, Occupational Therapy, Cognitive Behavioral Intervention, Qi Gong Sensory Therapy – while attempting to finish my dissertation and parenting my four-year-old daughter. That day, as we fell onto the bed, I was thinking about Aaron's eyes – how beautiful and full of light they were as he gazed into mine. He seemed open and alive. It felt good just to be together.

Then, unexpectedly, a neighbor showed up. This neighbor was very concerned that we weren't taking Aaron's autism seriously. In her view, people with autism behaved in certain ways, and we seemed to be ignoring all of the data and interacting with him as though he was not impaired. As she rounded the corner of the bedroom, I could feel her gaze assessing the scene. And literally, before my eyes, Aaron's eyes went blank, his laughter ceased, he stopped looking at me, and he curled up in a non-communicative ball in the middle of the bed – looking for all the world like her textbook notion of autism.

As I watched the change in him, a phrase came into my mind: *the spirit with which I gaze has the power to shape the reality in front of my eyes.*

I'd had enough meditation and quantum physics to know this to be true, to some extent, about everything. But it stunned me, the way it became literally evident in front of my eyes with regard to the life of this little being I loved. Walking alongside Aaron, I realized, was going to require sustaining a gaze from the Land of Love while simultaneously following the complicated mazes in the Land of Therapy and Diagnoses. They seemed like different universes. How to hold them together? All I knew was that I had a live-in teacher. Many years of trial and error have followed. The experiment is still running.

At the time, I had many practices as companions – mindfulness, Qigong, loving kindness, centering prayer. But these were not what I drew on most. Instead, I found myself developing new practices, out of necessity and by accident. Two in particular stand out. One was a practice of presence. For me it went like this: you let go of the list of the thousands of things to do, and you become present in the now, with no thought for past or future, no thought for what needs to be done or undone, no comparisons or distractions. You let yourself be in the moment, simply attending to what is in front of you – the light in their eyes, the dirt on their hands, their feet running on green grass, the chocolate on their cheeks, the words in their mouth. You attend so fully that the molecules of time open up and the sacred dimension of time that runs alongside regular time floats to the surface and carries you. In that space, there is a flow that feeds the energy of Love. There is presence enough to source the heart from an inexhaustible well. There, the heart can hold the complexity of seemingly irreconcilable opposites.

The other practice I stumbled into by accident. One morning, in the state of bleary exhaustion and spiritual desperation that comes with caring for someone with special needs, I reached for a stack of used poetry books, picking up one after another and reading until something happened – until I could feel my heart stir and my gaze soften, until the day seemed easier to bear. To this day, on many mornings, I pick up books of poetry and open them randomly and read until I feel some kind of shift, a movement, an opening in my heart. Often, I only have a few minutes. Sometimes it takes many poems. Sometimes just one word does it. I try to carry that one word with me through the day. Over the years I've collected volumes of poetry. I read poetry like my life depends on it – because it does.

***

When Aaron was about three, I was on the phone with a friend who'd called with great news: "You won't believe this, but I figured out why I have been having so many strange symptoms: I have celiac disease! The diagnosis explains everything!" I told her how glad I was. As I hung up the phone,

I thought about Aaron. His disabilities didn't fit neatly into any diagnostic category. There was no clarity about treatment or intervention. I was just beginning to half-sense the magnitude of what lay ahead – that there would never be a straight path forward. I could never call my friend and say, "If I just do X, it will all be better!" I was hit with the full force of what we were facing.

As I walked across our living room, an image suddenly dropped into my mind. I was in a dark cave, standing at the edge of a giant black abyss, perched precariously at the edge. If I looked down it was terrifying. But when I looked out across the chasm to the far side of the cave, I could see a semi-circle of lights. They were hovering, seemingly suspended in the air. I knew without thinking that they were the souls of the people who loved me, past and present. I stood there for a while in my living room, in the dark cave that had formed in my mind, taking it all in. The space named all that was true at that moment – the precarity, the deep uncertainty, and the fact that I am not alone. The presence of the lights did not make the chasm I teetered on go away. The darkness was still there. But I felt held, and drawn into the mystery of a spaciousness able to hold it all.

One week later while at the library, I happened to pull out a book on feminist anthropology. I opened to a page at random and was astonished to find almost the exact same image I'd seen in my mind's eye. The caption explained that the cave with a semi-circle of lights was a cross-cultural expression of the experience of *uncertainty*. "Yes," I thought, "and also its antidote." Finding the image again, so soon, made me pay attention more closely. I turned it over in my mind for years, like a rosary bead.

And then, while in Assisi three years ago, I stumbled across an art exhibit by the artist, Guido Dettoni della Grazia (n.d.), in the church Santa Maria Della Rose. I saw an installation as close to an exact replica of the image as I could imagine. I was stunned. The only difference was that the artist had rendered the semi-circle of suspended lights as small carvings of a maternal body – the body of Mary. The carvings were made from wood in multiple shades from light to dark, and their shape echoed the curves of a female body – nursing, praying, tending. The carvings appeared to be mysteriously hovering in their own light, each in a small glass tube, suspended in the dark cave of a church. The artist had chosen to make the semi-circle out of the Greek letters *Alpha* and *Omega*. On the floor, the *Omega* was created from soil, earth. The whole thing felt alive, vibrating. It communicated strength, tenderness, solidity, and delicateness. It was an embodied witness to Love as our beginning and our end, to the capacity of love to dwell in and evoke the Eternal, and to the suffering of maternal love. I sat in the dark and wept.

There have been many difficult moments as Aaron has aged. Imagine, if you will, having a strong, healthy 25-year-old male body, with all the hunger and hormones thereto appertaining, and being dependent on others to tie your shoes, get your food, and give you a shower. Imagine understanding about 90% of what people say, but only being able to express about 5%. Imagine navigating entire political, social, cultural, educational, and economic systems that, with rare exceptions, have engineered themselves around the idea that you are of no value. There are days, weeks, months so dark that the only thing that makes sense is to throw, hit, scream, take your clothes off, hold your breath every 60 seconds or all day until you pass out, or run away. Aaron has tried all of the above. Imagine being hit by your son so many times that you decide he can't live in your house anymore and you have to send him away to foster care until the wounds heal. Imagine how taking care of someone who needs help 24/7 for 25 years wears on a career, a marriage, a life.

Sometimes an image provides what other practices cannot – a multivalent symbol that's able to hold the complexities of questions we are barely conscious of asking, a pattern of movement the mind needs to traverse over and again to experience transformation. The practice of meditating on the dark edge of the abyss and the astonishing, beautiful semi-circle of lights – noticing, observing, being present to what is there and what arises for me – has sustained me.

**

I remember the day I first connected walking alongside Aaron to what was happening in my work with students. I was teaching a class on climate change and colonization, and my students were struggling. I could feel the despair, paralysis, and anxiety stalking the room. I stopped the class and asked them to talk about how they were feeling, to speak their questions out loud. Then, I asked them to name the questions behind the questions. We filled two white boards. We called them Live Questions. As I looked at the boards, I realized that their questions were like mine: How can I access joy and flourishing in the face of darkness, uncertainty, and despair? How can I strengthen my resilience and courage so that I can imagine new futures into existence and work to bring them forth? How do I care for self and community in the midst of climate crises worsened by trauma and systemic oppression?

I left the class thinking about all I had learned with Aaron. I realized that my students needed the same mixture of holding onto a vision of what is possible while doing the thousands of things that need to be done, all without a clear path forward. I knew how to do that. I'd been practicing it for years. And I knew that to sustain it, it was essential to find practices that tend to the spirit and keep the heart alive.

However, at the time, I thought of contemplative practices as something I did outside of the classroom, in my own community and life. I'd never heard of contemplative pedagogy, and no one at my university was doing it. I didn't know how to proceed. But I did know climate activists and policy makers who were deeply engaged in contemplative practices and intentional communities. It was clear to me that tending the inner life was vital to keeping their flames lit and their energy strong in this difficult work. I kept wishing my students could talk with them. So, I decided to interview them and publish the interviews as *Resources of the Spirit in the Race Against Climate Change* on the Millennial Alliance for Humans and the Biosphere blog (2019).

From these interviews emerged a series of core qualities that keep us vibrant in the midst of difficult climate justice work: equanimity/resilience, courage/truth-speaking, compassion/community, and joy/pleasure. I developed a new course organized around these themes and taught contemplative practices to accompany them. The development of the syllabus was multi-staged, collaborative, and student-centered and included a wide range of communities from across the university. *The Inner Life of Activism* is the first course at my university to deliberately and substantively engage contemplative pedagogies and is offered as part of the general education program. It is situated at the intersection of contemplative studies for social justice, the healing justice movement, and engaged compassion.

Students respond to the course with effusive feedback: "This should be offered to every student." "This class feels like the most important one I ever took in college." "I will use these practices in my work for social justice the rest of my life." The overwhelmingly positive responses underline the limits of traditional pedagogical approaches. Although a traditional liberal arts education has often been described as engaging the "whole person," in fact students often perceive they are supposed to leave their bodies and emotions outside the door. The reasons for this disembodied stance are many: outdated norms of supposed objectivity; an educational system increasingly shaped by the values of capitalism; the need to meet student and parent demands for career preparation. But the gravity and urgency of the ecological/political/cultural crises makes the disembodied stance increasingly difficult, and students manifest the stress of trying to hide their reactions and emotions. Contemplative approaches allow students to integrate body, story, experience, trauma, emotions, hopes, and fears together with ecologically focused content in a way that catalyzes transformation and engagement.

Several projects have flowed from this, most notably The Conversation Project at Willamette (n.d.), supported by the American Immigration Council's Center for Inclusion and Belonging and the Wabash Center for

Teaching and Learning. My colleague David Gutterman and I began the dialogue across difference project in response to the deterioration of campus conversational culture. As our national political climate has become more divisive and reactive, college classrooms and campus cultures across the country have become increasingly marked by polarization, fear, and presumptive resentment. Our students – like their peers elsewhere – too often lack the skills and disposition necessary for healthy democracy, including the capacity for bridging differences, the willingness to listen generously, the inclination to collaborate, the ability to "win" or "lose" graciously, and an abiding belief in the hopeful possibilities of democratic public life. The project's research results have been translated into curriculum, workshops, events, and training.

The course begins with a foundational unit "Preparing the Self for Conversation," in which we teach skills of listening, staying grounded, and cultivating curiosity and compassion for self and others. Next, students learn how to participate in and facilitate conversations across differences. Finally, they intern with community organizations. The curriculum centers dialogue and storytelling as vital means for recognizing and understanding the power that shapes our communities. We speak about approaching everyone as story-carriers. We ask how we can become worthy and adept at receiving other's stories. Students often say that the contemplative exercises are the most important part of the curriculum – and ones they would not have encountered otherwise. They are the first steps in asking the question, "How can we be community to each other?" My students love the joy and community-creating practices the most; how they cultivate joy as countercultural, how they challenge the values of productivity, achievement, and efficiency that dictate their google calendars and structure their academic lives.

Being present to Aaron's effusive joy has completely reoriented how I relate to the values that govern the academy. As Sandra Hendren (2023) has said describing her son, Graham, who lives with Downs Syndrome, "There is a kind of presence and enjoyment of presence and an accepting of the giftedness of life that is inherently wise. And it doesn't come from knowledge. It doesn't come from the mathematical accumulation of processing power and, therefore, the rendering of something that's monetizable." Walking alongside someone with intellectual and developmental disabilities is an every-day invitation into a new way of regarding wisdom, a new way of being in the world.

When we get to the section on joy practices in the course, I often tell them about my own practices that provoke me to ponder the questions posed above: How do you hold space in your heart for the coexistence of love and pain, joy and grief, hope and despair? How do you hold on to the most expansive vision of what's possible for the future, while simultaneously working in the weeds of day-to-day problem solving and the mind-numbing, never-ending details of care? How do you cultivate joy and flourishing in the face of setbacks? How do you care for yourself, loved ones, and community in the face of a dysfunctional, underfunded, and unjust care system? How, in the midst of all of this, do you grow resilience, compassion, courage, and energy?

And I tell them about dancing under the disco ball on music nights at Elphaba's House.

Practice: Mindful Poetry Buddy

I developed this practice when my children were small and I had little time for contemplation. The purpose of this practice is to soften and open your heart to love. It was inspired by a line from a Hafiz poem, "A Day Too Great a Force," which speaks about opening our hearts to weather our days.

The practice has two parts: a poetry exchange with a contemplation buddy designed to strengthen your sense of community and belonging, and a solo practice you can do anytime, anywhere.

Buddy Practice

This practice was inspired by a year I spent exchanging a Hafiz poem each day with a friend. We shared them in many formats: letters, phone messages, texts, emails, artwork. We lived apart, so there was always a lag time between when we picked the poem out and when it arrived, but it was astonishing how often the poem that arrived was just right for that day. Later, I used this buddy practice with my students and drew from a variety of poets. They loved it and some are still poetry buddies years later. I often wake up to poems texted to me from students in former classes, and very often they are exactly what I need to hear.

- Find a poetry buddy.
- Get to know what kinds of poetry they enjoy, or simply what delights them. Get to know what they are carrying in their lives, what is challenging.
- Look for poems that they would like, or ones that speak to their joys and sufferings. Think about what might help open their heart.
- Exchange a poem a day for a week – or longer.
- Find new ways to give them a poem, surprising them if possible. Use paper, texts, emails, voice messages, videos.
- Let the poems also speak to each other.
- Send your partner wishes for health, happiness, and ease along with the poems.

Solo Practice

Consider beginning your day with this practice, before you move out into your day.

- Gather poetry books in one place.
- Take a few deep breaths to settle your body. Become conscious of your state of mind. Find a word or two to name it. Put your hand on your heart. Become conscious of how your heart feels. Find a word or two to name it.
- Pick up the poetry and begin reading. You may read quickly or slowly, many poems or just one. Perhaps just one line or one word will be all you need.
- When you can feel your heart move, soften, shift, or open, pause and dwell on that word or phrase. Notice how your heart feels. Find a word or two to name it. Express gratitude for that poem and poet, that word or phrase, and for your heart.
- Take the word or phrase from the poem with you through the day. Return to it when you need to remind yourself how vital it is to keep your heart open.

Reference List

Boring, W. (June 12, 2019). *Resources of the spirit in the race against climate change.* Millennial Alliance for Humans and the Biosphere. https://mahb.stanford.edu/blog/resources-spirit-race-climate-change/

Dettoni della Grazia, G. (n.d.). *Maria: Permanent installation, assisi.* https://maria.tk/assisi/

Hendren, S. (Nov. 16, 2023). "Our bodies, aliveness, and the built world." On being podcast. https://onbeing.org/programs/sara-hendren-our-bodies-aliveness-and-the-built-world/#transcript

Willamette University. (n.d.). *The conversation project: An initiative to cultivate conversations across differences.* https://willamette.edu/arts-sciences/additional-academic-opportunities/tcp/

19
MY RHIZOMATIC AWAKENING

Steven Thurston Oliver

Rhizomatic approaches to learning allow for the fact that every individual has their own unique lived experience and brings to every experience a distinct context and frame of reference. As a reader, I came to this collection of essays with my own set of questions about how I might continue to do work in the academy, a space I find as beautiful as it is painful to exist within. I am a mid to late career Black Queer Identified man who has spent the better part of the last 30 years in various roles in four different higher ed institutions. Most recently, I was a tenured full professor and department chair at a regional public institution in New England. However, at a life and career stage when I should be settled and feeling positively about my accomplishments, I have found that it is increasingly difficult to be grounded and to cultivate a sense of wholeness and well-being. We are living at a moment of such tension in the larger world, within the United States, in all our cities and towns, and all that suffering finds its way into our institutions. The essays that make up this section offer powerful, insightful, tangible, and instructional examples of how we can move in the world while protecting our hearts, our sanity, and our peace. What follows is a reflection on how the essays contributed to a greater sense of clarity for me in a way I suspect they will do for many others.

In their essay *Our Skins are Membranes Not Walls*, the authors model the power of what can happen with an intentional sharing of contemplative practices among a community of individuals invested in the wholeness of one another. That leaning into wholeness is something we can do with and for each other is a powerful notion. The intentional connecting of contemplative practice with work as a safeguard against being fractured and disembodied is a powerful theme woven throughout this piece. Ahmed skillfully describes how she came to contemplative practice and the ways in which the search to become a more integrated human being was at odds with the pressure in higher education to compartmentalize our spiritual and professional selves. Chari highlights the paradox that is all too often the hallmark of institutions of higher education when she states that the educational space she inhabits "reproduces racialized and colonial violence even as they provide tools to critique it." An aspect of this violence, she argues, involves the loss of one's body in the name of intellectual legibility. No wonder so many in the academy feel that our health is faltering, and our sense of well-being is fading. The contemplative practices shared here seek to shed light on the ways that suffering, and loss of self can happen in the academy, while offering another way of seeing and being with ourselves and each other. Thompson provides thoughtful insight into the possibilities of learning in virtual spaces, posing the question "what if we understand the space between ourselves and those we talk to on the screen as sacred?" It is a haunting and beautiful question that has stayed on my mind as I grapple with imaging how I might convey this sentiment to students I teach online.

Wendy Petersen-Boring offers a beautiful story of lessons learned and contemplative practices developed as part of the journey of caring for someone with disabilities. It is a striking example of how our work lives and personal lives are not as separate as academic culture presumes. It resonates powerfully with me as she writes of climate activists and policy makers engaged in contemplative practices saying, "it was clear to me that tending the inner life was vital to keeping their flames lit and their energy strong in this difficult work." It occurs to me that working in higher education in this moment is exceedingly difficult, in ways no other generation has experienced. We are still dealing with the aftermath of the pandemic and a kind of resistance to naming the damage done by the collective trauma we all experienced. The very nature of our work has changed as higher education, along with the rest of the society, has slid into a perpetual hybrid reality that blurs the lines between home and work. Using this essay as a lens for making sense of a viable way forward has been extremely helpful. Specifically, the poetry practice Wendy describes is brilliant and something I will actively attempt to implement. The mind can at times take us to very dark places where it seems impossible to imagine how things might be different. And yet, we know that our thoughts are just arisings like waves that appear and subside. The practice of reading poetry until one feels a shift or an opening in the heart is so practical and something I can do for myself tomorrow in a continued effort to cultivate compassion.

Lela Mosemghvdlishvili's narrative offers both caution and hope as it reminds us of the possibility of burnout and the need to engage in self-care even if it means taking extended time away from the academy to facilitate our own healing. The practice of "Feeding Your Demons" as presented here resonates with my own contemplative practice of Zazen rooted in the Soto Zen tradition which highlights the need to be with things as they are. Lela writes that through this practice "the most challenging parts of us and our experiences are acknowledged and integrated through compassion." The wisdom presented here discourages the fracturing, resistance, and hardening that leads to disembodiment and suffering. By encouraging us to be with and examine parts of ourselves that are negative and draining of our vitality and life force, Lela's practice moves us in the direction of wholeness, curiosity, and non-judgment. It is a similar notion evoked in this essay as we are encouraged to be with and examine the parts of us that are negative and draining of our vitality and life force. Lela also emphasizes the necessity of congruence, a theme that runs through all the essays; the idea that our personal and professional lives are not separate but interwoven with our hearts and minds, and that both must be tended to.

Finally, Phyllis M. Jeffers-Coly encourages us to be open to a practice that allows us to engage the presence and wisdom of our ancestors as a source of connection, healing, and wholeness. She writes powerfully of the experience many of us have had in higher education being "on the edges and margins of higher education" when we are intentional about centering our efforts on Black people. Our scholarship is often not respected and our work with students is not on the institution's radar until there is a need to report on DEI efforts. She notes the ways in which we often internalize the hierarchical nature of the academy that does not respect and value our spaces and institutions to the same degree. I confess I have often felt the same way being based at a public regional institution and embracing the idea that I somehow did not measure up to my fullest potential that would have landed me somewhere with more name recognition, prestige, and resources. I sometimes feel this way despite knowing that the work I do is valuable and making a difference in the lives of students and colleagues. This kind of internal de-valuing can lead to burnout. Like Phyllis, I have at times found myself "collapsed on the floor and broke wide open." This essay shed light on the fact that higher education is failing Black people and reveals how contemplative practice can be part of sustaining ourselves on the journey. I had a powerful experience when reading Phyllis' description of the way that yoga supports her. I immediately took out my pen to mark this section writing in the margin "this is how I will stay well." So much of what she writes in this essay affirms inklings I have had about what I need to be doing now. This includes attempting to ground myself by connecting to those who cared for me who are no longer living. Phyllis suggests a personal self-care practice that is tied to our ancestors, allowing space for healing and restoration from race-based stress and trauma. This is a generative practice that affirms our worth, value, and our enoughness particularly when the space we occupy most days does not.

Thinking about the possibilities and limitations of this collection of essays, my hope is that others will find them to be as informative and affirming as I have. It is affirming to see that others are dealing with the same issues and, drawing on their contemplative practices, finding a way to meet the circumstances arising in their lives. The only limitations I see have more to do with the growing habit of many to not fully engage with the written word. I would love to see these stories offered in other modalities and platforms: a podcast or a video series. I really wanted to see the authors and hear their voices. The authors have offered readers a useful lens through which to clarify and make sense of their own lived experiences. It is easy to imagine a gathering of like-minded contemplatives using this collection of essays to do in depth reading together followed by discussion, bonding, and visioning strategies for moving forward collectively and individually. I am thankful to have encountered this collection of essays at this precise juncture of my career. Onward!

PART IV
Liberatory Relationality
Cultivating Collective Compassion
LeeRay Costa

The path to liberation is always one of both internal and external struggle, processes that inform and shape one another. In the following section, contributors explore and document their struggles for liberatory systems-change within higher education through the centering of their personal truths and the multiple ways they cultivate meaningful relationships across difference. This work, which could arguably be understood as a form of caring labor, inevitably begins with the embodied self as locus of experience, agency, and spirit and extends outward to ever larger circles of community. Imagine the contemplative practitioner as a small but weighty stone that, upon meeting the surface tension of a body of water – a pond, a lake, or a vast sea – creates a disruption that ripples outward in a series of undulations and movements that, over time, transform. This is the potential power of enlivened contemplative practices to liberate through relationality.

Engaging in contemplative practices requires us to begin with the self, and the process of going inward to observe and attend to a range of feelings and the critically important knowledge they give us access to, and to grapple with the discomforts, pain, and suffering that inevitably arise. In the experiences of our contributors, these include the discomforts of facing our own white supremacy, white fragility, and "settler moves to innocence"; our orientation toward "extractivism" and urgency; and our valorization of individualism over community, productivity over wellness, and separation and hierarchy over connection. Allowing ourselves the time and space to grapple with these discomforts enables us to better understand both our complicity in oppressive systems (even and particularly when they are unintentional) and our capacity to imagine and enact different ways of being in the world – what Ericka Echavarria refers to as "contemplative emergence" in her essay.

Angela Davis has written "we know the road to freedom has always been stalked by death." While this can be understood as meaning that the fight for liberation may require the tragic and literal loss of life, as is the case for so many movements fighting for decolonization and sovereignty, it can also be interpreted as referring to the necessary death of oppressive ideologies, narratives, and practices that maintain social inequalities and violence, as well as the death of individualism so central to white supremacist/higher ed cultures. Engaging in contemplative "inner work" is a crucial first step in liberating ourselves from the harmful stories and structures we have internalized and perpetuated, as well as a sustaining practice that comforts and vivifies in the face of resistance, especially when shared in community.

Our authors tell of their encounters with marginalization and devaluation, and their dedication to bringing into being a new vision of higher education. Drawing on the methodology of racial healing circles, Gusain invites higher ed professionals to share the stories of our hearts and to listen deeply to one another, while Loe invites colleagues and students to reimagine their notions of success and wholeness through the creation of accountable communities of care. The emphasis on accountability as a crucial element of relationship-building across differences of race, power, and privilege is taken up by Spragg. She offers the W.A.I.T. practice as a method for engaging white colleagues specifically in "a critical, self-reflexive process which illuminates internal narratives and challenges habitual impulses to speak from assumptions of unearned privilege."

Approaching the harms of white supremacy as she has experienced them as a woman of color, Ericka Echavarria shares the goal of transforming higher ed spaces "so that relationships and systems can heal from the toxic conditioning perpetuated by white dominant/supremist/normative culture." In her "I am Here" practice – "a blend of somatics, affirmation, and meditation" – Echavarria reminds higher ed practitioners to ground themselves in their own value, integrity, and wellness as foundational to building healthy, compassionate relationships and communities. Michael Yellow Bird and Holly Hatton offer yet another vision of systemic transformation through a decolonial mentoring relationship grounded in the lessons that Yellow Bird learned from his great-grandfather, Plenty Fox, an Arikara holy man. Together, mentor and mentee work to decolonize historically hierarchical relationships within the academy while simultaneously growing their skills in truth-telling, humility, and compassion.

I take these insights and lessons to heart as a cisgender white woman committed to transforming the relations of power that currently structure our academic institutions. I am inspired to think in new ways about how

I must both interrogate and leverage my own relative power in relationships with administrators and colleagues. Integral to this work is centering the experiences, voices, and visions of BIPOC and other marginalized folks within higher ed, as we do in this volume. As I strive to build trust, offer support, and receive necessary, critical feedback with humility, I think deeply about how I show up, the kinds of communal spaces I co-create, and the often invisible, behind-the-scenes work I can do in my roles as Director of Faculty Development, chair, and faculty member. These efforts, always grounded in my own contemplative practices and connection to spirit, are critical to fostering new ways of being together that I understand as compassionate relationality (Costa, 2019; 2020).

Cultivating more just, loving relationships remains at the forefront of these contributors' efforts and is made actionable in the contemplative practices they share. These stories and practices are precious gifts that can help us all become more liberated as individuals, and as members of organizational and systemic contexts within higher education. Indeed, it is in this dynamic, reciprocal movement between the individual and the collective that this transformative change is made accountable to our verbal commitments to justice and inclusion, and finds fertile ground for sustainability over the long term.

But ultimately, each one of us must embrace and own the work.

As you read the essays in this section, I invite you to consider the ripples and reverberations they create in *your* thinking, doing, feeling, and being. While reading I invite you to (1) pause and reflect on each author's story to seek its resonances in your own life and work, (2) interrogate the ways you have both contributed to and sought to challenge oppressive power dynamics, and (3) imagine what ripples you want to initiate in your own work practices and relationships in the service of creating a more liberatory and just academy. I hope that you will draw upon the practices offered here for inspiration and adapt them as needed for your specific situation and context as you seek to transform from the inside out.

May your journey of unbecoming lift your spirit

And may you nurture every relationship as a path to collective liberation

Reference List

Costa, L. (2019). *My Heart in My Hand: Spirituality, Compassionate Relationality, and Contemplative Feminist Pedagogy* (Plenary Keynote). Association for Contemplative Mind in Higher Education Summer Session, Smith College.

Costa, L. (2020). Peregrina. In S. Russo (Ed.), *Feminist pilgrimage: Journeys of discovery*, Stacy Russo. Litwin Books.

20
CULTIVATING BELONGING

Compassionate Practice and Pedagogy

Renuka Gusain

Part 1: The Practitioner and the Personal

> "But where are you really from?"
> "If you don't mind my asking, where are you from?"
> "Are you originally from here?"
> "I don't mean to sound like those people,
> but what's your back*ground*?"

These questions and variations thereof are questions I am often asked to respond to. Over the past few decades, I have responded in a variety of different ways, ranging from truths to avoidant half-truths, to absurd answers, depending on my feeling of safety in each situation and what my feelings of belonging are at that moment.

I was born in India and since the age of two, I was raised in different countries across the globe, moving from one country-language-culture-faith tradition-people to another every time my father got assigned to work in a different part of the world. Growing up I never felt that I belonged to any place in particular. Everything was transitory, including relationships (this was the age of snail mail before email). We learn about ourselves in relation to others but there never seemed to be enough time to be in relationship with people or countries. I sang along with one national anthem at the morning school assembly and another national anthem in another school assembly. I celebrated different national holidays depending on where we lived. No sooner had I barely passable proficiency in one language, we moved, and I had to learn a new one. I still recall getting a score of 3 out of 100 on an Arabic language test on the second day of school in Riyadh. Even as a third grader, I wondered why I was given that test. I had arrived in the country less than a week prior and didn't even know the alphabet. As an immigrant in the U.S. for the past twenty years, with a foreign passport and ever-changing visa status, I still remain without ground-home-land. I have taken to calling India my passport country and the U.S. my son's country. I do not know that I belong fully or am accepted entirely in either. I use different terms to describe the countries where I've lived, but have never used the term "homeland" because I feel I have none and it would feel inauthentic to claim. Sometimes I just reply that I am from everywhere. Implicit in that reply is the acknowledgment that I am from nowhere in particular.

Background. Back ground. Back home. The home that will take you back? The ground you came from?

Feelings of safety and belonging shift quickly when you do not have a place to call your home, no land that you can say you belong to. Immigration hoops further amplify my lack of safety and belonging. It has been difficult to not fully belong to one place, emotionally and logistically. The gift of having experienced life in so many different places does not outweigh the heaviness of not fully belonging anywhere and feeling incomplete, like a part of you is always missing. Like you are always trying to find the missing piece of the puzzle of yourself. Like you are always trying to define and explain your identity to others.

It is no surprise then that this absence of the singularity of home or an answer to where I am from, to which place I belong, has shaped my perspective and fueled my personal and now pedagogical striving for a kind of groundedness. Something to hold on to and perhaps an identity to claim. I thought that once I achieved this groundedness I would not be plagued by the absence and uncertainty of ground-home-land. Over the years, I have been actively and even enthusiastically seeking this groundedness in all sorts of contemplative practices that I had been introduced and reintroduced to in the U.S. Yoga – a practice my father has been doing for more than five decades – didn't work for me. Sitting meditation didn't work. Reflective journaling in a beautifully embossed leather-bound book with handmade pages didn't work. Loving-kindness (*metta*) didn't work. Body scans didn't work. Breathing techniques (*pranayama*) didn't work. I remember Whatsapping my mother who is a lifelong practitioner: "I don't see any benefit to your *anulom vilom* nonsense" (a type of controlled breathing). I so desperately wanted these practices to work for me, not fully understanding what that would *feel* like. Somewhere along the way I also wanted them to work for me so I could legitimately call myself a contemplative practitioner, a configuration of identity that I could then also put on my syllabi and my annual faculty review!

This absence and uncertainty was exacerbated by my simultaneous searching for belonging in the context of my professional life in academia. Having been an adjunct first, then a non-tenured lecturer for six years, and then finally a tenure-track faculty member, I was keenly attuned to the power differential that exists in academic hierarchical systems. The feeling these systems and structures perpetuate is of separation and othering, not community-building and belonging, at least not for all bodies. As an immigrant whose presence in this country was contingent on visa sponsorship which was itself contingent on a pre-tenure job, it felt even more risky to not get it just right. What would the student evaluations say if I tried out something that did not work? How would that affect my review? There are already biases that exist against minoritized peoples in the structure and processes of academia. Did I really want to risk becoming known as a contemplative practitioner professionally? What if that was not deemed intellectually rigorous? What if other academics thought I was skating on my cultural capital ("She's Indian so of course, she'll engage in these practices")? This was not a context that invites the whole self in. It is an environment that compounds and extracts emotional and invisible labor of certain bodies while also simultaneously effacing or diluting differences of those very bodies. The result is a fragmenting of the self which is to be expected in the absence of conditions that posit and nurture whole selves.

I reached a point of total exhaustion and frustration that contemplative practices, particularly in academia, didn't *work for me*. They did not make me feel grounded, they did not create a feeling of belonging in any context for me. And during that time, in a perverse way, I felt unburdened of the expectation I had placed on myself that I must be a contemplative practitioner. I let go of that identity and I let go of the idea that any of these practices had to work *for* me.

Work *for* me.

It was only after I let go of this construct – again, not out of enlightenment but out of exhaustion – that I realized how transactional and consumerist the language I used to frame this learning experience was. I was using the same extractive language that I had learned from academia. I had thought for years that these practices had to work for me, that there would be some kind of resolution after doing them enough times, that there would be a return, a payoff. I had a significant attachment to the results I was expecting and to the persona of a contemplative practitioner in academia that I grasped after.

I now realize that it was only once I let go of this attachment to a fixed identity that I also started letting up on my pressing need and yearning for belonging to a place. The curious consequence of being that exhausted and that unattached to a result was that I no longer had the energy to not show up in my wholeness. I did not have the bandwidth to perform someone I was not or to hide and protect parts of myself that I perceived as missing. I was not trying to complete my sense of self with an incessant and constant grasping for. Showing up in my wholeness meant showing up *with* this absence I had long felt and to acknowledge and articulate this feeling of perpetual lack of ground-home-land. Showing up in my wholeness meant embracing and befriending the absent or perceived incomplete parts of myself and acknowledging that I am a process. In my contemplative work I had missed out on self-acceptance and self-compassion. The irony of practicing loving-kindness (*metta*) without self-compassion is not lost on me. Self-acceptance was the ground I had been grasping for and I discovered that when I was too tired to continue grasping for and after.

I remember one of the earliest days when this realization dawned on me, I was in a classroom teaching a course on premodern global humanities and we were examining some Sufi poetry. As I started reading Rumi's "The Guest House," I got stuck on the first line. The poem begins, "This being human is a guest house…" It was not "human being," it was "being human." How many times had I read this poem and how many times had I taught it intellectually but not really felt it? I knew the meaning of the words and poem cognitively but feeling it and understanding it with intention, with every bone in my body as it were, was not something I had experienced before. It was a somatic experience I can only describe as a wave washing over me.

Being human. This *being* human. The poem is not about a finite, complete human being. The poem was about being human. Being open to all that the human experience brings. This being human is a guest house. A guest house, not a home, not a permanent, fixed abode. Between the "being human" and the idea of the self as a guest house, I felt something I had not felt consciously. I felt at home with myself. In myself and my being. The groundedness was not attached to a national identity or professional identity or a claim of some background I belonged to; the feeling of being grounded was within. My perception of the meaning of the words "practitioner" and "belonging" had long been stuck in their noun states. I started understanding them more as stative and dynamic verbs, like love and hope. These were ongoing states of being that began with self-acceptance and needed to be cultivated through practice and creating and nurturing community.

Part 2: My Practice and Pedagogy for Institutional Transformation

As I started to let go of using contemplative practices for the sole purpose that they would work for me and solve my puzzle for me, I also started thinking actively about inclusive models of being in higher ed that would acknowledge and invite all students and colleagues in their wholeness.

In my experience, structures in higher ed perpetuate othering and reward individualism. There is an absence of a communal feeling of belonging and relationality. At best, it might show up in silos that are organized by privilege and pre-existing hierarchies. How then could I create a sense of belonging within the structures of my educational, professional communities? How might I empower my communities to be intentional in their learning, growth, and relationship with each other? I knew that some contemplative practices would be a part of my practice and pedagogy, but I was not sure of the methodology and larger framework I could use or develop.

Around the same time, I was serendipitously introduced to the Truth, Racial Healing, and Transformation (TRHT) framework, designed and launched by Gail C. Christopher with the W.K. Kellogg Foundation in 2017. Racial Healing Circles (RHCs) are the centerpiece of TRHT and I participated in one such circle led by facilitators Mee Moua and Kohnee Harmon at my university. Racial Healing Circles are an invitation to experience individual and interpersonal transformation. They are experiences that engage the heart; require the heart to be open and expansive; reaffirm the humanity in all of us; acknowledge that unconscious bias lives in all of us; are the spiritual work of affirming and loving ourselves; and acknowledge (by "listening") the harms of the past through people's stories (W.K. Kellogg Foundation, 2016; 2018). Participating in that circle and bearing witness to our shared humanity inspired me to get more involved in TRHT. I was struck by two things in particular: (1) that the facilitators talked about the spiritual work of affirming and loving ourselves in an academic setting, and (2) the methodology they used in that two-day circle because it created a space that was not just safe but also invited participants to bring their whole selves in. In addition to careful listening and opening to different perspectives, a circle encourages us to grant ourselves the permission to be transformed and affected by the process of participation. It was powerful. I eventually underwent the training to become a Racial Healing facilitator myself and learned the circle methodology.

This methodology spoke to the heart of what I had been searching for: cultivating a community-centric approach to wholeness and belonging. It felt generative and vital, requiring work and participants to really see and hear and allow themselves to be seen and heard. This practice is explicitly about connecting to others, and the process of engaging in the circle enables us to see and acknowledge the barriers that create fragmentation and the othering of minoritized bodies. Seeing and acknowledging this is the first step to eventually dismantling these barriers. The connection created in these circles felt like hope.

During this time, I also became a Faculty Fellow at UNC Asheville's Center for Teaching and Learning and collaborated with our Office of

Institutional Equity to organize Racial Healing Circles across campus. Since 2019, we have had 109 participants (faculty and staff) and now have a total of 23 RHC facilitators on campus. We presented RHCs as educational and professional development opportunities for our faculty and staff that also promote equity-mindedness and robust community-building (UNC Asheville, 2021). Due to personnel changes in our administration, the work of officially hosting and facilitating RHCs was paused in January 2023. Nonetheless, as a Faculty Fellow my focus was on pedagogy in addition to inclusion and belonging and I did not see my efforts and engagement with one aspect as compartmentalized from the other. I saw intersections, points of generative connection and overlap. The heart of pedagogy for me has always been inclusiveness and belonging and I was situated professionally in a unique position to make these connections explicit.

After facilitating and organizing dozens of RHCs for staff and faculty in 2019–2020, I had started noticing that *how* I show up in meetings, with students and colleagues, was shifting and becoming more intentional. As I elaborate in the Practice section, following the RHC methodology I started offering a more structured way for engagement. For instance, I started utilizing storytelling as a practice for connection, deliberately weaving in personal narratives from my lived experience in different countries. The more I engaged in these narrative practices, the more I felt grounded in myself. I was sharing the fullness of my human experience, and this perforce also led to a deeper understanding of my students and colleagues as whole individuals.

Drawing inspiration from various contemplative practices I have engaged in over the years and the methods and structure I have learned from RHCs, I have been developing a model of pedagogy and engagement that I call critical compassionate pedagogy. I have led workshops at my university and presented papers on this pedagogy at national conferences. Critical compassionate pedagogy begins with centering and modeling an ethics of care and compassion <u>as</u> epistemology and ontology–as a way of knowing and being and doing. On my syllabi, I outline my intention and hope for our time together which lays the foundation for the semester:

> My intention is to help build and facilitate a *community of inquiry* together with the students in this course that is at once *compassionate*, *empowering*, and *rigorous*. I describe my teaching method and style as *critical compassionate pedagogy*. My goal and hope is to help you all achieve the course objectives listed below and encourage you to be generous, caring, and critical citizens of our shared world.

This intention remains constant inside of the classroom with students and outside with colleagues. The communication methods, deep dives in discussion, active and careful listening strategies, and grounding and reflective practices derived from RHCs help build and sustain a community of care and compassion. This intention makes all the difference.

It has taken a long time for me to call myself a contemplative practitioner and I still have days and weeks when that description does not sound precise to my ears. I think it would be more accurate to say that I practice showing up in my wholeness, whatever that might look like that day. I am at home with my identity as an educator and learner inside and outside of the classrooms. My guiding north star remains a focus on improving my pedagogy and sharing that and improving ways of creating belonging and authentic communication in my campus community. My logistical challenges and frustrations with immigration processes and paperwork are very much still present but my frustrations with what I used to perceive to be a lack and absence in my life do not have a hold on me like they used to. Undeniably, I still have those moments where I feel without ground. It is helpful for me in those moments to recite Rumi's phrase, "This being human is a guest house" and I am reminded that I am in process. I am getting better at appreciating that my ground is within and my ground is in and with community. In my better moments, I practice gratitude for that feeling of absence I often used to feel. It led me on a path that was frustrating and confusing but also serendipitous, where I discovered meaning and belonging.

Practice: Inviting Whole Selves: Planting Seeds to Cultivate Transformative and Sustainable Change

The practice I offer here has roots in my training as a Racial Healing Circle (RHC) practitioner. The goals of this circle practice are to create a space for authentic connection and sustainable community-building across perceived and real differences. Racial Healing Circles are not meant to "solve" racism, rather, they are an ongoing process, creating a shared ground from where we can engage in meaningful, non-judgmental perspective-taking. As the key element of the Truth, Racial Healing, and Transformation (TRHT) framework, these circles create and sustain a compassionate space for courageous conversation. The core of the RHC practice is attentiveness and seeing and hearing participants in their wholeness. In sharing our stories with each other, we enter a deeper heart space and affirm our common humanity. For a deeper dive into TRHT, please see their implementation guide.

The steps and method include Circle Opening, Touchstones, Prompts and Reflections for stories, Circle Closing exercise or ceremony. You are welcome to try out and adapt these steps as part of creating your own courageous community space. RHC practitioners often incorporate their own cultural or indigenous experiences in their circle practice. I almost always begin a new gathering and open the circle with a variation of a body scan that focuses specifically on our footing/sitting on the physical ground. I acknowledge the ancestral Anikituagi (Cherokee) land that I live on, its air that I breathe, and its grass that I walk on.

Following RHC methodology, I offer Touchstones or Group Agreements. The Touchstones guide participants on how to show up for and with each other, such as listening deeply and suspending judgment or maintaining confidentiality and honoring each other's vulnerability, or turning to wonder when topics get difficult. To begin conversation and storytelling, you may develop your own prompts and reflection questions that invite participants to share life experiences. For example, "Share a story about a moment when you moved/shifted from feeling harmed to feeling whole? What made this possible? What did you learn about yourself and/or others? What did this allow you to be or to do?" This is initially done in pairs. The next rounds of questions are invitations for deeper reflections, such as, "What did you hear in each of these stories that resonated with you, touched you, affirmed you and/or feels similar to your own life experience?"

Visualize the circle as a centrifugal movement of grounding and compassionate energy that is generated first by acknowledging and seeing each other as whole, carried forward through deep listening of narratives in small pairs, groups, or dyads, followed by reflections and moving outward to sharing and connecting with the entire group. Each step takes us deeper into meaningful engagement. The Circle Closing ceremony summarizes the experience and articulates the transformative and generative connections made.

Reference List

Diversity, Equity and Inclusion at UNC Asheville. (2021, November 8). *Racial healing circles.* https://diversity.unca.edu/equity/racial-healing-circles/

W.K. Kellogg Foundation. (2016). *TRHT implementation guidebook.* https://healourcommunities.org/wp-content/uploads/2018/02/TRHTImplementationGuide.pdf

W.K. Kellogg Foundation. (2018). *Restoring to wholeness: Racial healing for ourselves, our relationships and our communities (TRHT)* [Brochure]. https://wkkf.issuelab.org/resource/restoring-to-wholeness-racial-healing-for-ourselves-our-relationships-and-our-communities-trht.html

21
BELOVED COMMUNITY AS PRACTICE

Grounding Exercises, Care Teams, and Redefining Success

Meika Loe

How do we attend to the now, to be fully present with each other? How do we name and center historical and generational trauma? How do we collectively sit in discomfort, to grieve, but never become numb? How do we see each other as fully human? How do we simultaneously embrace student-scholar-activist identities, or lean toward radical hope and realistic collective solutions to social problems? These are questions we all have, especially in the context of disabling collective trauma, particularly in a time of global pandemic, climate crisis, and extreme race and class polarization.

My work in the classroom aims to center these questions, while also prioritizing a commitment to being fully human together, centering care as a practice, and ultimately generating social change efforts that reflect our complex human lives. I teach sociology and gender studies courses on health, the life course, and death and dying. My primary goals in these courses are to stay human, to redefine student notions of success, interrupt historical and generational silences, build, center, and sustain community care, and connect public issues to how we live our lives.

In a conversation with George Brosi and hooks (2012), bell hooks describes how building beloved community requires "radical openness," a sense of equanimity and integrity, being "willing to know one another," and valuing interdependency, even in a context of conflict. hooks writes: "There is no such thing as automatic community. Community comes not only from engagement and struggle but from a willingness to be open... I cannot really be with you in genuine community if I am not willing to know you. And to know you, I may have to know things that scare me or turn me off..." (Brosi & hooks 2012, pp. 79).

Much like for hooks, centering care at this stage of my career extends beyond classroom practices. I wonder, how might we, as faculty, staff, administrators, and students, extend these practices of beloved community beyond the classroom or the walls of the ivory tower, to create larger ripple effects in our campus cultures and beyond? Ultimately, centering care translates into being present for one another, and thus, attentive to both self and community. This essay details my personal, classroom, and community practices for centering care, redefining success, and creating and sustaining beloved community.

My Grounding in Contemplative Practice

As long as I can remember I have been a contemplative being, I have long enjoyed journaling, nature walks, witnessing, and deep listening. At the same time, I have often felt anxious and behind. Being present can be a powerful intervention, especially in this age of distractibility. Showing up fully with community, and with conflict, can be pivotal in transformation. For me this may mean looking the college president in the eye, and calling out racism. Or it may mean fully taking in the needs of my community, and engaging in authentic dialogue in the here and now. Or, being fully present with grief and loss in our community, and sitting with this together. In all of these cases, being present both shifts the energy in a room, and points to what an authentic and justice-centered institution might look like.

These days, the practice I focus on the most is being fully present. Perhaps ironically, it sometimes takes planning to be present; to intentionally re-center on the here and now. I want to behold that tree, look straight into my daughter's eyes, and immerse myself in discussion. A number of things help me, including: taking deep breaths, noting my surroundings, feeling gratitude, slowing down, taking a mental picture, making a cup of tea, and stepping back from technology. I find that my delight for being in the moment intensifies the more that I practice with grounding rituals. The most challenging moments – when my brain is scrambled and busy – occur the most when I'm on campus, such as during and after meetings, between class sessions, or catching up on work. Those are times when it may be impossible to slow down, but taking a break, and finding a way to ground myself can help tremendously. Recently, I did this in a parking lot. I forced myself to sit down and take three deep breaths in between meetings.

Classroom Practice in Praxis

In order to merge my personal practices with my teaching, I have made three major changes to how I teach. First, I have transformed my classroom into a space where we intentionally attend to beginnings and endings. We open, and many times also end class sessions with a grounding practice that centers us in our work, in our breath, in communities of care. Second, we center the practice of care through working in and through small care teams. My syllabus has a section on care as a practice, not just a theory. I let students know that they will be paired with two others, and they will dialogue and care for each other throughout the semester. Third, we collectively redefine success, interrupting white supremacist notions of success, and check in on this from the beginning of our time together to the end.

Beginnings and Endings

Robin Wall Kimmerer (2015) reminds us that in indigenous tradition, starting one's day involves a prayer of gratitude to Mother Earth. When we start class, we take time to be present, to be grateful, to connect. Some days this involves just taking three deep breaths, together. Some days we take five minutes for collective memorialization – remembering those we lost to COVID, or police violence, or trans-violence. We say the names, one by one, share an aspect of their humanity, and honor their lives. We do this for extinct species as well. Other days we connect with our breath and practice gratitude for Mother Earth. Or we key into moments when we felt cared for, then associate that caring energy with a texture and/or a color, and then send that energy out to those who need care – to refugees, care workers, friends and loved ones. As such, we build and belong to communities of care.

These grounding exercises are moments of collective effervescence that tie us together, in breath, and in grief. We can let everything else go. This daily ritual enables us to be fully present with one another, and to practice self-soothing, while also knowing we can build and belong to communities of care. We take turns leading these grounding practices, reminding ourselves that we can slow our pace, and intentionally and meaningfully curate our time together, starting with our beginnings.

Care Teams

For bell hooks, beloved community takes work; it takes being present with each other through conflict and joy. Calling one another in is crucial to communities of care, as I have learned from Loretta Ross (2021). I work hard to build beloved community in my class as a whole (usually no larger than 20 students). But most weeks my students also meet in care teams. You can call these teams what you want – accountability pods, or work teams. Ultimately, for me, these small groupings of students center and model the practice of care in the classroom, in the university, and in society. These are intentional communities – people you can count on and ask for help. These are smaller intimate spaces of trust and support, people who will call you in. Usually, they are randomly assigned peer groups of three.

In all of my classes we do listening exercises early on in care teams, to build strong relationships of care. And then, with regular ten-minute check-ins and a few small assignments, they take on a life of their own. In "Health" students interrupt silences to work through their own sex education. In "Death and Dying," they work together to normalize conversations about loss and grief on campus, and work collectively on a midterm exam on racialized mortality. In "Life Course" they work through internalized ageism and share stories of partnering with local elders. All care teams host dialogues with the class, and take time to imagine and dream with the lens of transformative justice. Trust-building requires work on the micro-level as well as with the class as a whole. I find that small efforts reverberate.

Redefining Success

The practice of redefining success allows all of us to begin to practice our own wholeness, presence, and beloved community. Redefining success and dismantling racism mean listening to bodies, health, and communities, and continually reflecting on white supremacist notions of success that may have led to unhealthy habits.

Tema Okun's short, easy-to-google document, "White Supremacy Culture," can inspire conversation about definitions of success in the context of our work (Okun & Jones, 2001). This document lays out how characteristics of white supremacy culture show up in our organizations. We can all admit that practices like perfectionism, either/or thinking, and individualism have dominated our educational years, and have led to unhealthy habits. What does it mean to redefine success for oneself while also attending to the larger community?

I created the following checklist in partnership with LeeRay Costa to spur reflection on what we mean by "success." We sometimes refer to this list as the "Whole Student Checklist." It reminds students that their wholeness matters, and details notions of success that many of us may not have thought about. I include this list in the class syllabus, and we review this list together at the beginning of the semester so that students may take ownership of their education, and set some practice goals for themselves.

Whole Student Checklist:

- Approach the task at hand with a beginner's mind (deeply curious)
- Question the single story and the binary
- Walk in as many shoes as possible
- Strive to acknowledge and bridge difference
- Listen deeply

- Pay attention to the voices that are missing
- Accompany one another in this journey
- Go to our edges, travel in the unfamiliar, embrace uncertainty, be radically open
- Be present
- Think macro and micro: hold institutions and individuals accountable
- Decolonize the mind
- Where/what you come from matters – attend to context and positionality, experience and embodiment – all forms of legitimate knowledge
- Prioritize self-care
- Remember that self-transformation and social transformation go hand in hand
- Reflect, reflect, reflect (reflexivity)
- Hold each other accountable/call each other in/forgive self and other
- Learn collaboratively, acknowledge and honor interdependency
- Practice community, practice care, strive to know one another
- Realize we are complicit in each others' joy AND suffering
- Put theory into practice
- Aim for mind/body/heart balance
- Imagine, dream, and strive for radical hope

I encourage students to discuss these notions of success, and focus on 2–3 goals on the checklist that resonate for them. Then, students work on these new practices in class and in care teams. In care teams, they can be accountable to themselves and one another, checking in at regular intervals in the semester on the following three questions: (1) How are these practices enabling health and presence? (2) How are these practices inviting new forms of community and belonging? (3) How might you want to redefine success in other arenas of your life and into the future?

By redefining success, all of us are transforming the academic project. We are creating openings for breath, for body, for community, and thus, for questioning what happens inside and outside of our classroom. The ripple effect is triggered, whether that means care for others is normalized, or radical hope is modeled in dorm rooms, on the quad, in the office, and/or back at home. We hear about these reverberations, sometimes months or years later; someone spoke truth to power, or cultivated an intergenerational relationship, or was simply present to hold space for another.

Closing

The end of the semester is bittersweet in a class that centers care as a practice. We take time to honor and reflect on the variety of successes we have had, as individuals, and in community. We take time to imagine communities and societies we aspire to participate in, and to transform. We have conversations about the care skill-set that students can now take into the world, and the ways in which they already have. We create collective rituals to honor our beginnings and bring our time together to a close, recognizing that the closing is also an invitation to accompany one another into the next chapter, and to continue to cultivate beloved community in other arenas of our lives.

When I honor my own beginnings in the academy, I remember my initial vow to cultivate beloved community and redefine success on campus. Thankfully, I have never been alone in this struggle to strive for life-affirming, fully human, liberating spaces; many faculty, staff, administrators, and students have contributed to a shared vision and struggle. Two decades later I can see how community organizing and persistence have paid off in negotiating and challenging static and oppressive structures within the academy. Without community and collective-action we would not have LGBTQ Studies, Women's Studies, Inter-Group Dialogue, and a Survivor Center on my campus. Above all, our common vision in beloved community grounds and sustains us, and thus sustains the university. These practices in community, transformation, and radical hope fuel my teaching, and investing in whole student success fuels my community activism, each and every academic year. As hooks reminds us, the "genuine stuff of life is our interdependency, is our capacity to feel both with and for ourselves and other people" (Brosi & hooks 2012, pp. 84).

When the semester ends, we all go back to living within our own structures. For me, this period is partly about resuming my practices for myself, and making that inevitable transition from looking outward, to looking inward and asking what I now need. Part of that is asking myself the questions I ask my students – about beginnings and endings, care and support, and personal notions of success. I check in with my mind, body, and heart. I connect with my self-appointed personal care teams, walk, journal, reflect, and bear witness. In a time of transition, this is the grounding I need, before it all begins again.

Practice: Redefining Success

How can faculty, staff and administrators assemble our own models of wholeness? The practice of redefining success allows all of us to begin to practice our own wholeness, presence, and beloved community. Redefining success and dismantling racism means listening to bodies, health, and communities, and continually reflecting on white supremacist notions of success that may have led to unhealthy habits.

Review the Whole Student Checklist shared in this essay. In community with colleagues (faculty, staff, administrators, as well as students), I invite you to discuss these notions of success as they apply to your work in higher education. Next, select 2–3 goals that particularly resonate for you. Then, work on these new practices in accountability teams or care teams, while checking in regularly. How are these practices enabling presence? How are these practices inviting new forms of community and belonging? How might you want to redefine success in the academy and in other arenas of your life and into the future?

Remember that change can unleash fear and trepidation. And yet, contemplative practices sustain us, keep us breathing, journaling, reflecting, and connecting with one another throughout the change process. We are transforming, and as we do, we are inching closer to life-affirming, liberating, and just spaces in the academy.

Reference List

Brosi, G., & hooks, b. (2012). The beloved community, a conversation between bell hooks and George Brosi. *Appalachian Heritage, 40*(4), 76–86. https://doi.org/10.1353/aph.2012.0109.

Kimmerer, R. (2015). *Braiding sweetgrass: Indigenous wisdom, scientific knowledge and the teachings of plants.* Milkweed Editions.

Okun, T., & Jones, K. (2001). "White supremacist culture," from *dismantling racism: A workbook for social change groups,* by Kenneth Jones and Tema Okun, ChangeWork.

Ross, L. J. (August 4, 2021). "Don't call people out, call them in," TED talk. https://www.youtube.com/watch?v=xw_720iQDss

22

WHY AM I TALKING? DISRUPTING DOMINANT NARRATIVES IN HIGHER EDUCATION

Deb Spragg

I identify as a white cisgender lesbian woman and turned 68 years old this year. Growing up during the Vietnam war era, my family attended a predominantly white liberal protestant church with Welch's grape juice for communion (taken only at Easter) and "world peace" as its main message. Thirty-five years later, in 2006, I became inspired by a Tibetan Buddhist teacher and went on to join another predominantly white congregation—the Western convert Sangha which had developed around him. For sixteen years now I've been meditating on a regular basis and have maintained my relationship with this teacher, his lineage, and this Sangha.

My contemplative life and practice have always been informed by my wish to be wholly present in community, meeting the messy world (outer and inner) with a relaxed attitude. In the context of teaching at a small university over the past ten years, I've begun to understand that "my wholeness" must include a fully embodied recognition of the ways in which my social location haunts my perception and shapes my actions. I've grown tired of the way most of our academic meetings unfold, for example, and hope to contribute to a shift in our meeting culture which will support more liberatory conversation. This means actually *feeling* my every impulse toward power and control and refraining from the habitual, often urgent centering of my own voice. In this chapter, I describe a practice which has been helpful for me, as a white woman, in my attempts to connect my actions with these intentions.

My initial turn toward Buddhist practice and involvement in Sangha challenged my primary relationship and was at times painfully disruptive to our family life. Contemplative practice did not save me from a legacy of white individualistic norms and a habitual pattern of stubborn disconnection in the face of conflict. My partner Stephanie had grown up outside Philadelphia, only an hour and a half from my hometown in suburban New Jersey, but her family background and life circumstances were worlds apart from my own. Ethnically, culturally, and socio-economically, our differences have impacted every aspect of our relationship and played a significant role in our co-parenting of three sons. When we met outside of Boston in 1989, we were both married (to men) and were parents of children in the same nursery school class. Our own marriage a few years later would not be legally recognized in Massachusetts until 2004. Even after thirty-five years, this crucible of love continues to provide transformative training in the context of our ongoing "embodied engagement with difference" (Walker, 2018, p. 30).

My personal development over these years, including my willingness to see into and beyond my dominant socialization, has been nourished by my teacher and the Buddhist teachings he fully embodies and genuinely conveys. But my attempts to bring conversations about whiteness and systemic injustice into my Sangha community have mostly fallen flat. While I can readily see the personal and interpersonal benefits of my practice, I cannot ignore the problematic aspect of my involvement as a white American woman in a Tibetan Buddhist religious organization. What part of my initial contact with this group in 2006 was exotification or orientalism? What part was (or is) my perfectionism, my attachment to some notion of Buddhism as a path to individual purity? How might this attraction have been an expression of what Tema Okun has termed "white supremacy culture" (Okun, 1999/2021)? These questions arose for me in the interplay of my practice and my work life at a small university in Cambridge, Massachusetts, where critical conversations were percolating.

Academia

In my marriage I have been challenged to interrogate my entitlement and the many assumptions of privilege rooted in my socio-cultural background. My work life as an intern supervisor, a university professor, and a faculty administrator has also called upon me to grapple with my unearned power and my positionality. When I left my job as a group therapist at a psychiatric hospital ten years ago and joined a predominantly white university faculty full time, the Buddhist teachings I had received around self-reflection converged with an academic culture of critical self-reflexivity. The habits and patterns of my interpersonal behavior began to be linked in my mind with considerations of power, influence, and color-blind racism. While university-wide efforts to challenge racism and bias were inspiring, my initial attempts to "join" these efforts were clumsy at best. Rather than truly collaborating in community, I got on my high (and very white) horse: independently trying to assemble race-based affinity groups without the necessary collaborative conversations; calling out bias and white racism in the meetings I attended; fighting loudly with colleagues on a faculty hiring committee about their bias; and challenging faculty members in my department in unskillful ways. I was enacting my interpretation of the role of a "good ally"—and also causing harm. Clearly, I needed more guidance!

In 2018, I found my way to an institutional DEI consultant, Dr. Liza Talusan, who also saw individual clients. Dr. Talusan's work on identity consciousness for educators and her challenging support were critical to my professional and personal development. I often spoke with Dr. Talusan about how to bring my contemplative practice into my community work. With her feedback, I eventually relaxed. I felt more genuinely connected to the people involved in social justice work at the university and joined the institution's "Bias Response Team." In this circle, I began to share more personally about my contemplative practices.

By 2021, the Bias Response Team had essentially been disbanded. What began as a collaborative and generative endeavor became absorbed into the institution's human resources "critical incident" process. Since that time, community members have been frustrated by the ebbing of the support for social and racial justice measures on our campus: the de-funding of student initiatives, loss of positions and structural supports, community efforts collapsing into the ever "centralizing" administrative maze, bad faith, and good people leaving every month. As sociologist Dr. Lori Latrice Martin (2022) points out: "…the words and deeds of far too many individuals and organizations moved almost exclusively by the killing of [George] Floyd or by social pressure to act were short-lived and non-transformational" (pp. 4–5).

In the context of this loss of momentum at our university, I want to focus on becoming a more relational, reliable, and accountable member of my community. The commitment to contemplative practice I'd developed prior to coming to the university is now wed to liberatory praxis within my academic life. My goal is to work toward a transformation of meeting spaces in higher education, which are so often characterized by white-supremacy-hetero-patriarchal values. White-identified faculty members can uplift and make space for new and unexpected conversations, they can readily and publicly acknowledge the scholarship of BIPOC community members, and they can be vocal in working toward equitable distribution of resources—including academic social capital. Regular opportunities for all of these arise in academic meetings, and contemplative practices can support the self-reflexivity that moves our good intentions toward transformation actions and may include both silence and speech.

"Right speech," as described by the Buddha, involves abstaining from speech that could be harmful: "And what is right speech? Abstaining from lying, abstaining from divisive speech, abstaining from abusive speech, abstaining from idle chatter: This, monks, is called right speech" (Magga-Vibhaṅga Sutta, n.d., SN 45:8). A definition of "right speech" for our own time might go on to name the habitual impulses which spring from the assumptions of unearned privilege. "Harmful speech" would surely now include silencing, gas-lighting, microaggressions, and other expressions of white superiority—all of which can be seen as forms of "lying" or "abusive speech." To understand these levels of harm, I need to dig beyond my personality and behavior into the systemic and historical assumptions of white hegemony.

The W.A.I.T.? Practice

There is a practice I believe can open a space for this kind of self-reflexivity. The practice has a simple scaffold—an acronym which my colleague Angela Crawford Ervin shared with me a year or so ago. "*W.A.I.T.?*" stands for "*Why Am I Talking?*". In my position of power and privilege as a white female faculty administrator, this is the most helpful acronym I have ever heard. *Why Am I Talking?*—always such a good question!—because the word "why" implies a reflective action step. In meetings and conversations, noticing a habitual impulse to speak, this acronym brings awareness to my physicality, and to the urgency I may find there. In the wake of this bodily awareness, discernment around my inner motivations, and how my social positionality is interacting with them can also arise.

The outcome of this practice might be a more intentional sharing, or it might involve amplifying the comments shared by a colleague. It may guide me toward no sharing at all, allowing more airspace for alternative viewpoints and narratives, and for synergy which can connect us. My choice to *not* share might also contribute to a collective silence which fosters something completely unexpected. As Barbara Applebaum (2013) reminds us, "witnessing involves listening not simply to confirm what is already known but rather listening to hear something new, something that is beyond our frameworks of comprehension" (p. 19).

W.A.I.T.? as a reflective contemplation can help develop meeting spaces where differences interact and impact each other but need not conform to a dominant narrative. Perhaps the *W.A.I.T.?* practice can cultivate a community which embraces the creative potential forever present in our differences, rather than relying on "Roberts' Rules of Order" to reinforce the white supremacy norms of the academy (Puckett, 2023).

A Brief History of the Practice

As it turns out, use of the *W.A.I.T.?* acronym has been widespread. Why Am I Talking? has been applied in different ways by various people and organizations—and the goals and values of these groups do not always align. As a tool for social justice, it has been used in anti-racist work for many years. The author of a blog post about the "brilliant new acronym" thanked colleagues at Coalition of Communities of Color (CCC) (2023) for sharing the *W.A.I.T.?* tool with her (Okun, 2016, February 18). In a TikTok comment about this tool (2021, November), the writer states that they "learned WAIT from Urban Bush Women," a renowned dance and BIPOC performing arts group in New York which offers a summer leadership institute rooted in social change. In 2016 the title of a journal article headlined the acronym: "W.A.I.T. (Why Am I Talking?): A dialogue on solidarity, allyship, and supporting the struggle for racial justice without reproducing white supremacy" (Leonard & Misumi, 2016).

In recent years, the *W.A.I.T.?* tool has been incorporated by several practitioners of Non-Violent Communication (NVC) (2024), a model developed in the context of 1960s civil rights activism. A 2018 NVC book on "mindful communication" included a description of the acronym; the author, it turns out, had previously been a member of Ajahn Chah's Thai Forest Buddhist lineage (Sofer, 2018). Perusing the website of the Thai Forest community, I found a 2008 blog post describing the "many little signs" posted around the grounds of the Metta Thai Forest monastery in California including one that said "*W.A.I.T.?*" (Amaro, 2008, November).

That 15-year-old blog post was the earliest reference to the *W.A.I.T.?* acronym I'd found. It brought me full circle, returning me to the Buddhist precepts on "Right Speech." These precepts and the disruption of white supremacy culture are the two main streams which help me frame the *W.A.I.T.?* practice in my own life and in my work in the academy. Right speech is at the heart of it; when informed by critical reflexivity, this practice can open a space for deeper engagement to disrupt our self-narratives.

Personal Practice

This year, I have taken the question *Why Am I Talking?* off the sticky note on my desk and into the virtual meeting spaces at my university. It's a work in progress, as my participation in meetings has often been propelled by urgency, or by a sense of individualistic self-importance. Working with the

W.A.I.T.? practice has helped me find a quieter, more thoughtful engagement in our community—a welcome shift.

I recall a conversation from several years ago: a cisgender male member of a white affinity group had spoken about how he felt he should not speak in open meetings, to "allow space for other (BIPOC) members of the community" to speak. I'd felt that there was a certain position that the speaker non-verbally conveyed, as if it was his personal job to "be inclusive" of others, and that he would do this job faithfully. But in his earnest sharing, I primarily sensed his strong identification with being a "good ally." It's not hard for me to spot, given my own troubling history!

The thing that distinguishes the *W.A.I.T.?* process from that speaker's somewhat dualistic stance is that the question requires your self-reflection. It asks that you get into the nitty-gritty of your own urge to speak. That you do not simply keep your mouth closed, but that you scrutinize your impulse—what you *might* say—and listen inwardly for your self-narratives. Embodied contemplative work lets us notice what is happening at this moment: Where is this pressure coming from? What's my motivation? This process tends to disrupt one's identification with being "a good ally" and is more likely to lead to feelings of chagrin.

What Was I Thinking?

I am mostly working remotely, and opportunities for *W.A.I.T.?* practice come around with regularity. These "opportunities" take place within relationships: when my body grips in the face of a small but somehow threatening encounter, my potential for inflicting harm on other people increases—and a moment for practice arises. But remote work and virtual meeting formats can disconnect me from the somatic information that might otherwise help me to curb an unexamined impulse. In this way, the virtual practice opportunity requires closer attention to problematic inner narratives and more awareness of my physical state.

A while ago, during a Zoom meeting, a recent hire was enthusiastically sharing her ideas. Her facility in my own narrow area of expertise got to me. Without being able to honestly name it to myself, I felt disrespected by this young Black colleague, and I was suddenly caught up in an unexpected streak of jealous insecurity. I instantly felt old and vulnerable, unrecognized for my years of work. I felt territorial. I had not taken a breath or checked in with myself, so none of this was clear in my mind at the time.

Without an inner conversation or a practice that disrupted my unspoken narratives, what emerged was a competitive, fast-talking "expert." I believe this move was an expression of an underlying racist attitude where I relied on my "whiteness as property" (Harris, 1993). I used this property to re-establish dominance in a moment of anxiety. Since my comments were designed to protect my personal house of cards, they were delivered with an energy which prevented them from being metabolized (who would eat that food?). Whatever the literal content was, my behavior, including my paraverbal behavior, was harmful. The message was a disconnect which had aggression and rejection in it. In retrospect my cover-up is obvious—not only the cover-up of my feelings, but also of disturbing racist tropes that hovered below them. My tone and pace were a sure sign that I'd "forgotten" what "I" am made of—my socialization as a member of the dominant culture. More importantly, the empathy that might have disrupted my self-narrative was nowhere to be found.

After the meeting, my young colleague told me she did not experience my expression as problematic, and she accepted my apology. I wasn't sure; had I overreacted and simply been mired in shame due to my own politeness protocols around "not speaking nicely"? Or had I actually broken trust in a way that prevented a more open conversation? Whether my colleague experienced harm or not, I do not know. But another person might well have.

Psychologist, speaker, and author Maureen Walker teaches that in the process of looking inward and disrupting our narratives about self and other, "good conflict" can arise (Walker, 2018). In the example above I denied my feelings of territoriality, jealousy, disrespect, and white entitlement; I denied my racism and stuck to my unspoken internal narratives. Had I been able to access it during that meeting, the *W.A.I.T.?* practice would have allowed me a place from which to notice and disrupt my habits and patterns.

Why am I talking? The reflection that this practice involves can also foster more intentionality in speaking up in support of my colleagues. Dr. Shardé M. Davis (assistant professor of Communications at the University of Connecticut and creator of the hashtag #BlackintheIvory), encourages white faculty to engage in positive "microbehaviors" such as highlighting the ideas of Black colleagues by repeating them with attribution. Women on President Obama's White House staff used a similar process they called "amplification": when a woman spoke up, another would repeat her point, and say the first woman's name to give her credit. This same strategy could serve to head off the poaching behavior I've witnessed (and spoken to) in academic spaces. With the support of "amplification," there would be no way for someone to take credit for re-stating another person's idea. I can use my energy to acknowledge and support BIPOC colleagues, de-centering the dominant voices in the space.

Building community by honoring BIPOC contributions during real-time meetings sounds like a promising practice. But it first requires me to slow down and refrain from participation in the competitive urgency of white supremacy culture in academia. This is the very essence of the *W.A.I.T.?* practice, rooted as it is in the contemplative mind. It involves a learned skill for those of us who have been socialized over generations to grab, to extract, and to exclude.

Conclusion

From what we might call my "sole-proprietor activism" (a.k.a. white savior behavior) to recognizing community as the true agent of change, I have seen the way contemplative practice has slowly, pervasively, changed my approach. Instead of relying on self-righteously calling out the powers that be, I am becoming a *W.A.I.T.?* practitioner. And I can share this practice with other white colleagues in academia who are interested in disrupting the norms and inner narratives that dominate our communication.

When, as a member of the dominant culture, I ask myself the question, *Why am I Talking?* I open a door to wholeness—to full participation in community, and to the possibility of recognizing and disrupting my habitual narratives around self and others. This practice invites the brilliance of my colleagues, supports the sense-making of things difficult to name, and honors our embodied humanity, even in the disembodied world of virtual meetings.

> "To create a silence in which another voice may speak is at the heart of community transformation. It doesn't sound that hard; in fact, it sounds like just the kind of thing we say we want to do. But we would do well to recognize from the outset that making a space for other voices is in fact a disruptive process".
>
> *(Walker, 2018)*

I am inspired by this 2018 keynote talk by Dr. Maureen Walker, in which she quotes from a poem by Paul Williams (1990) titled, "How to Tell the Truth." The theme of the poem is listening. *Listening*, meaning residing in uncertainty, not knowing where the truth lies. Without naming them, the poem recognizes the mistaken assumptions that often crowd my own listening.

"How to Tell the Truth." The words of the poem land and echo within me. A sensation sweeps up my body for a second, starting at my solar plexus. I feel vulnerable; the words bring fear and discomfort. I understand this sensation as a doorway and a welcome signpost.

Practice: W.A.I.T.? *A Reflective Practice*

The object of the *W.A.I.T.?* practice is to disrupt patterns of white dominance in academic and professional meetings. The practice invites white community members into a critical, self-reflexive process which illuminates internal narratives and challenges habitual impulses to speak from assumptions of unearned privilege. To build further accountability, move the practice into the collective, share it with colleagues, and introduce it during an academic meeting space. Process your experiences together and build capacity.

The practice itself has a simple scaffold–the acronym "*W.A.I.T.?*", which stands for "*Why Am I Talking?*" Here's how the personal practice might go:

- In meetings and conversations, notice your impulse to speak.
- Attend to the sensations in your body.
- Bring to mind the acronym *W.A.I.T.?* and its meaning—*Why Am I Talking?*
- Pause to listen inwardly for your motivation, for any emotions that arise, and for any narratives about self and others which may be associated with your urge to speak. Notice if these feel habitual, or fresh.
- Again, notice your somatic experience, and breathe into it.
- Make a decision. The outcome might be
  - More intentional sharing
  - Amplifying the comments of a colleague, with attribution
  - No sharing, allowing more space for alternative viewpoints and narratives
  - No sharing, allowing for the distillation of your own ideas
  - No sharing as a contribution to some much-needed silence, perhaps helping to foster something completely unexpected

Reference List

Amaro, A. (2008, November). Why am I Talking? Beginning our day, Vol 2. In 2014, the original blog post became part of an online collection, which can be found at the following URL https://www.abhayagiri.org/media/web-books/beginning-our-day-volume-two/index.html

Applebaum, B. (2013). Vigilance as a response to white complicity. *Educational Theory*, *63*(1), 17–34. https://doi.org/10.1111/edth.12007.

Coalition of Communities of Color (CCC). (2023) https://www.coalitioncommunitiescolor.org/

Harris, C. I. (1993). Whiteness As property. *Harvard Law Review*, *106*(8), 1707–1791. https://doi.org/10.2307/1341787.

Leonard, G., & Misumi, L. (2016). W.A.i.T. (Why am i talking?): A dialogue on solidarity, allyship, and supporting the struggle for racial justice without reproducing white supremacy. *Harvard Journal of African American Public Policy*, 61–74.

Magga-Vibhaṅga Sutta (SN 45:8): (Thanissaro Bhikkhu, Trans.). (n.d.) https://www.dhammatalks.org/suttas/SN/SN45_8.html

Martin, L. L. (2022). Black out: Backlash and betrayal in the academy and beyond. *AAUP Journal of Academic Freedom* (13). https://www.aaup.org/JAF13/black-out-backlash-and-betrayal-academy-and-beyond#.Y5z2-rLMIqc

Non-Violent Communication (NVC). (2024). https://www.cnvc.org/

Okun, E. (2016, February 18). W.A.I.T.—*Why am I talking? The Fakequity Blog.* https://fakequity.com/2016/02/18/w-a-i-t-why-am-i-talking/

Okun, T. (2021). White supremacy culture—Still here. https://www.dismantlingracism.org/uploads/4/3/5/7/43579015/white_supremacy_culture_-_still_here.pdf

Puckett, K. (2023 February 28) B-Sides: Reading, Race and "Robert's Rules of Order" in Public Books. https://www.publicbooks.org/reading-race-and-roberts-rules-of-order/

Sofer, O. J. (2018). *Say what you mean: A mindful approach to nonviolent communication.* Shambhala.

Walker, M. (2018). Transforming community through disruptive empathy. In C. Gunderson, D. Graff, & K. Craddock (Eds.), *Transforming community: Stories of connection through the Lens of relational-cultural theory* (p. 30). Whole Person. Note: This volume is based on transcribed works from a conference in 2016, including Dr. Walker's keynote address.

Williams, P. (1990). How to tell the truth. In *Nation of lawyers* (pp. 41–48). Entwhistle.

23
CONTEMPLATIVE EMERGENCE

How My Contemplative Practices Have Supported Transformative Change in a Higher Education Space

Ericka Echavarria

Introduction

Contemplative emergence is an integrated, embodied, and transformative change process cultivated over time from a deep reflection of lived experiences supported by a series of daily contemplative practices to build self-awareness, accountability, and capacity to steward justice. The process has allowed me to (1) transform harmful experiences by helping me see my experience as one connected to patterns of greater collective harm, (2) reflect on my values and inner resources, and (3) curate more generative ways of producing and sustaining resilience while cultivating fairness and mitigating harm. My specific daily contemplative practices include activities of meditation and stillness, movement, affirmation, and journaling to reflect, release, and realign with my values. Moreover, my practices support and resource me through moments of difficulty and uncertainty, and also infuse joy and gratitude to keep me grounded and able to meet all that arises. The foundation of my practices is zazen meditation. I was first introduced to the Zen Buddhist practice of zazen or sitting meditation (Chogye International Zen Center of New York), which focuses on counting the breath, while I was going through a particularly painful period in my life which included both a personal and professional transition. Since then, I have slowly added a list of generative practices to my contemplative toolbox: a journaling practice where I free write thoughts, feelings, and sensations, affirmations, somatic practices, (includes a blend of yoga, aikido-jo kata, clinical somatics, walking, Qigong, and 5 Rhythms) to tend to, notice, and release areas of physical discomfort and return to a feeling of confidence in my own body's expression, shape, and wisdom. Additionally, I intentionally engage in joyful activities such as spending time with family and friends, writing, cooking, singing, dancing, reading, and resting. These practices help me tap into internal wisdom, sustain personal capacity, and result in positive benefits to the communities where I live and work.

What drives my practices is the desire to embody justice, first from within and then shifting outwardly. Personal justice for me is living from a place of wholeness or being in alignment with my values, and not causing harm to myself or others. This way of living also supports my commitment to critically think about ways to bring a change of the transformative nature into spaces so that relationships and systems can heal from the toxic conditioning perpetuated by white dominant/supremist/normative culture. When I lean into my work with this intention I am better able to hold space for myself and others without judgment, and be in a *well* body, mind, and spirit. I strive to abolish a conditioning which says I must use violence to create change and desire to embody new ways of relating to change in myself first, so that I may hold space for others to do the same.

Suffusing Contemplative Practices into My Higher Education Role

I currently serve as an administrator and adjunct faculty at a prestigious school of social work. In my full-time role as Associate Director in the Office of Practicum Learning, I identify, vet, and secure educationally appropriate practicum opportunities for our students so that they may engage in experiential learning outside the classroom and meet residency degree requirements. As an adjunct instructor, I teach and support students in deepening their understanding of their different dimensions of identity, how it impacts their practice, and how to build tolerance and capacity to bear witness and hold space for the identities and inequities of the communities they serve. In both roles, my ultimate goal is to mitigate harm to the communities served by our students. As an Afro-Dominicana mid-management level administrator and non-tenured faculty member, I do not always feel safe or belong in academia. Furthermore, as my values are not aligned with the structurally oppressive culture of power, productivity, and non-accountability, I often function outside the edges of the academy's boundaries.

Prioritizing my humanity as well as that of others with whom I interact, is a value which steers how I work and lead in academic spaces. For example, pausing to discern and analyze why a student or their Practicum Instructor is facing challenges, refusing to send a student to a particular practicum to mitigate harm, declining to add more responsibilities to my plate, and requesting adequate support to succeed in my current responsibilities is not the norm in academia. Slowing down, being more intentional and less reactionary, and prioritizing individual relationships over transactions are actions in direct opposition to white supremacy/dominant cultural notions, including ideas of urgency, paternalism, binary thinking, productivity, individualism, defensiveness, and fear of open conflict (Okun, 2021). Furthermore, when interpreted by those unfamiliar with and actively complicit in preserving the status quo, these actions can also appear to be insubordinate and have contributed to personal experiences of alienation, lack of belonging, questioning, criticism, and disposability within the academy. The impact of those experiences has led me to feel disconnected, burned out, frustrated, resentful, vengeful, afraid, dismissed, unsupported, and resolved to resign.

The contemplative tools I use offer a space to metabolize and process these heavy emotions rather than holding onto them or misdirecting them at others. While those experiences cannot be minimized, I realized that responding to my pain can often perpetuate patterns of harm and contribute to a toxic work environment. My practices support a transformative and more generative way of working in academia.

For example, because my practices allow for another perspective to emerge, I am better able to separate my own narratives about my non-belonging from the larger systemic patterns of oppression. This frees me to move with integrity and focus on what would most serve, rather than respond defensively or transfer shame or blame to another. I can then critically discern my complicity, listen and bear witness with no judgment or personal agenda, and better collaborate with others (e.g. students, Practicum Instructors, community partners, colleagues). Additionally, I can often transcend the identity of "victim" or "oppressed" because I am empowered to remember my values and choices and not respond from rage or overwhelm, thus mitigating self-harm and/or harm to others. I then have more capacity to engage in compassionate action in relationships, which is desperately needed in higher education spaces to dismantle oppressive structures.

Contemplative Emergence

While these practices support my own self-awareness and capacity, they also support and send ripple effects of change throughout the academy as an emergent strategy which begins to chip away, albeit slowly, at the structural mountains and walls of oppression holding up power in the academy.

According to adrienne maree brown (2021), "emergent strategy" is a strategy for building complex patterns and systems of change through relatively small interactions" (pp. 2). brown defines the elements of emergent strategy as having a cognitive and embodied understanding of (1) fractals (relationship between small and large patterns of existing), (2) adaptation (how we change to integrate patterns of being), (3) interdependence and decentralization (who we are in relationship to one another and how we care for one another), (4) change as nonlinear and iterative (the key to change lies in understanding what we are already practicing, and how we translate successes and failures into lessons), (5) resilience and transformative justice (how we move through conflict, repair harm, and transform), and (6) creating more possibilities (how we curate generativity, hold complexity, and move with natural ebbs and flows).

What Brown shares in her book resonates because I have found that the strategies which emerge after a period of contemplative reflection regarding experienced harm can often lessen the pain and provide new perspectives of being in relationship with oppressive structures and/or perpetrators, as well as, with oneself.[1] This transformative process has evolved into what I call "contemplative emergence." As defined earlier, contemplative emergence is a change process that includes the integration of harm through supportive contemplative practices to build self-awareness, accountability, and capacity to steward justice. From this perspective, I was able to reflect on my experiences of harm in academia, connect them to patterns of institutional harm, temper my emotions, and leverage my inner resources and values to curate more generative ways of working in the space. Below I will share one such experience of harm and the teachings that arose from the aftermath.

During the height of the pandemic in January of 2021, my mother who had been living in a nursing home and had recovered from COVID, transitioned. I was on a webinar and giving a presentation when her nursing home called to report she was transitioning and that it would be incumbent on our family to be on FaceTime with her soon. I took a pause and spoke with my family, then finished my 30-minute Zoom presentation in time to say our farewells to my mom. It was an unbelievably heartbreaking and cherished moment. She transitioned a few hours later.

When I spoke to my direct supervisor to request a bereavement leave, I was told that urgencies would be managed but there would be an expectation that I keep my workload and pick up upon my return. After finishing the call with my supervisor, I was distraught and determined to resign. I felt pressured to take a shorter leave, or work while I was on leave, and was enraged that such choices or double binds were subtly presented to me during such a difficult time.

I resolved to take a two-week bereavement leave and face the consequences of my unattended work upon my return. I dove deep into my grief process and spent a great deal of time unpacking the multidimensional layers of grief and resourcing myself through my contemplative practices and seeking refuge in my spiritual and supportive communities. The feeling of loss was compounded by physical separation during the pandemic, and not being able to be with or see my mother while she was ill, or during her transition.

Engaging in my practices, and unplugging from my work obligations, allowed for new observations to emerge regarding my relationship with myself, others, and the academy. After my mother transitioned, I had *transitioned* as well and could not return to the status quo. The more I reflected on my personal loss, the more I was able to connect with the overall sense of grief in the collective space, specifically, the loss of a former way of living, the feeling of having no autonomy over external circumstances, and the overwhelm from the lack of support from our institution despite the realities of the pandemic. I knew from my supportive community spaces that many folks were feeling similarly and seeking new ways of being in their lives, in their relationships to others, and in their work.

It took several months to feel whole again. I titrated between rage, sadness, apathy, surrender, and the desire to resign from my role. Out of the rubbles of these intense emotions emerged equally provocative questions: Why was my supervisor unable to support me? Was this about her capacity or more about institutional lack of capacity? Why did I feel like I was "caught between a rock and a hard place"? Was I the only one feeling this way? How could I continue working in a place that did not support my values? How could I take care of myself if the institution refused to do so? What was the way through this situation? What was I not seeing? What could I do differently?

Time and space with my practices during my leave, and in the months that followed, birthed contemplative emergence, or a shift around responses to these questions. First, I realized that my experience of harm was parallel to others' experiences, and, being placed in double binds were inevitable consequences of living and working in oppressive systems. Furthermore, since the oppressive nature of the academy elevates productivity over wellness, and does not acknowledge that regeneration is necessary to sustain one's capacity, folks are often positioned between choosing one's self-care against the needs of the institution. This dynamic can lead to shame and guilt on one hand, or burnout, or lack of capacity and/or accountability on the other hand. When my supervisor announced she was taking a medical leave to heal from a post-COVID-related condition that was not improving several months later, the memory of my own double bind surrounding my mom's transition was activated. As she shared the struggles around her decision, I felt we were one and the same, and that our struggles in the academy represented the larger collective impact of systemic oppression. I was also reminded that the pandemic did not create these situations, it only highlighted the patterns of harm, their frequency, and impact. Knowing this affirmed my necessity to lean into my contemplative practices as an adaptive strategy to create spaciousness and find some resting place in between. Taking a pause and a leave from work created spaciousness for me. Spaciousness allowed me to zoom out to the macro level, depersonalize, be present without judgment, and discern how to best serve in my role and mitigate harm.

This allowed for more ease and freed up energy to face other difficult aspects of my roles, including having critical conversations about power and privilege and oppression dynamics and managing a caseload of 100+ students with various identities and needs. Spaciousness supported my healing and the integration of lessons I learned and consequently boosted my resilience.

Second, I became more honest with myself about what I needed, reflected on where I needed to set boundaries, and honored my capacity. This reflection also led me to examine where I had contributed to my own double binds. In the academy, which perpetuates hierarchies of power based on degrees and titles, access to knowledge and resources is often hoarded by a select few. The result is that only certain people can manage certain tasks and are responsible for doing so, while lower-tiered employees are expected to simply do what they are told and are unable to offer any new or different perspectives on how to work more efficiently. Such a separation of people based on illusory competency or expertise creates an oppressor/oppressed dynamic by affirming the power of one group through the taking of the power from the other. This relationship further disregards the humanity of both the holder of knowledge and the lower-tiered worker because in maintaining the status quo, one is forced to continue to manage tasks despite what realities may be impacting their work. Simultaneously, the co-worker, feeling devalued, loses interest in their work and will only do what they have authority to do through their given role. This power structure ultimately impacts innovation and motivation on both sides and thwarts collaboration.

When I was on bereavement leave I was unable to manage a program which fell under my scope of leadership. Because I was the only person who had knowledge of how things should be done, this added more stress and unnecessary work to my plate. While I had unknowingly followed the status quo and hoarded information and knowledge simply because I replaced the person who had done the task before me, I had contributed to an unhealthy codependent dynamic and had simultaneously oppressed myself and those under my management. I could not see this clearly until I had some space to reflect on the structural dynamics. In order to decentralize and shift this power play, I created a manual for the staff I managed, trained them on how to do some of the things I did, and began holding them accountable for specific duties. I also recruited a new colleague's support in managing the program. While it did not necessarily decrease my workload immediately, it allowed for more space to improve upon other aspects of my job and curate more time to plan and intentionally prioritize tasks according to real urgency.

Through these revelations also emerged new practices to ease the discomfort from the resistance I felt from my institution in holding this transformative stance. "I am here" is a practice born out of the confusion, grief, and rage I felt after my mom transitioned. In this practice, I composted those intense emotions into a blend of somatics, affirmation, and meditation to be used prescriptively as well as, proactively. "I am here" serves to remind me I am not just another cog in the wheel, that I have and can offer something of value, and I have integrity and accountability around how I uniquely show up in this work. This practice, along with others, has supported my own change process to well-being, and hopefully has laid the groundwork for greater collective transformative change. Below are some of the ways "I am here" has enabled me to enact individual change and pivot to greater collective change:

1. When I pause, take a breath, drop into the body, feel my feet on the ground and back supported against the chair, I am regulating my nervous system while also reminding myself I am supported. This allows me to discharge energy, be less reactive and depersonalize what is happening, and connect to a larger dysfunctional pattern, rather than provide a triaged or band-aid response to the smaller or presenting issue.
2. When I am regulated I can then discern what is really urgent and prioritize an order of response because while everything in the academy is seen as urgent, the reality is some things are not as urgent as others. We do not have capacity to thoughtfully and effectively respond to several things at one given time. Being able to discern allows me to be intentional about what I can and cannot control and temper expectations about a specific outcome.
3. When I say "I am here" I recall my intention, and I remember who I am. I can take accountability and move toward collaboration with others. I can be more transparent about where I have made mistakes and need support and my level of capacity. These choices allow me to honor the reality that what I do impacts others, and vice versa, and affirm that in order to curate alternative and more efficient processes, I cannot do it alone. These actions open doorways to communication and authentic relationships and honor our interdependence.
4. The repetition of the words and the breath serve to disrupt my conditioned response and generate a new, adaptive response.
5. The words "I am here," remind me of my values to serve and mitigate harm. I know I must seek outside accountability/processing pods for further resourcing, validation, support, and authentic feedback because not everyone in the academy understands how working in this oppressive structure has impacted how they work.

Conclusion

Contemplative emergence has helped me articulate and visualize how my practices are shaping a different way of being and operating in this space, so that I feel more empowered and "free" while I choose to remain in this institution. It evolves moment by moment, depending on personal and institutional context. I accept I need regularly scheduled time and space to pause, metabolize, and integrate lessons learned from wisdom which has organically emerged from everyday experiences. While the incident I describe in this essay happened nearly two years ago, the writing of this manuscript has also served as a process of contemplative emergence.

Experiencing personal loss, as well as connecting to a greater collective loss during the pandemic helped me see how my experiences of dehumanization are parallel to others' experiences, and symbolize the quality and weight of oppression in the collective sphere. I have less judgment towards others who have adapted to the toxicity of the higher education space in ways that align with the status quo, knowing that their adaptation, though different than mine, is motivated by a similar human desire to belong and be valued. This understanding allows me to offer compassion, respect their humanity, and work alongside them in ways that honor who we all are in the institution. Modeling self-awareness, self-regulation, self-care, accountability, and rest, are ways we can responsibly care for ourselves while also caring for each other and building community during times of change. Taking regular periods of pause and/or longer rests can help us better see the patterns of harm and make different choices. Healing ruptured relationships and focusing on what connects us to the work helps breed transformative justice, or notions of relating to one another from a sense of respect for our shared humanity and connectedness. Decentralizing knowledge and power cultivates self-determination, improves morale, and can lead to innovation in finding more sustainable solutions to challenges in the work.

Lastly, through contemplative emergence, I am able to more clearly see, feel, and know what oppression really is. Oppression, no matter who wields it, is still oppression. Causing harm to undo oppression is another iteration of oppression manifested and internalized in the oppressed who are overwhelmed by their rage, hurt, desire, and power. This way of being cannot lead to anything sustainable and merely cultivates fertile ground for more harm. I seek liberation and transformation for myself and others from the confines of white supremacy, patriarchy, cultural hegemony, and all oppressive systems, and believe possibilities for change include an untethering from old ways of being and working in these institutions. I see the use of contemplative practices as a force which can help resource, sustain, and nourish the deep, exhausting, and often disillusioning and painful work that fighting for transformative change can be. Through these practices, we are more able to wield our personal and collective power to work from values which center our humanity and move with the often slow rhythm of change.

Practice: Contemplative Emergence

I am here

Sitting or standing…
Feel yourself supported in a chair
Bottom on the seat, spine against the chair
feet on the floor making contact with the ground
and rooting down into the earth.
Feeling all parts of your foot as you root into ground.
Toes, then balls of feet, heels.

> Deep breaths,
> in and out. (3x)

Right hand on heart left hand on belly to
connect with your essence.

> Deep breaths,
> In and out. (3x)

While touching your heart, recall your
wisdom and your intention and remind yourself
of who you are:

> "I am here" (3x)

Pause deep breath in and out
I am Here
Pause
Deep breath in and out
Pause

> I AM HERE

Note

1 See for example Echavarria (2022). This is another example of contemplative emergence.

Reference List

brown, a. m. (2021). *Emergent strategy: Shaping change, changing worlds.* AK Press.

Echavarria, E. (2022). Ode to woman on the train and my sistahs: Healing and reimagining loving relationships with black, indigenous, and women of color (BIWOC)". *Journal of Contemplative Inquiry, 9*(1), 246–247.

Okun, T. (2021, May). *White Supremacy Culture.* White supremacy culture. https://www.whitesupremacyculture.info/

24
ENACTING AN INDIGENOUS DECOLONIAL CONTEMPLATIVE MENTORSHIP IN HIGHER EDUCATION

Meditations on the Legacy of Plenty Fox

Michael Yellow Bird and Holly Hatton

Michael

I am the Dean and Professor of the Faculty of Social Work at the University of Manitoba, Canada. I live and work on Treaty One territory which is the traditional lands of the Anishinaabe, Dakota, Cree, Oji Cree, and Dene Peoples and the homelands of the Métis. I am an enrolled tribal member of the Mandan, Hidatsa, and Arikara (MHA) Nation in North Dakota, USA. I have been a social work and Indigenous studies scholar and administrator at six different universities (two in Canada and four in the United States) for more than 30 years. I have been practicing mindfulness meditation since 1975 and have been involved in Indigenous contemplative practices for much of my life. I have served as an Indigenous decolonial contemplative mentor to white settler academics, such as Dr. Holly Hatton, who have an interest in promoting justice using contemplative approaches.

Holly

I am a white settler woman who grew up in Northern California. I am an associate professor in child, youth, and family studies at the University of Nebraska–Lincoln and an Early Childhood Extension Specialist. I live and work on the past, present, and future homelands of the Pawnee, Ponca, Oto-Missouria, Omaha, Dakota, Lakota, Arapaho, Cheyenne, and Kaw Peoples, as well as the relocated Ho-Chunk (Winnebago), Iowa, and Sac and Fox Peoples. In my time in higher education, I have come to understand that the dominant narrative is often not about compassionate leadership and mentoring. However, I have discovered that through contemplative practices, truth-telling, being mentored by Dr. Yellow Bird, and allowing for vulnerability, higher education can be a place where mindfulness engagement can lead to transformative change.

In this chapter, we begin by discussing Michael's role as an Indigenous decolonial contemplative mentor and how the teaching and contemplative life of his great grandfather, Plenty Fox, enabled him to embrace this duty as an Indigenous decolonial contemplative mentor to Holly and others. We next share how we have used contemplative practices to disrupt settler power and logic in the academy and integrated these practices into our academic lives to maintain our wholeness. We discuss some of the contributions we have made to bring contemplative practices into the academy, share a decolonial contemplative practice that we use with our students and colleagues, and end with a call for action for decolonial contemplative mentoring, decolonizing contemplative practices using neurodecolonization, and bearing witness "to connect with and serve those who are suffering" (Harris, 2023, para. 1).

Dismantling coloniality and colonial systems and relationships in higher education through decolonization and decolonial praxis is a challenging and ongoing process due to the settler logic and power that is deeply embedded in social and political forces such as white supremacy (Ansley, 1989), settler colonialism (Hurwitz & Bourque, 2014; Wolfe, 2006), and the coloniality of power (Quijano, 2000). White supremacy advances the belief that white people have an inherent superiority over other races and thereby should rule over them. Settler colonialism is a system of oppression that displaces and eliminates Indigenous Peoples and replaces them with colonizers. The coloniality of power includes the continuation of colonialism in contemporary society, social discrimination, the support of hierarchical relationships between different ways of knowing, and the privileging of certain groups and knowledge above others (Quijano, 2000).

Dr. Michael Yellow Bird

Indigenous Decolonial Contemplative Mentoring

Being an Indigenous Decolonial Contemplative Mentor is a demanding métier. In this role, I regularly share with mentees the painful, traumatic histories and contemporary circumstances of Indigenous Peoples, provide context to the stories, point out the effects of different types of settler logic and power, suggest solutions, and share decolonized contemplative practices to help individuals prepare to engage in resistance and anti-colonial activities. Despite all my years of contemplative training, helping others go through these stages and processes takes an emotional and spiritual toll on me. However, I am not alone in this place. The decolonial contemplative mentee must also struggle to bear witness to the challenges and trauma that I am describing. In the Zen Peacemakers Order, "to bear witness is to embrace both the joy and the suffering we encounter. Rather than simply observing the situation, we become the situation. We become intimate with whatever it is – hunger, poverty, discrimination, disease, or death" (Harris, 2023, para. 2). Bearing witness means to "identify a person or a group who is disenfranchised or who is suffering (para. 10)…to spend meaningful time with them," (para. 11) and to "serve the situation" (para. 13) on a personal and systemic level (Harris, 2023).

Bearing witness is not easy since it can trigger adverse responses such as white fragility (discomfort and defensiveness) or what Hurwitz and Bourque (2014) describe as "settler moves to innocence" which can involve denial of responsibility, justification of what happened, and the desire to be morally absolved of what has or is occurring. As a mentor, I must exercise patience and compassion, and gently and continually move the conversation and actions toward understanding, acceptance, and reconciliation.

The Legacy of Plenty Fox

I credit my ability to thrive in the Western academy and serve as an Indigenous decolonial contemplative mentor to my great grandfather, Plenty Fox, who was a traditional Arikara holy man, contemplative, and a prominent figure in my contemplative lineage. I have used his teachings and contemplative practices to maintain my wholeness, identity, compassion, and resilience, and to be open to challenging ideas, beliefs, and people. Although I never met grandpa Plenty Fox, my father's stories about him described how his contemplative life endowed him with humility, compassion, strength, non-judgmental behavior, the willingness to teach others, and the courage he needed to maintain his integrity and wholeness in the face of dramatic change, racism, and colonialism. He embodied a special kindness and unconditional love that he held for all people and sentient beings and an enduring respect for the sacred that he brought into his everyday life. I have used his contemplative legacy and teachings to inspire my work as a dean, professor, and decolonial contemplative mentor.

My father always said how fortunate he was to be raised by grandpa Plenty Fox, since he bestowed upon him special stories, prayers, songs, love, patience, and the sacredness of meditation and silence, which my father passed on to me. Contemplative rituals were deeply embedded in my grandfather's life, and he held a deep empathy for all life since he believed that while the world was filled with beauty, it was also a place of suffering, struggle, and confusion. Upon waking, he would begin his day by thanking and lighting the sage he had gathered from a special place that was watched over by the spirit guardians of the plants. To him, plants embodied spirit and sentience. Closing his eyes, he began shaking his sacred gourd which rattled rhythmically in the early morning light as he sang a prayer song to thank his dreams for speaking to him. This was followed by him going outside, standing in silent meditation, and then singing a song to give thanks to the sun for life, for light, and the blessings it bestowed upon all the creatures of the earth. It was at this time when he bid farewell to the stars that were gently fading in the presence of the rising sun. In my contemplative practices, I continue to sing my grandfather's songs, express his prayers, sit in quiet meditation, and practice humility.

My academic career has focused on decolonizing social work (Gray et al., 2013), the effects of colonialism and methods of decolonization, Indigenous Peoples, Indigenous contemplative practices, decolonizing mindfulness approaches, and decolonial contemplative mentorship. I have supported students, faculty, and administrators in the neoliberal, western academic landscape to mindfully question and confront systemic racism, white supremacy, and colonialism. I have focused my efforts on helping others to understand how painful, destructive, and brutal colonialism, settler colonialism, and coloniality have been for Indigenous Peoples, and how contemplative practices can be used to open spaces to disrupt colonization and provide a path of healing, truth-telling, reconciliation, and transformation.

To disrupt settler logic, power, and communication protocols in the academy, I have started meetings by burning sage or sweetgrass and offering sacred words in my tribal language to create a safe, decolonized, and open space. I have invited Indigenous elders to our events and meetings to offer traditional prayers and have led or asked others to lead short mindfulness exercises to help set a positive, respectful tone. I have created undergraduate and graduate mindfulness courses to help students build resilience, decolonize the mind, reduce stress, improve emotional and social learning, and their ability to take care of themselves and others. Since the early 2000s, I have introduced mindful decolonization practices in the academy to assist students and faculty to reflect on the effects that colonialism has on marginalized groups, to assess their own level of colonization, and to envision decolonizing methodologies that will create insights and pathways of practice to address colonialism. I have organized and led early morning mindfulness practices for students and faculty to build a positive and more caring environment, and I have shared with others my belief that contemplative practices can serve as a counterbalance to racism, marginalization, hostility, and colonization.

One of the main contributions in my role as a decolonial contemplative mentor and scholar has been the development and introduction of a neurodecolonization framework that I created to help Indigenous Peoples and settlers to decolonize and heal from the effects of colonization using mainstream mindfulness meditation and traditional Indigenous contemplative practices (Yellow Bird, 2013). Neurodecolonization enables one to understand how we can mindlessly use the words, memes, concepts, and values of colonization in our everyday lives, and how each has become entangled in our actions, subtly reinforcing white supremacy, coloniality, and racism.

Neurodecolonization involves training the mind to overcome the destructive thoughts, feelings, emotions, and behaviors associated with the traumas of colonization (Clarke & Yellow Bird, 2021; Yellow Bird, 2013). Neurodecolonization enables an individual or community to engage in the processes of mindful activism, mindful anti-colonialism, truth-telling, and compassionate decolonization, which involves respectful reconciliation between Indigenous Peoples and colonizers to build alliances to resist colonization.

Neurodecolonization begins with a period of *cleansing* where one uses contemplative purification practices to strip away the harmful and invasive thoughts, beliefs, and values imposed by colonizing structures and processes. Next, is the restoration and *renaissance* of cultural practices, thinking, beliefs, and values that have been forgotten or abandoned due to colonization, but are relevant and necessary for survival and well-being. These practices include traditional or contemporary spiritual songs, dances, prayers, symbols, ceremonies, rituals, stories, dreams, and the prophecies of Indigenous communities. The final phase involves practices that can lead to *enlightenment* and raise our creativity to birth and use new ideas, thinking, technologies, lifestyles, and relationships that contribute to the advancement and empowerment of humans and all sentient beings.

Neurodecolonization practices and processes have been invaluable to my Indigenous decolonial contemplative mentoring of Holly and others since they provide a means to engage in difficult conversations regarding white supremacy and privilege, settler logic and power, racism, coloniality, and decolonization. Neurodecolonization practices provide a safe place to begin acknowledging and healing the traumas of colonization, a time for renewal through engaging in ancient contemplative practices that are important to healing and restoration, and offer a space to dream of enlightened futurities for the sake of all humans and sentient beings.

Dr. Holly Hatton

How Compassionate Mentorship Can Heal and Transform in Higher Education

My personal journey with mindfulness began in graduate school during a time when I questioned my ability to be an effective academic. Everything seemed centered on the future, and I had a great deal of fear – fear of failing, of not fitting in, and of not being enough. It seemed that the philosophy was to do more, to accomplish more, and I started to lose my sense of purpose. I was stressed, felt that I did not fit in, and was told by one professor that I may not be suited for a PhD. I considered leaving the program with my Master's Degree. It was at this time of uncertainty that I was offered an opportunity to participate in a Mindfulness-Based Stress Reduction (MBSR) eight-week in-person course. MBSR was created by Jon Kabat-Zinn (2003). Those eight weeks changed my life, personally and professionally. I felt part of a community that gave us permission to feel and that appreciated the humanness of being vulnerable and not feeling okay. I also learned helpful ways to manage my stress and reactive emotions. After such an enriching experience I found myself wanting to learn about the science of mindfulness and how it could support my well-being. At this time, I was immersed in the literature on the individual and interpersonal benefits of secular Western forms of mindfulness. My scholarly focus became mindfulness.

In 2016, I accepted a position at the University of Nebraska-Lincoln (UNL) as an assistant professor. Within the first two weeks of working at UNL I was told that I should change the focus of my research. Mindfulness was "religious" and would never be accepted in the academic community as a "real world evidence-based science." I found myself once again questioning my place in the academic community. A few weeks later after meditating, my uncertainty shifted. I felt grounded in my decision to study, teach, and practice mindfulness as a professional. However, I also felt a bit unsettled in how to best teach mindfulness as I was learning that my understanding of mindfulness and how it was being researched was shaped by many colonized influences. I found myself struggling with bringing mindfulness into academia in a way that would not be alarming to people who feared I was teaching a religious practice in a secular institution. I maintained that mindfulness includes spirituality but I still did not know how to research and teach mindfulness. I also struggled with not culturally appropriating important mindfulness practices while wanting to share these practices with students and others in the community. I sought ways to teach mindfulness that were culturally responsive and not used to silence people of color.

These struggles and uncertainties continued for two years, and then I had the great opportunity of meeting Dr. Michael Yellow Bird in 2018. I was familiar with and inspired by his work prior to meeting him. I was invited to join the Zero to Three Mindfulness Advisory Committee; after just one virtual meeting listening to Michael talk about mindfulness and decolonization, I felt I had more guidance and conviction to bring mindfulness into my academic work in a way that felt relevant, fulfilling, and authentic. I began to identify ways to think about science in a more meaningful and impactful way. A lovely statement that captures this holistic understanding of mindfulness is that we should live in an academic world where we are, "guided by lens of stories rooted in the revelations of science and framed with Indigenous worldviews-stories in which matter and spirit are both given voice" (Kimmerer, 2013, p. 346). With Michael's mentorship, I felt uplifted to engage in truth-telling as I learned about, researched, and taught contemplative practices. Soon after I was invited to co-author with Michael an article for Zero to Three which gave me an opportunity to engage in difficult conversations with Michael about my belonging in this space of decolonizing mindfulness; as a white woman, what is my place and value?

One of the formative mentoring experiences I shared with Michael was an invitation to co-author a book chapter with him in 2021. Through our collaborative writing and many Zoom conversations, my understanding of the decolonization of mindfulness deepened. Although the chapter centered on the importance of decolonizing mindfulness for the field of social work, I learned how mindfulness has been used as a way to "pacify feelings of anxiety and disquiet at the individual level rather than seeking to challenge the social, political, and economic inequalities that cause such distress" (Carrette & King, 2004, p. 22). Through our discussions, I learned how mindfulness could be used to bring about systems change in my academic work, and I embraced the value of not knowing, and of paying attention to different ways of knowing in my mindfulness scholarship. Michael shared readings with me and then took the time to reflect and dissect their meanings. It was through these important teachings and discussions that I felt I could be an ally and an academic who acknowledges that I have a lot of growth and learning to do to decolonize Westernized notions of mindfulness. I also learned that I have a place to both be a voice and to listen and be quiet when needed, and to discern when to lift up the voices of others. Through these conversations, I was beginning to learn the importance of bearing witness.

What does it mean to be an ally in a decolonized mindfulness? This is a question I often ask myself and through Michael's supportive listening and mentorship I have been able to sit with this question and confront the pain and hurt that emerges knowing my White privilege sits upon the structures and processes of systemic racism and settler colonialism. When I take notice and acknowledge this truth, it can feel overwhelming and painful; there can be guilt, anger, and sadness. In particular, I find that running meditations are a helpful practice. It was not until I received mentoring from Michael that I learned how running can be a powerful way of using meditation to feel strong, healthy, and empowered to address issues of equity and inclusion in academia. It is a way that I'm able to confront difficult feelings, be present with them, and then make meaning and understand their root causes. This way of practicing mindfulness helped me deepen my own sitting practice, furthering my own healing and self-compassion. I have found that students also appreciate and value mindful movement practices when sitting still can be too overwhelming.

Michael has taught me other practices that garner self-compassion and compassion for others. These practices allow me to feel held and provide the strength to serve as an ally in the decolonization of mindfulness. There is one practice we created that is particularly helpful in allowing oneself to observe and confront the colonialism that has influenced my conceptualization of mindfulness – Observing and Confronting Colonization Practices – which we share here. I offer this practice to the graduate students I teach so that they can begin to understand how mindfulness can be a practice of individual and collective change. For me, this mindfulness practice strengthens my activism by having me take notice of my feelings and thoughts and identify the ways that my actions perpetuate harm. This noticing then allows me to be intentional in making choices in how I learn, teach, and research mindfulness.

In addition to engaging in these mindfulness practices I also intentionally teach contemplative practices, such as journaling, art, and meditation, as ways to plant seeds and engage in truth-telling, which is often difficult when discussing anti-biased educational practices. In research, I examine whose voices and cultures get represented in our definitions of "effective mindfulness practices" and work to ensure that those practices do not harm others. Most recently, I collaborated with Michael to lift up this perspective for a program we created at the University of Nebraska-Lincoln called Cultivating Healthy Intentional Mindful Educators (CHIME, Hatton-Bowers et al., 2023). This eight-week professional learning program aims to bring mindfulness, compassion, and social-emotional learning practices to early childhood educators. Through Michael's mentorship, wisdom, and guidance, we continue to grow the CHIME program in a way that is culturally responsive and not solely centered on the individual "fixing" themselves or figuring out how to deal with stress caused by systemic inequities.

Although I have much to learn, I am grateful for this opportunity to have a mentor such as Michael who allowed me to be vulnerable in an academic relationship. Through his teachings, truth-telling, and keen ability to listen to me, he fostered my own healing and gave me the knowledge and strength to be an ally in this journey of decentering Western ways of knowing in higher education with mindfulness, compassion, and humility.

Call to Action

In Western academia, inequities and marginalization exist for some, while others enjoy privilege, power, and entitlement. It will take a community of enlightened administrators and academics to bring about a willingness to use contemplative practices to engage in truth-telling and enact needed systemic changes. And if this feels overwhelming or there is uncertainty about where to begin, those of us who are committed to bringing contemplative practices into higher education can provide mentorship to others to initiate these changes for a more compassionate academy.

In order to do this, we recommend that contemplative leaders and practitioners in institutions of higher education commit to the following:

1 Create mentorship programs: work toward creating formal decolonial contemplative mentorship programs for students, staff, faculty, and administrators.
2 Disrupt settler logic and power: create and use decolonizing contemplative practices that are aimed at disrupting various forms of settler logic and power.
3 Explore and take care: explore the use of neurodecolonization practices to open up safe spaces to begin truth-telling, acknowledging and healing the traumas of colonization, creating a time for renewal and restoration, and a space to dream of enlightened futurities. We also need to be responsible for shifting academic thinking away from doing more and more and more, and instead pause and engage in activities that nourish us. Part of renewal and restoration is taking the time to engage in our spiritual practices, eating well, sleeping, and taking time to exercise.
4 Bear witness: encourage and teach students, faculty, and administrators how to bear witness and act against the travesties of colonization, racism, and White supremacy. To bear witness means to be intentional in exposing ourselves to the suffering and systemic inequities that exist in academia and to do so with compassion.

Contemplative practices have a critical place in higher education. They can bring about an understanding of, and a connection to, the sacredness of all life and can change the trajectory of the colonized realities in the Western academy. As the legacy of Plenty Fox teaches us, the contemplative life can endow us with what we need to maintain our integrity and wholeness in the face of dramatic change, racism, and colonialism.

Practice: Observing and Confronting Colonization, Suffering, and Oppression

Find a comfortable sitting position. Relax your body, sit up straight, lay your hands on your lap, gently lower your gaze or close your eyes, and silently and mindfully repeat to yourself:

"I am meditating in order to decolonize all oppressive systems and to end the suffering of all sentient beings."

Repeat this several times, deeply sensing what it feels like to meditate on the meaning of colonization, suffering, and oppression.

Reflection

When you finish, take a minute to settle in a moment of silence. This meditation can be deeply moving. For many of us, we may experience difficult, painful, and challenging feelings. We may also experience feelings of strength and feel grounded to confront colonialism. After settling, note what emotions, thoughts, and sensations came up for you. We invite you to journal your experience, draw, move your body, or whatever is needed as you tend to what arises during this practice. Consider sharing your experience with a mentor and talking through your observations and questions.

Reference List

Ansley, F. L. (1989). Stirring the ashes: Race class and the future of civil rights education. *Cornell Law Review, 74*(6), 993–1077. https://scholarship.law.cornell.edu/clr/vol74/iss6/1.

Carrette, J., & King, R. (2004). *Selling spirituality: The silent takeover of religion.* Routledge. https://doi.org/10.4324/9780203494875

Clarke, K., and Yellow Bird, M. (2021). *Decolonizing pathways towards integrative healing in social work.* Routledge. https://doi.org/10.4324/9781315225234

Gray, M., Coates, J., Yellow Bird, M., & Hetherington, T. (2013). *Decolonizing social work.* Ashgate Publishing Company.

Harris, J. S. (2023, November 12). How to practice bearing witness. *Lion's Roar: Buddhist Wisdom for Our Time.* https://www.lionsroar.com/how-to-practice-bearing-witness/

Hatton-Bowers, H., Clark, C., Parra, G., Calvi, J., Bird, M. Y., Avari, P., & Smith, J. (2023). Promising findings that the cultivating healthy intentional mindful educators' program (CHIME) strengthens early childhood teachers' emotional resources: An iterative study. *Early Childhood Education Journal, 51*(7), 1291–1304. https://doi.org/10.1007/s10643-022-01386-3.

Hurwitz, L., & Bourque, S. (2014, June 06). Settler colonialism primer. *Unsettling America: Decolonization in theory & practice.* https://unsettlingamerica.wordpress.com/2014/06/06/settler-colonialism-primer/

Kabat-Zinn, J. (2003). Mindfulness-based interventions in context: Past, present, and future. *Clinical Psychology: Science and Practice, 10,* 144–156. https://doi.org/10.1093/clipsy.bpg016

Kimmerer, R. W. (2013). *Braiding sweetgrass.* Minneapolis: Milkweed Editions.

Quijano, A. (2000). Coloniality of power and eurocentrism in Latin America. *International Sociology, 15*(2), 215–232. https://doi.org/10.1177/0268580900015002005.

Wolfe, P. (2006). Settler colonialism and the elimination of the native. *Journal of Genocide Research, 8*(4), 387–409. https://doi.org/10.1080/14623520601056240.

Yellow Bird, M. (2013). Neurodecolonization: Applying mindfulness research to decolonizing social work. In M. Gray, J. Coates, M. Yellow Bird, & T. Hetherington (Eds.), *Decolonizing social work* (pp. 293–310). Ashgate Publishing Company.

25
CONTEMPLATIVE RESISTANCE AMIDST THE FIRES OF GLOBAL SUFFERING

Jennifer Cannon

I join this dialogue from Western Massachusetts, from the unceded homelands of the Pocumtuc Nation. The town I live in is Amherst, Massachusetts – named after Lord Jeffrey Amherst who is responsible for biological warfare against regional Indigenous nations. For decades countless activists have tried to change the name of our town, and Amherst College, without success. In 2016, the Town of Amherst voted to recognize Indigenous People's Day, and eliminate reference to Columbus Day, but has been unwilling to acknowledge Lord Jeffrey Amherst's complicity with genocide. As we continue to think about what it means to decolonize mindfulness and other contemplative practices, let us stay vigilant about the concrete realities of settler colonialism. How can our contemplative justice movements directly connect to efforts in higher education toward reparations and the rematriation[1] of Indigenous land and stolen goods? Many higher education institutions are being called to accountability, beyond the verbal or written recognition a land acknowledgment might offer. As we reflect on the essays in this section, let us hold this question prompted by Michael Yellow Bird and Holly Hatton: what does it mean to decolonize our practices?

A brief note on positionality: I enter this dialogue as a cisgender white woman, feminist, Buddhist, scholar and practitioner of liberatory mindfulness, antiracist educator, social justice activist, mother, grandmother, and daughter of the Earth. I am also someone who has spent many years on the margins in higher education, as a doctoral student later in life, as adjunct faculty and Visiting Lecturer in multiple institutions, and as a contemplative educator and leader.

DOI: 10.4324/9781003416777-30

What a privilege it has been to engage these essays, which are on fire with a collective spirit of rebellion and resistance! It is impossible to read these essays and not be moved by the shared longing to break free of tired habits that keep us bound to oppressive institutions, structures, ideologies, and ways of being. Calling us to move boldly into a stance of courage and integrity, these essays remind us of our agency and our mutual imperative to manifest the healed and whole communities we have been yearning for. These authors do not waste time explaining and defending why and how contemplative practices are needed in liberatory struggles – this foundation is already known. Embodiment, stillness, awareness, reflection, grounding, witnessing. These somatic practices help provide the foundation from which we move into ethical action for collective liberation. Through diverse contemplative practices, the contributing essayists ask us to resist colonization, dismantle racism, disrupt patterns of white dominance, and redefine student notions of success.

In the wake of George Floyd's murder and the Movement for Black Lives there was a surge in antiracism initiatives in higher education. Gaining momentum from a reactionary place of crisis, these initiatives were not designed with an eye toward depth and sustainability. DEI and antiracism programs, endorsed by our colonized and colonizing institutions, will not get the work of freedom done. Not surprisingly, these efforts are often reduced to superficial measures to ease discomfort, or appease demands for structural change. Antiracist language, utilized (or co-opted) by an institution for funders or promotional material, must be matched by consistent antiracist practices at every level of operation.

Amidst our institutions full of brokenness, can we still move toward wholeness? Can we live within the brokenness with eyes wide open, hearts attentive, and full of the requisite faith that "we are the ones we have been waiting for" (Jordan, 2005)? We are the ones to employ emergent strategies of resistance at the local and micro levels, rupturing oppressive systems designed to reproduce and reinforce hierarchies of power and privilege. We are the change that comes from embodying justice (Echavarria), decolonizing our practices (Yellow Bird & Hatton), and enacting critical compassionate pedagogy (Gusain). We are the change that acknowledges collective grief and stands shoulder to shoulder with radical hope (Loe). We are the change that weds contemplative practice to liberatory praxis (Spragg). This section's authors do the work of disrupting complicity with systems and structures that do not recognize our humanity, support our wholeness, or serve our freedom.

Renuka Gusain aptly challenges the transactional extractive language of academia and also the extractive and transactional approaches to contemplative practices. She sheds light on the futility of antiracism efforts in the absence of honoring each other's humanity and building solidarity across lines of difference. Through the practice of storytelling and Racial Healing Circles, Gusain moves toward wholeness by being witnessed and truly heard by her colleagues. How simple and profound is this revelation!

Meika Loe urges us to dismantle white supremacist notions of success by redefining and reclaiming what success means to us and uplifting practices of community care. Loe creates public space for students to grieve – to collectively memorialize those we have lost to police violence, COVID-19, and violence against trans communities. Modeling this ethic of community care, Loe asks how we might extend care practices beyond the classroom or the walls of the ivory tower to create larger ripple effects in our campus culture and beyond.

As a white antiracist educator, I find that contemplative practices are a foundational step in disrupting white dominance. Critical antiracism skills include awareness, discernment, and humility – skills that can be cultivated through dedicated contemplative practices. Deb Spragg's thoughtful WAIT practice teaches white people to notice and disrupt white dominant habits and patterns by pausing, using honest self-reflection and critical self-inquiry to examine one's motivation for speaking. This practice of careful discernment can interrupt white savior behavior and lead to a conscious choice to remain silent so others may speak, and BIPOC voices are amplified.

We can balance Spragg's practice with the understanding that white silence can also be used to collude with oppression (DiAngelo, 2012). There will be times when it is essential for white allies to speak to an issue, strategically leveraging white privilege, when it is unsafe or emotionally draining for BIPOC colleagues to speak. As Spragg discusses, it is important for white folks to be in a grounded space of listening, witnessing, and presence to the situation at hand – not taking up space with our own agenda. Accessing a rigorous self-reflection process is critical to discerning when silence is complicity and when silence is needed to make space for marginalized voices.

Structural change is most sustainable when all stakeholders are involved and invested in the process, especially those who are most impacted by racism and white supremacy culture. As Ericka Echavarria points out in her essay, we must learn how to decentralize knowledge and dismantle hierarchies of power based on illusory categories of expertise. By inviting the wisdom and experience of all workers in higher education, Echavarria affirms that we are all knowledge keepers and have something valuable to offer the collective. Arguably, this is a radical contemplative practice, recognizing and utilizing the skills and talents of all members of a community, regardless of rank or status. Echavarria also shows us how to resist white supremacy culture by "slowing down, being more intentional and less reactionary, and prioritizing individual relationships over transactions."

As someone who consciously chooses not to collude with dehumanizing practices, Echavarria teaches us to work from values which center our humanity.

Michael Yellow Bird and Holly Hatton introduce contemplative practices in a framework of disrupting settler colonialism. Their mentor/mentee relationship provides a living example of what decolonial mentoring can look like in higher education. Yellow Bird talks about the emotional and spiritual toll that this work takes as he shares the traumatic histories and contemporary circumstances of Indigenous Peoples, and the patience and compassion required to work with a white settler mentee who is coming into a deeper awareness of colonization. The authors purposefully move from bearing witness to engaging in resistance. It is not enough to bear witness alone – courageous action is required to end colonization.

Additionally, Yellow Bird and Hatton model the critical importance of decolonizing mindfulness. Mindfulness must not remain a neoliberal tool to be peddled in higher education in order to reduce stress, or boost one's ability to focus and excel in athletics or academics. Mindfulness, rather, is presented as a collective form of healing which leads to mindful activism. Dismantling white mindfulness (Fleming et al., 2022; Karelse, 2023), and the commercial mindfulness industry, is an important part of the decolonial project. Michael Yellow Bird strategically links mindfulness, from Asian Buddhist roots, with traditional Indigenous contemplative practices, for the purposes of radical recovery from the brutality of colonization.

White supremacy culture teaches us to speak from a rational or analytical framework, to erase human suffering by using sterile data and scientific measurements. Alternatively, as these essays demonstrate, contemplative practices encourage us to uncover and access multiple forms of knowledge. For me, wholeness is only possible when we are telling the truth about our pain, grief, and fears when we are acknowledging the brokenness, rather than finding band-aid solutions or academic language to cover it up. In order for me to feel whole, I must be able to speak from my embodied experience and utilize embodied knowledge as a guide or reference for teaching, advocating, healing, and agitating within the academy.

While our institutions may remain protected enclaves of privilege, inequality, and oppression, it is simultaneously true that higher education is alive with transformative change, seeded by our collective grief and longing for another way to be in this world. As Arundhati Roy (2003) has written, "Another world is not only possible, she is on her way. Maybe many of us won't be here to greet her, but on a quiet day, if I listen very carefully, I can hear her breathing."

Note

1 "Rematriation is Indigenous women-led work to restore sacred relationships between Indigenous people and our ancestral land, honoring our matrilineal societies, and in opposition to patriarchal violence and dynamics" (Sogorea Te' Land Trust, para 1).

Reference List

DiAngelo, R. J. (2012). Nothing to add: A challenge to white silence in racial discussions. *Understanding and Dismantling Privilege*, 2(1), 1–17. https://robindiangelo.com/wp-content/uploads/2016/01/Nothing-to-Add-Published.pdf

Fleming, C. M., Womack, V., & Proulx, J. (Eds.). (2022). *Beyond white mindfulness: Critical perspectives on racism, well-being and liberation.* Routledge, Taylor & Francis Group.

Jordan, J. (2005). Poem for South African Women. Poets.org. *https://poets.org/poem/poem-south-african-women*

Karelse, C.-M. (2023). *Disrupting white mindfulness: Race and racism in the wellbeing industry.* Manchester University Press. https://doi.org/10.7765/9781526162076

Roy, A. (2003). *War talk.* South End Press.

What is Rematriation? (n.d). Sogorea Te' Land Trust. https://sogoreate-landtrust.org/what-is-rematriation/

26

AFTERWORD

A Ritual for Resisting

Michelle C. Chatman, LeeRay Costa, and David W. Robinson-Morris

> Breathe.
> Take the deepest breath you have taken all day.
> You are here. We. Are. Here.

The narratives and practices offered in this volume are a testament to the courage of our contributors, and to their hope for a more humane and just academy. Their essays envision a world that does not yet exist—but must be made manifest—if we are to achieve wholeness, repair the planet, and heal ourselves and the system of higher education.

We have called forth transformation.

Transformation is an unpredictable undertaking. It is multi-directional, multi-dimensional, messy, and often chaotic. Transformation requires release—letting go—to receive an unknown state of being, knowing, and doing. It is hope undergirded by fear in an unknown but imagined future, those fears conquered by love, and prophetic imaginings made manifest by determined collective action. It asks us, much like certain schools of contemplative practice, to be both nothing and everything, simultaneously.

To be transformed, we must engage in acts of resistance. Resistance catalyzes transformation from potential to kinetic energy; dissolution and creation; a future always already in the making. Resistance is opposition to the current flow, the present milieu, and the current context in refusal of oppression, violence, inequity, and inhumane behaviors and actions. It is not by coincidence that resistance in scientific terms is measured in ohms. In Hindu, Buddhist, Jainist, and Sikh cosmology, Ohm is a sacred mantra—the primordial sound of creation—an onto-triadic rheomode connecting past, present, future, nature, and all living beings in the cosmic dance of the universe (Barad, 2007; Ramose, 2002; Robinson-Morris, 2019). To resist is to (re)direct energy, alter the flow, and make perceptible a new, different reality.

We have asked you to resist.

Resistance looks, feels, and is different for each human being. For some, it might be treating others with loving-kindness within institutions that have become inhumane or speaking up for those who are unable to speak for themselves. It might mean sharing this volume with friends and colleagues. For others, it might be researching, teaching, and then applying what they have learned about decolonization or critical theory in service of systemic, institutional, social, and personal transformation. Resistance might look like engaging in the peaceful protests that have erupted on college and university campuses across the country, or providing water, food, and support to those who choose to protest. Ultimately, the fruit of our individual acts of resistance is produced through collective efforts toward justice that make manifest transformation.

The whole of the Earth aches for liberation and yearns for the transformative enactment of love. Again, at the time of this writing, our students and colleagues are engaged in protests on campuses across the country. They are advocating for peace, an end to war, and a recognition of humanity over the power of the state. They are squarely engaged in the disruption of systemic white supremacy that, philosopher Charles Mills (1997) remarked, is the unnamed political force that has shaped the globe. Our students are mapping new futures and are showing us and leading the way toward a new world. Our students are birthing the world many of us conceived in the fertile womb of our imaginations in our own youth, and in our scholarship and teaching as professionals. Contemplative resistance always compels us toward justice, humanity, community, and recognition of our ecological kinship.

We have asked you to commit to carrying it forward, together.

Liberation, a fruit of resistance, is a collective undertaking. The path to transformation is expansive, always.

We insist that you share this work and carry it forward into your respective communities. Volume contributor, Steven Thurston Oliver, offers one possible way of carrying this work, our work forward. He imagines, "a gathering of like-minded contemplatives using this collection of essays to do in depth reading together followed by discussion, bonding, and visioning strategies for moving forward collectively and individually." Remember the old resistance adage: don't agonize, organize! We suggest organizing communities of practice to read and reflect on the stories and ideas shared in these pages. Engage your imaginations to blossom the new.

We invite you to share this volume and its intention with colleagues and administrators who may not yet be familiar with contemplative practice, scholarship, or pedagogy. Organize small discussion groups, faculty learning communities, or other events that create space to discuss alternate ways of being and doing within the academy.

Like education, healing, resistance, and liberation require community and most importantly, for us to remember joy.

We summon joy.

Joy, too, is a method. Joy, like Christina Sharpe's (2023) bold assertion of beauty in *Ordinary Notes*, is a method. Perhaps, it is by the experience of joy we should gauge the fullness of our humanity and the wholeness of our lives. Suffering is inevitable; therefore, in a world of saturated with suffering, the shock of joy is to be relished. The contributors of this volume share with us their lived experiences of being and doing within institutions of higher education. They share with us their pain, glimmers of happiness, moments of powerful realization, and offer access to portals of ancestral communion. Largely, however, they do not explicitly lift up joy. You might ask, how do we emote joy when we are not well, not whole, amid such overwhelming suffering? We re-member.

Imagine sitting with your Ancestors. Ask them the question just raised to you.

They endured every manner of hardship; experienced every manner of event in the spectrum of the human condition. And were, in the intensity of suffering, able to conjure a prophetic joy, and when it rose up in some and descended upon others they savored the taste of present joy. We, like them, are being asked to practice prophetic joy, to create moments of joyfulness in the midst of it all. We are them.

Joy is a method and method is always a decision about how we choose to *be*.

We offer to each of you deep bows of gratitude.

No matter how you decide to carry this work and the wisdom of the contributors forward, we thank you. We thank you for your generous time and for embracing these offerings. We thank you for witnessing the personal stories shared here, for engaging with the ideas of the contributors, and for the creative ways you will place these ideas and narratives into service of resistance, transformation, and collective liberation.

We acknowledge and bow deeply in gratitude for those who remain engaged in the work of higher education, the education of students, and who each day, without fanfare or recognition, model the way for students and colleagues. Please know that you are seen and supported.

A Ritual of Resistance

Find a place of safety and comfort, alone or in community.

Breathe.
Take the deepest breath you have taken all day.
You are here. We. Are. Here.

Locate the anger. Lean into the pain.
Let it flow. Grasp nothing.
What are you resisting?
In its touching, your salvation.

Feel the ache of liberation.
Soften into the nourishing embrace of love.
Wipe tears. Unclench jaw. Loosen fists. Release sound.
Breathe.

Smile into joy. Laugh in hope.
Where does it feel free?
Convene with yourselves in the free places.
Free zones are the nascent spaces of liberation.

Breathe.
Imagine.
Imagine community.
Imagine freedom.
Imagine new futures.
What images are painted on the canvas of your mind?

Sit in gratitude.
Breathe.
Breathe in the manifestations of your resistance.

Hum: Ohm.

Rise.
Be what is not yet, that you have called forth.
Resist.

May this volume, an incredible gift to our liberated and healed future, encourage you to embrace wholeness through contemplative practices and help us cultivate a more inclusive, just, and compassionate academia and world.

Reference List

Barad, K. (2007). *Meeting the Universe Halfway: Quantum physics and the entanglement of matter and meaning*. Duke University Press. [Database]

Mills, C. W. (1997). *The racial contract*. Cornell University Press.

Ramose, M. B. (2002). The philosophy of ubuntu and ubuntu as a philosophy. In P. H. Coetzee & A. P. J. Roux (Eds.), *Philosophy from Africa* (2nd ed., pp. 230–238). Oxford Press.

Robinson-Morris, D. W. (2019). *Ubuntu and Buddhism in higher education: An ontological rethinking*. Routledge.

Sharpe, C. (2023). *Ordinary notes*. Farrar, Straus and Giroux.

INDEX

Note: Page references in *italics* denote figures, in **bold** tables and with "n" endnotes.

academia 23–24, 30, 32, 37, 50, 73, 86, 120, 195, 209–211; colonial 42; equity and inclusion in 233; harm in 221; and marginalized people 11; and mindfulness 232; and people of color 11; social space of 118; transactional extractive language of 238; Western 234
academic social capital 210
accountability 19, 45, 59, 68, 218, 221–222, 224–225; and higher education institutions 237; institutional 2; and relationship-building 190; teams 207
activism: civil rights 212; community 206; contemplation for 139–140; mindful 231, 240; "sole-proprietor activism" 215
administrators 1, 7, 12–14, 60, 82, 85, 97, 114, 191, 198, 206, 209, 211, 219, 227, 230, 234–235
African American tradition 127
African-centered rituals 128
African-descended tradition 127
Ahmed, Zahra 144–145, 156, 157–159, 185
Ajahn Chah's Thai Forest Buddhist lineage 212
Amherst, Lord Jeffrey 237

ancestral knowledge/heritage 40, 43–45
ancestral violence of colonialism 159
Anthropocene 38
anti-Blackness 18, 24, 78, 159
anti-Black racism 148
antiracism programs 12–13, 163, 237–239
Anything We Love Can Be Saved (Walker) 150
Anzaldúa, Gloria 74
Apple, Michael 158
Applebaum, Barbara 211
Arbery, Ahmaud 158
The Artist's Way: A Spiritual Path to Higher Creativity (Cameron) 112
Asians: decolonization for 43; immigrants 42; as a monolithic "model minority" 42
Association for Contemplative Mind in Higher Education conference 81
Association for the Study of African American Life and History conference 152
Ayahuasca ceremonies 167

Baldwin, James 3
Barbezat, Daniel 9
Beer, L. E. 56

beholding 30, 79, 134
belonging: cultivating 193–200; institutional transformation 196–199; Inviting Whole Selves: Planting Seeds to Cultivate Transformative and Sustainable Change practice 199–200; pedagogy for institutional transformation 196–199; practitioner and the personal 193–196
beloved community: beginnings/endings 203; care teams 203–204; classroom practice in praxis 202–205; contemplative practice 202; as practice 201–207; redefining success 204–205, 206–207
Big Quit 8
BIPOC 13, 109, 191, 239; community members 210, 213; performing arts group 212
Black feminism 24, 58–60, 159; and contemplative practices 56–61; and fellowship 59; in practice 58–59
Black Feminist Thought 59
Black Lives Matter 160
Black Magic: Religion and the African American Conjuring Tradition (Chireau) 127
Black men: and Buddhist resonance 134–137; and illusion of togetherness 137–139; and meditation 137–139; multiplicity of 133–140; state-sanctioned terrorism of 156
The Black Shoals: Offshore Formations of Black and Indigenous Studies (King) 39–41
Black Studies 129
Black tradition 134
Black women 17–18, 27–31, 59–60; contemplative practices 57; gendered racism 56; and higher education 56–58
Bland, Sandra 158
Boal, Augusto 105
The Body Keeps the Score (Van der Kolk) 148
bodymind 92–93, 96, 98–99
bodymindspirits 37, 40, 45
body oppression 91–99

body sovereignty 92, 93–95, 129; Native American 95; overview 93; and systemic oppression 94; toward decoloniality 95; and universities 97–98
body without organs (BwO) 144
The Book of Delights (Gay) 163
Born for this Mission 78
Bourque, S. 229
Brazil 65
"Breathing-Drawing-Meditations" 64
Bridging Self and Other through Mind and Dance seminar 169
Brookings Institution 72
Brosi, George 201
brown, adrienne maree 220–221
Buddha 211
Buddhism 44, 75, 168
Buddhist: contemplative practices 159; resonance 134–137; tradition 134
burnout 8, 19, 23, 83, 166–174, 185–186, 222
Bush, Mirabai 9
Bush, Nana Lawson 154n4
Butler, Octavia 8

"cajitas" 18, 24; as contemplative practice 47–55; journey 47–49; practice 53–55; as "sacred boxes" 51, 53; as situated and intergenerational 51–53
Cameron, Julia 112
Candia-Bailey, Antoinette 20n2
capital: academic social 210; cultural 23, 56, 195
capitalism 38, 161, 180; racial 63
care teams 203–204
Center for Contemplative Mind in Society (CMind) 133, 134, 140, 148
Chari, Anita 144–145, 156, 159–161, 185
Chatman, Michelle C. 133–140
CHIME program 234
Chireau, Yvonne P. 127
Chow, Rey 41
Christian higher education 63, 66
Christianity 65, 66, 151
Christopher, Gail C. 197
civil rights activism 212
classroom ancestral knowledge 162
classroom practice in praxis 202–205

Clifton, Lucille 3–4
Coalition of Communities of Color (CCC) 212
collective compassion 189–191
Colman, F. J. 143
colonialism 40–41, 48, 94; ancestral violence of 159; internalized 38, 44; settler 63, 66, 69
coloniality 231
coloniality of power 228
colonization 39–41; of North America, and Asians 42; observing and confronting 235–236; scientific 43; space of 45; wounds of 43–44
community activism 206
compassionate decolonization 231
compassionate listening 67
compassionate mentorship 231–234
conjure/conjuring 127–128
Conjuring Transformation 127–130; cultivating wholeness 129–130; institutions of higher education and wholeness 129–130; possibilities/limitations 128; practices as service of self/systems 128–129
connection 143–145
consciousness justice 18, 77
"consejos" 52
Contact Improvisation (CI) 92, 95–96; relationship with own body 96–97
contemplation: for activism 139–140; for healing 139–140
contemplative dance 101–107
contemplative education 73–75
contemplative emergence 190, 226n1; contemplative emergence 220–224; and higher education 219–220; overview 218–219
contemplative justice movements 3, 20, 237
contemplative life 169
contemplative practices 1–20, 134; benefits of 168; "cajitas" as 47–55; colonial shadows of 36–45; instant mindfulness 6; for liberation 59–60; as onto-epistemology 5; and racial oppression 19; of relational flourishing 63–70; risks associated with 16–17; sustaining forms of 57–58; through Black feminist lens 56–61; transformative change in higher education 218–226

contemplative resistance 243; and global suffering 237–240
Contemplative Teaching Fellowship program 134
The Conversation Project at Willamette 180
Convivencia 64, 66–67
Cooper, Anna Julia 31, 33
Cosmotheandric Vision 64
Costa, LeeRay 204
CourageRISE model 72, 73–75
COVID pandemic 1, 7–8, 64, 156, 158, 161
Creative Envisioning 18, 109–117, 129; engaging in 115; impact of 113–114; impact on work/community 114–115; overview 110–112; practice 116–117; as spiritual practice 112, **113**
Creative Visualization (Gawain) 113
critical antiracism skills 239
Critical Race Black Feminism 59
crow 28–29
cultivating belonging 193–200
cultural appropriation 45
cultural capital 23, 56, 195

dance 92, 98; contemplative 101–107; as mindful practice 102
Davis, Angela 17, 190
Davis, Heather 38
Davis, Miles 75
Davis, Shardé M. 214
"A Day Too Great a Force" (Hafiz) 182
decolonial contemplative mentorship 230
decoloniality, and body sovereignty 95
decolonization 39–41, 44, 230; for Asians 43; Native 42
decolonizing mindfulness approaches 230
Deepening Belonging: a Contemplative Practice of Relational Flourishing 66–69; accepting 70; befriending 70; checking in 70; discerning next steps 70; extending gratitude and blessing 70
deep witnessing 67
DEI 186, 210, 238
Deleuze, Gilles. 143–144
della Grazia, Guido Dettoni 178

Diaz-Mendoza, Virginia 129
Dillard, Cynthia 13, 56
disjunctures: defined 49; and formal education 52; in higher education 49–50
double bind 86, 89n7
double consciousness 48, 52
Du Bois, W. E. B. 48

Eastern philosophy 134
Echavarria, Ericka 190, 226n1, 239–240
education: Christian higher 63, 66; contemplative 73–75; higher (*see* higher education); profit-driven model of 72
embodied reading 41–43
embodied ritual-making 67
"emergent strategy" 220
endarkened feminist epistemology 56, 59
enlightenment 44, 195, 231
Envisioning a Future that Works for All: Characteristics of the Visioning Process (Wahl) 115
epistemic violence 148
epistemology 73–75
Ervin, Angela Crawford 211
"extra-neural" learning 73

faculty 1, 5–7, 9–14, 16, 18, 53–54, 81–82, 97–98, 114–116, 195, 206, 209–211, 219, 230
Feeding Your Demons (FYD) practice 167–168, 169, 171–172; becoming the demon 173; feeding the demon and meeting the ally 173–174; finding the demon in the body 172; personifying the demon 172; resting in awareness 174
fellowship: and Black feminism 59; as contemplative practice 58; overview 58; in practice 58–59
feminism *see* Black feminism
Floyd, George 8, 156, 158, 159, 160, 163, 238
Flunder, Yvette 66
food insecurity 103–104
free writing 162
Fritzsche, Lauren 102
Fugitive Pedagogy (Givens) 60
fugitivity 3, 60–61

Gawain, Shakti 113
Gay, Ross 163
Givens, Jarvis 60
global suffering, and contemplative resistance 237–240
Grant, Bradford C. 133–140, *141*
Grant, M. 58
gratitude 244–245
Great Disengagement 8
Great Resignation 8
grounding in contemplative practice 202
Guattari, Felix. 143–144
"The Guest House" (Rumi) 196
Gumbs, Alexis Pauline 2, 69
Gusain, Renuka 190, 238–239

Halifax, Roshi Joan 88n4
"harmful speech" 211
Harmon, Kohnee 197
Harrell, Sharon 150
Hart, Tobin 121
Harvey, Stefano 7
Hatton, Holly 227–236; call to action 234–235; compassionate mentorship and higher education 231–234
healing 1–3, 5, 7, 11–14, 18–20, 23–24, 58–59, 74, 83–84, 110, 120, 149–151, 225; ancestral 44, 64; communal 157; contemplation for 139–140; healing 159, 161, 167; indigenous 114; and living 166–167; and mental narratives 83–84; racial 148, 153, 190, 197–199; sacred 148; spiritual 65
Healing Higher Education: Racial Reckoning, Racial Justice (2022) 148
Healing Wisdom of Africa (Somé) 150
Hendren, Sandra 181
higher education 37; being contemplative in 118–126; and Black women 56–58; and compassionate mentorship 231–234; and contemplative practices 218–226; disjunctures and application in 49–50; Indigenous decolonial contemplative mentorship in 227–236; institutions, and wholeness 129–130; oppressions within Christian institutions of 18;

and Racial Healing Circles 20; transformative change in 218–226
Holmes, B. A. 75, 150
holographic co-becoming 45
hooks, bell 122–123, 201–203, 206
"How to Tell the Truth" (Williams) 215
hunger 103–104
Hurwitz, L. 229

identity 75, 82, 219–220; construction 121, 124; immigrant 87; negotiation 119–120; politics 16; sexual 138; shared 24; shared racial 59; social 124
illusion of togetherness 137–139
Indigenous communities 231
Indigenous contemplative practices 230, 240
Indigenous Decolonial Contemplative Mentor 228
Indigenous Decolonial Contemplative Mentoring 228–229
Indigenous decolonial contemplative mentorship 227–236
Indigenous peoples 37, 45, 228, 230, 240; genocide of 38; neurodecolonization 40
individualism 162, 197
inner power 86–88
instant mindfulness 6
institutional transformation 196–199
intentional communities 203–204
inter-being 68, 75
intercorporeal field 160
Interior Castle (St. Teresa of Avila) 110
internal conflict 48
internalized colonialism 38, 44
ishvara pranidhana (surrender to the divine) 149, 152
Islam 151
Islamic teachings 18

Jeffers-Coly, Phyllis M. 144, 186
Jesus Christ 65
Jim Crow 78
Jordan, Valin 104
jo staff 87, 89n9
joy 244
Joy Unspeakable: Contemplative Practices of the Black Church (Holmes) 150

justice 2–3, 11–12, 15; consciousness 18, 77; contemplative 3, 20, 237; racial 210, 212; social 11, 42, 60, 63, 122, 124, 180, 210, 212, 237; transformative 204, 221, 225

Kabat-Zinn, Jon 232
Kimmerer, Robin Wall 203
King, Tiffany Lethabo 39–41
Kloppenberg, James 93
Kuo-Deemer, Mimi 43

LaDuke, Winona 14, 163
Lama Tsultrim Allione 167, 168, 171
land sovereignty 94
Latin America 65, 66
Learning from the Future: How to Make Robust Strategy in Times of Deep Uncertainty (Scoblic) 115
Lectio Divina 110
Lectio Visio 110
Lerman, Liz 102
liberation 14; commitments to 64–66; origins to 64–66
lines of flight 143–145
Liu, Michael Shiyung 43
living and healing 166–167
Loe, Meika 239
Lone Dog, Leota 162
Lorde, Audre 37, 162
Lucchesi, Annita 94

Machig Labdron 167
Maison des Esclaves 149
Maroon communities 144
Martin, Lori Latrice 210
Marxist theory 159
Maynard, Robyn 115
meditation 6, 12, 14, 57, 81–83, 87–88, 120, 134, 162; and Black men 137–139; and illusion of togetherness 137–139
Menakem, R. 148
meritocracy 162
Metta Thai Forest monastery in California 212
Meyer, Manulani 45
"microbehaviors" 214
Mills, Charles 243
mindful activism 231, 240
mindful anti-colonialism 231
mindful communication 212

mindfulness 6, 120, 123–124, 135, 162
Mindfulness-Based Stress Reduction (MBSR) 232
mindful practices 122
Moore, Langston 103
Moraga, Cherríe 162
moral distress 83, 88n4
Morrison, Toni 3
Mosemghvdlishvili, Lela 144–145, 185–186
Moten, Fred 7
Mother Earth 203
Moua, Mee 197
Movement for Black Lives 238
multiplicities 144; of Black manhood 133–140
multiracial feminism 156–164
multiracial feminist conversation 156–164
Mural by Michael Rosato 154n5

"narrative history" 48
Native decolonization 42
neurodecolonization 40, 44, 231
Non-Violent Communication (NVC) 212

Okun, Tema 204
On Intercorporeal Perception (Anita Chari) 159–161
oppression 48, 239; body 91–99; within Christian institutions of higher education 18; observing and confronting 235–236; racial 19; systemic 82, 94, 158, 222
Ordinary Notes (Sharpe) 244
othering 197
Our Skins are Membranes Not Walls 184
Owens, Lama Rod 83

Panikkar, Raimon 64
Parker, G. 148, 150
Patton, L. D. 56, 61
Paxton, Steve 95–96
pedagogy: for institutional transformation 196–199; of power 157–159
Pedagogy of the Oppressed (Freire) 105
Pentecostal Christianity 64
Petersen-Boring, Aaron 175–183

Petersen-Boring, Wendy 144, 145, 185
Plenty Fox 229–231
poetry 16, 18, 24, 37, 44
point of contact 98–99
Porter, C. J. 59
postcolonial feminism 159
power 6–7, 14–15, 18–19, 31, 83–84; inner 86–88; institutional 85; of non-judgment 68; pedagogy of 157–159
practice: beloved community as 201–207; for institutional transformation 196–199; of redefining success 206–207; of seeing and being seen 29–31; as service of self and systems 128–129
Practicing Liberation in Virtual Space (Becky Thompson) 161–163
prayer 40, 47, 57, 101
Prescribing Colonization: The Role of Medical Practices and Policies in Japan-Ruled Taiwan, 1895–1945 (Liu) 43
Prichard, Robin Raven 128
profit-driven model of education 72
psychological safety 67–68

qigong 38; ancestral knowledge and heritage 43–44; cultural appropriation 45; embodied reading 41–43; tuning body, breath and mind 38–39

racial capitalism 63
Racial Healing Circles (RHCs) 197–199, 239
racial hierarchy 24
racial inferiority 38
racial oppression 19
racial reckoning 1, 8
racial trauma 148, 154n1
racial justice 210, 212
racism 231; anti-Black 148; gendered 56
Radiant Rest: Yoga Nidra for Deep Relaxation and Awakened Clarity (Stanley) 150
Radical Dharma: Talking Race, Love, and Liberation (Williams, Owens and Syedullah) 84
"radical openness" 201
radical presence 166–174

Ralph, Sheryl Lee 30
Reagon, Bernice Johnson 163
reciprocity 93–94
redefining success 204–205
reflexive praxis 58
Rehearsals for Living (Maynard and Simpson) 115
relationality 197
relationship with own body 96–97
the remaining life 169
resistance 237–246; and contemplative dance 101–107; contemplative practice as act of 1–20; and inquiry 74; internalized colonialism 44
Resources of the Spirit in the Race Against Climate Change 180
rhizomatic awakening 144, 184–187
rhizomes 143–145
Rice, Tamir 158
Richardson, Bernard 140
"right speech" 211
Rinpoche, Dzigar Kongtrul 75
ritual of resistance 242–246
Robinson-Morris, David. W. 1, 9, 13–15, 16
Ross, Loretta 203
Roy, Arundhati 240
Rumi 196, 199
ruptures 143–145

Salyers, Candice 128–129
samadhi 151
Samora, Julian 50
scientific colonization 43
Scoblic, J. Peter 115
self: -compassion 122–123; practices as service of 128–129
sentipensante pedagogy 48, 55n1, 72
settler colonialism 228, 237, 240
Sharpe, Christina 244
Simpson, Leanne Betasamosake 115
sitting meditation (zazen) 81–84, 87–88
slaveholder religion 66
Smith, Barbara 162
social justice 11, 42, 60, 63, 122, 124, 180, 210, 212, 237
sole-proprietor activism 215
somatic trauma-informed practices 159
Somé, Malidoma 150
Soto Zen 82
SOUL culture 148–150, 154

spaciousness 31–33, 87–88
Spragg, Deb 239
Stafford, Barbara 160
Stanley, Tracee 150
state-sanctioned terrorism of Black people 156
Stopping the Clock Grief Series 154n4
St. Teresa of Avila 110
student(s) 168–170, 180–182, 219–220; Black 33; of color 51; and contemplative pedagogy 44; and COVID 161; holistic growth 10; hyper-marginalized 59; mindfulness practices for 230; protests 7; resistance 102
suffering: confronting 235–236; observing 235–236
svādhyāya (self-study) 149, 153
systemic oppression 82, 94, 158, 222

Takaki, Ronald 48
Talusan, Liza 210
Taoism 44
tapas (devotion) 149
Tatum, Beverly 59
Taylor, Breonna 158
"Teaching *Who Killed Vincent Chin?* 1991 and 2001" (Wu) 42
Templeton, Emerald 8
Thai Forest community 212
Theatre of the Oppressed (Boal and McBride) 105
Thich Nhat Hanh 68, 75
Thompson, Becky 144–145, 157, 161–163, 185
Thompson, S. 58
A Thousand Plateaus: Capitalism and Schizophrenia (Deleuze and Guattari) 143
Thurman, Howard 3, 140
Tibetan Buddhist religious organization 209
TikTok 212
Todd, Zoe 38
transformation 67, 242: Conjuring 127–130; humanity-centered systemic 2; institutional 7, 9, 15, 60, 115, 196–199; liberatory 20; ontic 145; systemic 190
transformative change: and contemplative practices 218–226; and higher education 218–226

transformative justice 204, 221, 225
Trump, Donald 114, 160
Truth, Racial Healing, and Transformation (TRHT) framework 197, 199
truth-telling 231
tuning body, breath and mind 38–39

The Undercommons: Fugitive Planning and Black Study (Harvey and Moten) 7

violence: ancestral 159; epistemic 148
A Voice from the South (Cooper) 31

Wahl, Daniel Christian 115
W.A.I.T.? practice 211–212, 239; brief history of 212; object of 215–216; personal practice 212–213
Walker, Alice 88, 150
Walker, Maureen 214, 215
Wapner, Paul 101, 103
Waziyatawin 39–40, 42
We Got Soul, We Can Heal 151
Western psychotherapeutic methods 167
white fragility 229
white mindfulness 240

"whiteness as property" 213
white silence 239
white supremacy 190, 228, 231, 240
"White Supremacy Culture" (Okun) 204
wholeness 34, 84–85; cultivating 129–130; and institutions of higher education 129–130
"Whole Student Checklist" 204–206
Why Are All the Black Kids Sitting Together in the Cafeteria? (Tatum) 59
Williams, Paul 215
Wilson, Shawn 162
Wilson-Hartgrove, Jonathan 66
witnessing as love 31–33
W.K. Kellogg Foundation 197
writing 57–58
Wu, Jean 42

Yellow Bird, Michael 39–40, 42, 44, 227–236; Indigenous Decolonial Contemplative Mentoring 228–229; Plenty Fox 229–231
Yoga 162

zazen 81–84, 87–88
Zen Peacemakers Order 229

For Product Safety Concerns and Information please contact our EU representative GPSR@taylorandfrancis.com
Taylor & Francis Verlag GmbH, Kaufingerstraße 24, 80331 München, Germany